MACHIAVELLI
Rage

2nd Edition

Ylond Miles-Davis

ISBN 978-1-950818-99-0 (paperback)
ISBN 978-1-950818-40-2 (ebook)

Copyright © 2020 by Ylond Miles-Davis

All rights reserved. No part of this publication may be reproduced, distributed, or transmitted in any form or by any means, including photocopying, recording, or other electronic or mechanical methods without the prior written permission of the publisher. For permission requests, solicit the publisher via the address below.

Rushmore Press LLC
1 800 460 9188
www.rushmorepress.com

Printed in the United States of America

Stand up to the miracles of the author's storytelling, and I think you will agree that it is a passionately realistic novel of many voices in the world awakening social conscience.

The Clans From Mint of Zeb

THE BIGGEST MYSTERY ever confronted by the living, the dead, and the un-dead was Mint of Zeb, the city of all eternity. The region near Memphis, south of Cairo, was where dusty plains and thorny shrubs cuddled stripped stick figures and sand charms. A perfect Egyptian endorsement was bound to set things that had not been seen for a mighty long time. Mint of Zeb was also a dwelling where misfits played shadow games with nomadic herdsmen, near sites of worship. Burial grounds honeycombed with tombs ruled like gods rule under the sun that never dies. Inside Mint of Zeb's catacombs, very few grieved for lost faith. They desired the good life, one that never absorbs a tragic definition. Like a lasting wedding song, a few of them outside the catacombs traded passive belief for active faith. The region was sparsely populated but attracted many travelers. The year was 1945, and it mocked progress inside a blood pool of a ditched phenomenon. Time in this place was as indefinable as an ancient offering to graze the land of Jews, a required condition for decadent courts. Staged shadows, forced-fed lip theatrics, and distinctions among tribes determined whether anyone was truly free.

The lofty and proud Sa were craft makers. They carved and sold statuettes to promote idol worship. Stretched neck Sa women worshiped Egyptian sex gods, and they were funky with pride. Devotion to demigods was as rampant as black -eyed slaves trading souls for the successful prosecution of one's master. The ruling elders' strongholds were so maddening that it hooked this place under a pledge to liberate their people from burdens of depravity. Among them lived the Yu, who took pleasure in their poise with unflinching resolve. These mystical warriors managed a lifestyle where luminous eyes rarely gazed on sacrificed carcasses left to the sun. They were a mystery to the desert people, like honor, and it angered the Sa tribe that God could bless another with treasure and riches. The blessings included supernatural defense agreements. The Yu tribe's presence was a free flowing necessity, and so was their combat intelligence. Their gravitational pull was infinitely powerful. They could survive anything amazing, and altogether they were unmatched. For these reasons the blood of long wars rarely covered the dry but thirsty terrain. When blood did pour, it was a blood offering or leakage from smacked or switched sacrifices that fed the area appetite for fresh desert sand trails, holding out hope to get the blood that it needed.

The ageless sun, teeth of cold sand dunes, and bark of yellows and browns called desert winds to blow on all life. The Yu considered this call free under one God. They believed blood spoke, and that human bloodshed emptied by ill will might yield a curse on humanity.

The Yu often wondered why humans hunt people like they are hunting for animals to eat. It was their duty to protect and initiate goodwill. Some called it, *Duty Free.*

Duty Free, was a merciful condition prearranged by their one God. The gnawing anger of the Sa could never bind or push them out into other world powers which included the catacombs where fresh, edgy, and original Vampires lived. The definition of their body did not embrace vain war or needless bloodshed. The customs of idolatry repulsed them. Like reincarnation, their secrets would die to resurrect a power that existed in the faith of Yu exclusivity. The Sa were covetous, but not completely foolish. They shared Yu fortune. And so it was, mercy did not permit the secret region to destruct inside the biggest mystery ever confronted.

Like a healthy bladder infected to purge, the Yu tribe observed excess. Nonetheless, they judged the Sa and the *Temple of Essen.*

The remote Temple, made for recreation and revival, sat between two special domains. It was created to gulp the desert sun and fiery moonlight. Two T- shaped mosaic pillars enclosed a narrow gateway; the pillars sucked in dry wind that brushed against decorated walls. The Sa mystics believed that on windy nights wall scenes performed like souls split into tiny pieces. They told of unusual musical notes luring the winds, assuring painted images of something more than thirst. In time, if permitted by the God of the Yu, the throat of the desert would be eager to drink up the Nile. The ancient site was a place where culture fueled flames with happy slaves of rhythm. Like a construction team of skilled artisans, the Yu believed one day these enslaving sounds would reach the other side of the world, and like vessels escorting tenors down the river, a fiery bill would one day meet a great sword.

Essen priestess guardians, musicians, and temple maids were bound to servitude by temple gods for centuries. Before Christ, few were paid. Among those employed were tinted –skinned, blue twins. These mysterious ancient doubles have preserved an unusual but powerful legend among the Sa and Yu. It is believed that the twins' sky -blue skin and artistic endowments were altogether supernaturally superior, surpassing most human understanding.

Their cloak of sky- blue pelt, unusually elongated fingers, beautiful, willowy arms, and fine white locks afforded them great prestige as cloistered sculptor makers. Neither time nor season has ever marred their uniqueness. Both have provided honor and exclusivity. Their public manifestations were as rare as meeting twin ghosts holding diamonds and pearls. Those fortunate enough to have gazed into their black oval-shaped eyes have never returned to an ordinary existence. The twins are beautiful gods, in a great galaxy of *Those Who Must Be Kept*. They are an army of the Nazarene meriting influence of many spheres of glory, including their favorite, a sphere in music. The legend claims it is by beautiful sound and exceptional unknown powers the twins could animate corporeal crystal sculptures. On full moon-lit nights, the mystic region's casts of shadows of the Valley of the Kings gave the figures a human dimension.

In times past, while engaged in precious stone making, the cloistered Essen's choir wooed the twins' flexible movements. The privileged choir and chosen offspring observed the command of creation from the cradle to the grave. Like loose flowers bagged up in exchange for black diamonds and pearls, their works were extraordinary and rare to behold. The great Essen crystal statue Alia especially responded to the sound of melody, and the fastest dances under moonrise.

On the eleventh hour, hereditary princes offered blood sacrifices. On midsummer's eve, people gathered around the statue, and a willing elder offered blood. The offering was poured into the mistress gold cup. Afterward, her lovely skull exuded hues of sky blue. This assured the Sa and Yu that Alia's rage was pacified. The blue twins foretold that in the generation of Darius Yarbaba, blood through her cup would not be obligatory. A new cup could offer a blood ransom for the salvation of souls, the Nazarene.

It all started before the cup of Christ was offered. A Sa girl named Alia was born to a royal Sa prince, Ali Yarbaba. The child's beautiful mother, Nuit, was born into a glove full of honest, tough, and vigilant, humans, and the ancient Yu. The glove full of humans were the supporting casts. When the prince discovered her, he took an immediate liking to Alia. It was more than a feeling, similar to a crawler toward a bee with many tentacles making a mystery. Their union was special due to the extraordinary actions of each tribe putting tribal differences aside for the sake of unborn blessings. Everyone embraced the union, between opposites.

After their first-born Alia was born, she fed on wolf's milk and matured quickly. Before her mortal end, the Sa tribe held a great expectation in her future. They determined that she would hold the high position of a temple priestess.

While she ripened with the silky sand dunes, her splendor grew, and her reflection drew upon everything. Later, the supernatural power to absorb the essence of anything before her became manageable. Like a terrestrial goddess, she only took in and reflected glory, then drew upon her angels. Her unusual qualities were most understood by the blue twins, and two elite elders, one from each tribe.

Both tribes decided that she would be beholden to masters who came from the sky. Her energy was harnessed in a mystical dome inside the *Temple of Essen*. Once a year a powerful midnight ceremony was invoked under the starry sky. A golden chair engraved in Lapis Lazuli, alabaster, and rubies placed on the shoulders of attendants, traveled from one abode to another with Alia seated comfortably. Before concluding the beautiful ceremony, it was placed in the middle of a magnificent crystal chamber. Egyptian wall paintings colored in dusky red, black, and yellow paint decorated the beautiful chamber. Alia, peacefully mounted inside of this seat rejoiced while incense sprinkled, and an untouched water source from the Nile flowed underground. She was a mystery, and many of them were unable to satisfy their minds of her true identity. As the Essen choir and crowds of people took their places in front of her, the echoes of their beautiful songs fed her soul, the chamber, the bottom of the Nile, and a silver moon. At that time of year, it all bloomed a mysterious firmament above the dome. Yu and Sa priests went around the beautiful crystal chamber reciting prayers while the blue twins inside an eternal Galaxy carried mysterious powers which dissolved and removed back into space.

Julius Florian, a strong, imposing temple Vampire warrior from an unknown tribe, had different plans. *Those Who Must Be Kept* call him Julius, The Handsome. He shuddered with reverence, howled by night, and could not tolerate the indecencies of temple prostitution, taxes, and indulgences for sex slaves that also occurred at the Temple. Night after night he envisioned generations of human trafficking which sought to involve Yu women among the traditional elite. He used their light to guide his way, and the heavenly blood of the Yu pleased him most. Human trafficking born into a new world would be a great abomination, for it was through Yu grace that the secret region did not fall into poverty or get swallowed into obscurity. This potential doom-haunted his thoughts. One night, while Alia was preparing for a midnight ritual, he crept behind her like a fog on turtle's feet. His ebony heels merged with the quiet of midnight. Julius whispered, "When a Vampire loves a woman."

He bit into her lean neck and left her sapped for the blue twins to discover and later treasure. The flagstone floor beneath her body was covered with wrongdoing. Exposed was one drop of blood that shimmered like red mercury. This deep-crimson blood mark was as striking as the best part of humanity. Her still corpse had made living hell worse. With the silver moon hanging under the black sky, the twins immediately dedicated her to the idea that all people should be free. They swiftly immersed her face and body in a unique quartz resin cast and kept her inside of them for another time when she could return to a sea of organic society's maintaining pride and sovereignty.

Julius swiftly turned down sandy rolling, and swelling aisle then doubled back and covered his tracks. In the pitch-dark of the night, he disappeared and hadn't been seen in Egypt since. After his disappearance many crystal statues were hidden, others have vanished. The crystal statue of Queen Alia has flawlessly endured with the path of the stars. And so, the blood custom continues. Offerings remain secret, inflicting retributions on those that hated her vital energy.

In the summertime of 1945, Darius Yarbaba was a descendant of the royal Sa and younger brother of Lazarus. Darius was a slave owner, privileged temple keeper, craftsman, and wise warlock. He did not restrict his craft making to molds, digging inside the royal crates, or making statuettes which he called *Peppi*. His craft had great measures in the supernatural and holy prostitution, which enhanced poor women's glory. For centuries, willing temple whores sexually catered to strange travelers and locals. The ancient temple had stayed well preserved on the shifting sands of Egypt. At its height, the temple was considered a vessel of ritual, wealth, and power. A place that has only heard of change, but never saw it, until the morning star and a pale moon gave birth to the horizons of the sky and super moon wooing its gazers into submissions. All works and profits went to the advancement of the temple and the quality of life. Neither time nor the Yu had convinced the Sa of their bedlam. The labors of Darius Yarbaba mimicked the great harlotry of his ancestors. The Yu also continued to benefit in the ease in which they gained access to a well-endowed lifestyle. The bond between them was similar to the heads of blue & black twins. They also were long and silent in the Kingdom of *Those Who Must be Kept*, where their well-remembered God reigned. It was so amazing the clay pots exuded perfumed glory. One bird emerged from a pot, spread his wings, and flew north.

In the *Temple of Essen* major lessons in shapeshifting were taught by two- thirds of their finest mystics. They called it finesse, toasted to the good life, and used clay to battle.

Darius had a warped view of most women. His view was worse than a methodical desert god sitting on a throne grasping for scorecards. He'd promise poor travelers daughters of free women, and poor newcomers' employment. He never followed through. Instead, he'd offer them tarts and bid them rhinestone leashes until their snares became their freedom. Many women were attracted to his well-kept ginger beard. It represented the age to be feared with issues and conflicts presented as artistic. His leashes truly possessed promises, and as a ghostly pact with cultural possession, he re-enslaved free women into a modern lifestyle of his ancestors' spoil. The temple's tiny world of drawn shades and teeth chattering prosperity continued.

Through it all, the Yu maintained allegiance to their ancestral practices, particularly the tradition of bloodline exclusivity. This vital practice held; however, for the last hundred years, their desire to breed was only occasional, leaving them afraid and in danger of extinction. Cultural decadence kept them from breeding. On so many levels the region was morally polluted, and like a dragon crawling through wet sand, their will to reproduce nearly died.

Darius kept hope alive. His eyes began to hunt with the prowess of wolves. Eventually, his sight landed on his highest discovery. He could see his brother's love for a beautiful Yu girl named Devora. Not completely hardened by the ancient customs his heart sung with ancient Egyptian lyrics. A singing dog gifted with soul also thundered with the course of their love. Lazarus and Devora's love appeared living to the open air of Memphis. In many ways, the occurrence replicated the old love story between Nuit and Ali.

The Yu and Sa elders could not forget Nuit's tragic demise and quickly put all tribes in remembrance of the one drop of blood. Like bumblebees in a trap, it was maintained that Yu and Sa must never marry again. The pursuit that all people should be free remained critical, but the elders warned that Lazarus and Devora's union might yield a wave of destruction to Memphis, or even worse, risk the ancient ritual offerings dedicated to the great Alia statue.

The rituals brought lavish measures into the temple. Their union could threaten the core values of their ancient society. Eventually, whispers convinced the tribes to discourage their union. The special guests of untainted love might never have a chance to walk with the familiar. The ugly head of history might interrupt their journey. So, like an obtrusive blimp, murmurs advertised dread.

Darius despised unmerited whisperings. His eyes refused to lie to his soul as he gazed on the couple's splendor. For him, their love was the jungle. It will play harmonies for you if you let it. Their love began to impact his understanding of the meaning of love, and after a few months of observing their public virtues, Darius became repelled by dumb idols and primitive habits. Before long he took an unusual turn. Even secret blood offerings to the cup of Alia felt as empty as a pour of cosmic rules. He'd pondered, what was the point of saving the desert if the sound was gone? Hearing does not believe, however seeing reveals layers of harmonies through their relationship. This witness impacted Darius' humanity.

One night, while Darius was bathing and meditating on his brother's love and happiness, an eagle showed up and snatched a short white glove. A pair was lying on a limestone bench. Immediately stirred by the sight and strangeness of the bird's action, he screamed, "Oh mighty one, what sign might this be, as these gloves belonged to the temple Virgin Alia. They are as white as snow and as spotless as an untroubled heart."

The eagle replied, "Couldn't you spare one? You have seen what I did to the Egyptians, and how I bore you on eagles' wings and brought you to myself."

Darius perceived the lover of his brother to be carrying a promise of twins inside her belly. He slowly descended into the water. While submerging his body into the heat of silky water, he accepted the visitor as a sign from heaven. He concluded the eagle's voice was for the coming of something greater than bloody temple sacrifices, idols, and desecrated tombs. Quickly emerging from the water and standing upright, like an iron rod, he gazed across the atrium into Alia's life-like eyes. Darkened edges disclosed days with another nation and time in Memphis without reproach.

In the same hour, Lazarus and Devora walked through a maze of hallways. The smell of incense wafted through the air. Soon, they encountered Darius in the atrium. Their presence stopped his breath.

Suddenly, tenors of choirs awakened four black jasper statuettes hidden like DNA in a pit beneath the temple's courtyard. Darius whispered,

"Can you feel it?"

He stared deeply into Devora's eyes.

"Of course we can feel it. It has been directed externally. Let my enemies be scattered, and the sons of God arise!" answered Darius.

Devora cried, "Death shall swallow us up if you do not help us! We beg your magical order. Hypnotize the region, for they must accept our union. We shall pay any price for their night of ignorance to be forever removed; it is a snare against true love."

"What say you, the Yu ask such a thing. We beg your magic? The mighty Sa stink of dung to your celestial nostrils. I have pondered many nights while watching the two of you. How is it that your lovely thin arms embrace my brother's colossal Sa frame? It reminds the Yu tribe of a planet thrown into the ice age. I, on the other hand, have been shown a wonder," said Darius.

Devora's soft voice bled through her sheer veil.

"You understand, I am on fire for Lazarus. I love him, more than the Yu or Sa honor the spark of the blue twins Galaxy. What is the point of saving the armies' galaxy, if the sound of love is gone?"

"Might you be asking me to deceive and manipulate the tribes for personal gain? Or even use ancient symbols to translate your message to go forth into a new world in your likeness?" Darius asked.

A long silence fell, on a plot bent on sin.

As air blew through her thin veil, it failed to hide her glory. Like a mystery never answered, the opening to her soul reflected the strength of a million men marching. If by chance the veil had fallen, her glory would have caused Memphis to mourn.

Darius quickly looked to his brother.

"Brother Lazarus. Your hour has brought more than a love offering. Your lady carries special twins within her womb. They reflect the revelation of *Those Who Must Be Kept*s' very own blue & black twins. From Devora's womb, they have discovered the truth about the law of supply and demand. This very night, I heard an eagle talk. It came within reach right here in the atrium. I was bathing when the words from its beak spoke. We are to prepare for the coming of things that were bought with a price."

He handed the glove to Lazarus.

"The eagle took the other one, and then with high speed ascended into the sky, down a long brown road before him."

Darius replied, "My brother, it is true Devora is pregnant. How could you have known? When the tribes find out, they will say an omen shall harm *Those Who Must Be Kept*. You must grant Devora her wish. Use your magic to hypnotize them. For our sake, lure them to sleep and make them forget the old ways of those who have passed on. We desire to be together in peace without reproach and our twins welcomed! If not, we shall end it, right here in front of the great Statue of Alia. Devora will tell the statue, drink her milk for Memphis, but instead offer teardrops beneath its feet. We will not even offer a carnival song. I promise you we shall always think twice for the eagle's assurance of our double blessing within Devora's womb."

"Beloved brother Lazarus, one must not become a victim of blackness, it is the fall of man, and magic can only go so far. My practice of it might propel me to fall off my stool. We shall prepare for the coming of the twins, and mysteries bought with a price. What these mysteries are and what price this is, I will come to learn in another land."

Darius instructed Lazarus. "Put this glove inside Alia's hand. Her substance is sleek, like red sticks. Until now her darkened eyelids have revealed a remote past, banished and altered. The eagle's message sparked a loving concern for what belongs to the future. His voice was something glorious. I have not experienced anything of this outward speed before. It's going to find us, like composed magnetic fields. Furthermore, the power yields a red lining that exists between my hand and *Those Who Must Be Kept.*"

"I do not understand! We need your magic," Devora insisted.

Conflicted between the Sa magic and the mercy of Yu, she sighed, "We will be covered in mud by the tribes."

"Devora, you are the only woman in the world who escapes atrocity. It humbles even me," Darius whispered.

"My dear Darius, this is because there is only one woman in the world with many faces. I am not ashamed of them. When you look at me, you experience them all." She slowly removed her veil.

"No, this can't be true! I see most women as whores and breeders for our ancient courts. Hurry, cover yourself quickly, now!"

She protected her face like an outsider.

"Fine, let's block out all the chatter. I will give you your wish Devora, and use my magical order to hypnotize the tribes. Hand me the rot inside Alia's shell. The scarabs inside are in search of residue. With the promise of eagle wings, I bind the crawlers. Now an ancient funk of forty thousand seasons shall cradle a brand new human race which your womb holds."

"Thank you, Darius, for the sloping walls on these royal courts shall hide our secret," she answered.

"Clap for it, Lazarus, you very well know the secrets of the Sa." Darius decreed.

One clap by Lazarus prevented Mint of Zeb from one night of wonder in the pristine natural night sky. Lazarus affectionately whispered, "Just to be close to you Devora, Spirit made light."

"Cover Devora's bottomless eyes with this wrap. You're now dealing with the boss of a lady whose destiny is to produce royalty. All of the lights have deadened for the sake of your twins. They are the light of the world, with no excuses or apologies," said Darius.

"Now, Devora sit in front of the great sculpture while the patron of craftsmen intertwines the midnight hour with the hum of Essen. Life throughout the universe will awaken decades of epic sounds. We all are aware of the terrestrial sound books of forty. They preserve the secrets of the undead. The portion is sealed within Alia's gold cup. Hand me the Virgin's glove, while I sing of the future," Darius ordered.

Lazarus stood silent and stared. Her movements were quick and desperate.

"I can wait all night long. Light the torch." She answered.

"It is lit, slow down; you know you can't touch this torch." Meanwhile, his other hand sloped onto the statue's belly.

Afterward, Devora's movements slowed down. She perched on the granite bench. Using Cobra magic, Darius placed the glove on Devora's lap and quickly removed the veil from her black silken-capped skull. Standing in her shadow, he whispered, "There's only one woman in the world my lady, and every plot that has ever existed rests within our pact this night."

She replied, "On this very evening, under the skies of Mint Zeb, my eye paint will display something more than thirsty skin. Cover my lids quickly and block out the light of the moon."

Darius sang, "Get thee back Crocodile and depart from the Yu, she is Devora."

Devora answered, "Get thee back alligator, depart from the Sa, our treasure is on an island with eight tribes sitting on eight seats of understanding.

The imperishable one is near eight scales with angel haircuts. Beautiful, elaborate, and free lacking nothing that does not decay or tangle with trouble. A flying bird cherishes my womanhood. A beast thought it belonged to his song and dance. After a breath, I put away his sorrow while blood and water kept keeping on from different points of views one wrinkle at a time." Her brow frowned.

"Relax Devora as I tie the knot of the veil tightly. Only for a manner of time, our time is a mythic time it shall hide your earthly status. Indeed, the veil rests beautifully against your olive skinned neck."

Darius dug below the great statue's feet. He cupped some wet soil together with the rot and residue from Alia's cup. Massaging the moist soil in his palms, he gently wedged the concoction into her ears and whispered, "A little-sacred soil from under the throne of Alia has discovered a new resting place. Tonight is the night among mortals that our Essen choirs will diminish. Like roots escaping the burning sun, the deepness of soil within your ears will help our choir's hum fade away which is essential. For now, your attention must rest on Lazarus and the double blessing within your womb."

Moments later Darius called to man-made gods, fly high free bird. Soon he was in a deep trance. Suddenly, four Jasper sculptures beneath the temple's courtyard began reflecting` signs of decades seeking justice. Their ebony arms stretched towards Alia's direction. Although obstructed by a stone ceiling, their gaunt arms supernaturally danced through dimensions. They stretched toward her seated throne. In the vein of a public discussion on bounty put on someone's head, members participated like a reckoning. A trusting Devora sat frozen in time. If Darius were to have stuttered his petition would be faultless as Lazarus' confidence in Sa magic never wavered.

Devora's hope was not in Sa spells. Certainly, their tribe was involved. She believed, the mercy of the Yu tribe compelled the visitation of the talking eagle, and at whatever cost their fight was to win souls lost to the ages for what is still a nebulous notion.

Suddenly, two priests wearing decorative headdresses entered the atrium. They immediately interrupted Darius' trance and demanded ceremonial rights. The angry priests began shouting in an ancient Egyptian tongue. Lazarus became uneasy. In a manner of seconds, a Yu priest initiated a ritual. He snatched the cup of Alia. His breathing and chanting were strong while fiercely whistling into the charcoal sky. The tone must have reached a bright north star, as its form instantly disappeared into the darkness. Shortly after, he grabbed a golden hilt from a rare white jade statue facing Alia. The statue was topless, without greaves, or a defense helmet. Her hilt was prized by Yu and Sa, and available to only the two masters. With the ease of falling dust, he aimed the scepter at Lazarus' jeweled turban. A bolt flashed across the midnight sky, and a powerful might appointed rain to pour down. Muddy water rose from beneath the great Alia statue.

Lazarus demanded an explanation for their actions. Instead, he found himself under his turban and transformed into a Staffordshire terrier. In chorus, and in Egyptian tongue, the priests proclaimed, "Our privileges know of your request through secret means.

Supernatural defense supersedes your magic to hypnotize the tribes. Devora's appeal is against all laws. The unseen realm has given birth to the physical realm, setting the stage for a startling move."

The Jade statue looked towards Lazarus. While hard drops of rain hit Lazarus' fur, clipped ears, and wet nostrils, he became conscious of the corporeal change. So far his mental abilities were still in place. Unwilling to be an offer or sacrifice to an Egyptian idol, his four new paws bolted him out of the atrium.

The priest continued loudly, "Devora is absent and in a deep trance. The sacred mud taken from the seated throne has lured her into a bottomless sleep. The mud has potent ingredients. Introducing this set apart mud into her ears was an act of great rebellion. This self-interested appeal meddled with a higher will. Now there shall be room for *Justice*! Priests from both tribes have read about this on sacred shards. The Sa do not understand it, but what we all understand is that her attention must garner something greater than an end which justifies the means."

"What will you do?" Darius asked.

"According to these sacred writings, you will discover this truth in a new land. The process based on a mixture of our interest, and how we reached our means based on values will speak to us on how we are to feel. Take Devora to America and never speak of the pact with anyone."

Darius kept silent about the eagle.

"We shall see to it that you leave this land safely, with precious jewels and bullion. Your royal inheritance ensures financial well-being. Quickly, feed this tobacco to her," they demanded.

Darius' eyeballs moved toward Devora. His stomach felt like a disaster area. The Sa elder pulled out a strange brown plant from a small pouch. He placed it in Darius' sweaty palms.

"She is in a deep trance with a dark Lord who is showing her signs that mimic illusions and the devil's horns. You must unite the veil from around her eyes. Slit a dry leaf from this root and feed two seeds to her. Destroy the leftovers. We trust that you realize the importance of its destruction. Now quickly put the seeds under her tongue before it is too late. She will remember very little. From this point on, every time she sleeps, the pleasure spirit will gain more control of her body, its core attached to the crystal statue. Regrettably, your magic has released power from the golden hilt. We demand that you do not continue with any rituals from this day forward. Magical powers can not dislodge this pleasure spirit."

"What should I do when the spirit has gained full control?" Darius asked.

"After the shadows have parted like curtains, the seeds will help, and we shall go fishing in the sea, but both of you will be far from this place!"

Within twenty-four hours, Devora did not remember her great lover Lazarus, the magical ritual, or the rage she held against the tribes. To the great surprise of Darius, she remembered him, the twins inside her belly, and the words of the great eagle.

"Darius, a woman does not create a baby she receives a baby. I am like a seed to bloom wherever I am planted. The other two seeds that I hold within me guarantee flower bombs, for I have immaculately conceived twins."

"What are flower bombs?"

"They are warriors and overcomers holding the fragrance of love for the light of God's kingdom. Like pink- tinged wings and dazzling color on checkered floors, truth was on its way back to me already."

Darius held his secrets and gave Devora the blessings of an untroubled heart. He never once mentioned their wish to vacate the minds of all men, women, and children. He placed their deal with magic behind them and credited time in Egypt to a journey holding a mysterious promise. He believed in the eagle's words, deciding these words would bring to pass more than drained sacrifices, jewels, and a trove of silver and gold coins given amid a meeting room exodus. They prepared to leave South of Cairo and never return without the very least, wisdom and supernatural treasures in the spirit of jubilee.

The Black Box

A VESSEL FROM Europe carrying supplies for neighboring regions reached the port the next night. Darius was unable to sleep and was pre-occupied with getting Lazarus to the ship unnoticed. Devora had been in a fetal position for a few hours. Her body looked graceful on top of an ancient Persian rug marked with hand sewn pomegranate designs. The treasured rug covered a small area in Darius' chamber. The sight of her face shining with sweat compelled Darius to slump over her body.

"Lay your weary head to rest Devora. After dripping for hours, the warmth has ripened the pomegranates. They glisten and look pleasant enough to eat."

"Don't miss the jet, don't miss the jet," she mumbled repeatedly.

Darius knew he had little time to hide her delirium. The heat was blazing. He peeled off her sheer veil.

"Dream always our beloved princess, one day you will be my sister-in-law. We will arrive in a new land soon. Now I must go to the ship with Lazarus." He smiled thinly.

His eagerness to reach the ship moved with the quiet growl of Lazarus. To get ahead of the problem, Darius hid him in an extraordinary box called *Lux*. This special box challenged reality, time, space, and gravity. Devora had given the box to Darius. It belonged to her tribe, the Yu. The box consisted of interlocking planks and time capsules made by the blue & black twins. These amazing planks were held by grass with a kind of sewing that in so many words sparked the birth of the four thousand four hundred -year -old Yu Empire. The *Lux* could even shed Holy blood, and select mystics saw the blood. Devora insisted that under no circumstance the box should remain in Egypt. The Yu believed the *Lux* was also a time vessel which could be used in the afterlife to visit anywhere in time. Its size was just right for transporting Lazarus.

Despite its mass, Darius repeated, "New life awaits us all in America! We shall not succumb to your new corporal form, Lazarus. You are safely hidden in a boundless box, it floats like a butterfly. Do not worry you can't ever be contained."

It was about 11:00 p.m. when Darius and Lazarus reached the seaport. Darius surveyed the surroundings. Some were strangers, and a few spoke Latin. He took note of a ten-day language course. Soon a gust of wind brought in a strange odor. The tones of voices closing in triggered him to loosen his knife before turning towards them. The strangers were afraid of the knife's round rock- crystal nob and jackal's head. It compelled them to speak of aberrations on high seas. Darius spoke several languages and understood a little Latin. The strangers had referred to incidents before reaching the seaport. The exact nature stayed sheltered behind Stonewall language barriers. Within seconds, he turned to the Egyptian rebels, who were encircling him, and shouting about stockpiling and defense. Darius was not sympathetic, but grateful that the ship's arrival on Egyptian territory would serve as a timely escape for him and Devora. Like a handshake between two people who are in no way ordinary, the perceived traitors would soon voyage onward. Caution followed the next day. Their walk to the seaport was shamelessly quiet. Devora broke it when her eyes fell on tradespeople fleeing the area like trout en route for worms. A couple of Sa women were hovering over a pool of blood. It was no doubt a sacrifice was slit. Devora politely smiled.

One woman said, "How did you get those pretty teeth?"

Devora answered, "You all did not get to those. Sit close and keep your master warm, as we breaststroke to our living regalia."

With pronounced agitation, Devora slowed down behind Darius and cried, "Bloody events are unfolding, before us. My eyes have never gazed upon bloody sacrifice. The Sa look as if they have been to hell and back! Ordinarily, they make their sacrifices near the temple. Many of the strangers are crafty and have disguised themselves as tradesmen and herdsman. Their influence will quickly become a threat to Sa & Yu territory. I overheard some plotting. They left wallets and blood- stained clothes at other ports near the Nile. Identities are being stolen."

Darius stopped to look over his shoulder. "We have just reached this port. How is it that you have overheard anything?"

"When seeking the truth like the melt of frost, mangled finds will surface. Traitors and their smuggled images of killed captives made room for memories. The source spoke old Latin and shouted about signs, wonders, and foul odors. Many entities shall come on cramped boats; smugglers blamed intruders. More shall come in from Europe."

Darius nervously gripped Devora's head. "We shall need helpers along the way. But you do not understand Latin!"

Adjusting her head cover, she answered, **"In nomine Patris et fillii et Spiritus Sancti**. Last night I was filled with spirits of time. I lit a few candles, burned them slowly, blasted my nostrils, and then traveled through the *Lux* our chamber of wisdom. During the night, spirits spoke in thunderous chant and rain poured on shrinking footprints of ancient monuments. Wise voices filling the sanctuary of my womb understood."

Darius' mouth flattened. He felt like he was in a dream that would one day face an unknown empire. "Foreign schemes cannot hide long in the seaport of Alexandria. The Sa run this place economically. They also have always recognized the quiet sneak that lurks with their prey."

"My response might disgust you," she said dryly.

"Please speak your mind," Darius insisted.

"A bathing place for Vampires has brought forth an odor off the coastal slaughterhouse. Like a rat-infested ship, with some still in cages abandoned by humans, its drift towards shore is timely.

Nosferatu elders do not reek; however, a Vampire alone is a Vampire destined. It never misses blood until it's absent, then it travels, and at whatever cost will even pass through unguarded human egos. It pretends to be a part of something else and may be responsible for unspeakable horrors. The Yu have always known of the undead military involvements. They are numerous, nursing in many countries around the world. A great evil prowls within this brood and death shall flood the sewers. Alas, the ancient Sa are to blame! For centuries, their territory has turned a blind eye to the power of how the Vampires trap light. However, like an undiscovered black hole with fleeting horizons, my progeny's light escapes them. My light found in the aftermath lifted out of its horror and darkness. More significantly, our knowledge, wisdom, and wealth supersede the Vampires. Enough, I say! If not stopped, the most deadly will cause the sun to wane. As many as there are tongues, an agony will plant a flag in this brood. The Yu recognize that fire and the sun are the best disinfectants."

Taken aback by her understanding of the sun power of *Those Who Must Be Kept*, he noted, her memory must be to a certain degree returning. Could it be her memory was the sound of a gibbon, who some say calls the sun to rise? Or, an undiscovered black hole, after death, leaving valuable materials for an escape. Darius was not exactly sure. It could be ructions from the pleasure spirit. Her discernment was astonishing. Reconciling to be watchful, and unwilling to fall prey to evil, he decided not to mention what happened in the temple. At nightfall, he saw two priests and a rebel carrying a swathed figure. The moonlight barely exposed the thing. Initially, he thought it was a dead body wrapped in hot towels. However, after a closer examination, he noticed it was not human.

"Failure is twin failure," Darius said to himself.

Lazarus stayed quiet while Darius shifted his bare chest away from the *Lux*. "Danger, Danger!" He claimed to be holding a wooden box of human feces. The tradesmen passed him. As expected, the distractions helped camouflage his doings. Continuing toward the men, it was not long before he was on the opposite side of the deck. Darius watched them suspiciously from the southern section. Hidden from their view, he could not believe his eyes. Two priests and a rebel were working together around four large barrels. The back of the ship just about concealed their actions. Darius was spying from a particular angle. Suddenly, it occurred to him they were not just ordinary clerics, they were the priests who expelled him and Devora. How could he ever forget their hawk noses and steely slit eyes? One destined to cry I told you so, the other looking for someone to blame so they could use Lazarus as a scapegoat. Quietly setting the box down, he stooped behind it. The suffocating dry air almost stifled his breath. A heavy wheeze nearly propelled his frame into a hushed wave. He refused to believe a rebel was helping the same priests who expelled him and Devora unload life into the sea. Right before his eyes, pieces of unusual winged life and smashed slabs of ancient stones flung right off the port into the sea.

"It can't be so; their involvement would be sacrilegious," Darius said under his breath.

One priest slowly swung a green lantern. Darius cried, "Ancient statues from the temple, thrown to the celestial Nile, preposterous!"

Shadows around the priests' ceremonial robes started to snake around the white jade statuette. As Darius watched the priests dance with stars, he desired to fly away. Curiosity held him in place.

While the rebel continued to toss remaining portions of stone like catacomb bits, the priests raised the statuette. With the strength of a spotlight, the statues rock-solid arm plunged into the rebel's neck. The bloody rebel fell on top of a few barrels and then to the ground. His beefy 5 foot 10 -inch body rolled towards a puddle of martyr's blood.

The Yu priest threw the white jade statuette into the sea. Darius hoped that it might rest on a wave until rescued. The Yu priest pulled an ancient book from his robe, and then placed it on the rebel's heart who then cried, "Nawart Masr," which means welcome to Egypt. The rebel immediately recognized the ancient writing on the book, and shouted, "The seed of the truth, grace, and a mission to make people know each other better."

The priests hurried, in a march for life towards an unrevealed mission. Darius stood up clasped the box tightly and headed toward the vessel. There was cargo stored in the hold beneath and between an area on the ship. Each night he needed to go down to visit Lazarus. The maximum height in the storage was just slightly less than the height of a standard sarcophagus. There were also three limestone caskets and tall unusual barrels inside.

Darius gently caressed each casket whispering, "I woke up like this! Royal mummies, Egypt's indestructible. Oh, hell no, I shall not disturb our royal elite. Timeless shrouds are preparing for another journey. When their unseen procession reaches the shore, horror shall increase for a modern audience. These ceremonial mummies advance. Removed from the order in which they once belonged, they now must travel to deep places that shall be fabulously sexy. They will not be coming to play but to slay a casserole of many doctrines of deception. The Sa shall offer them pregnancy clay, fragrant spices, and herbs. The Yu will understand their need to survive because of their need to preserve what is real. I will do a new thing. Like lime mortar in the putty form, I must hold us together for our very best outcome. When the Yu talk through Devora, I'll act! The royal mummies are the apple of my eye. Tonight under the moonlight, the eye of Horus rest peacefully. Your grinding shall summon a twisted gourmet of mysteries which helps earth and heaven to increase daily in all good things. Heaven shall rise parts inside theaters of warriors and overcomers. Upon our landing into the new world, I'll gain more fortune, power, and wisdom. Power shall back our cries for virtue in the new land. But we shall not arrive crying; we arrive with power. Osiris has already liberated us. These conditions never change. Later we shall return to a new Egypt. Upon my return, all mummies from Mint of Zeb will be called out of the catacombs to oblige me in the security of eternal *Justice*, wisdom, and renewal. I stand tall on the truth, with a voice of wrath."

Darius wedged a tall barrel open. It contained a special compound of Nicotiana Tabacum, another barrel carried ground up bitumen.

Gently placing Lazarus on top of one sarcophagus he whispered, "Tomorrow at 3:00 p.m., I will bring bread and water. You're suffering, and injustices shall not be forgotten. My brother, the priests, responded wrong and helped put you in this shape. Later, I shall help you gain a generous table. The Most High God ordained bounty for our loving people."

When Darius left the ship, he seriously pondered Mint of Zeb's history. He began feeling more at home with the Yu beliefs about peace, order, and preservation. The tribe reminded him of what was special about spiritual battles.

His tribe, the Sa, and their obsession for ravenous forces invaded his fast walk. He reached a courtyard, east of a waterway covered with blossoms. Meditating on his encounter with the eagle, he recalled a small gold box that he picked up from the temple. The eagle had left it for him. The box, slightly protruding from under his vest, poked into his chest bone. He opened it nervously. Within the box were unusually small skulls from ancient times and fragments of a papyrus scroll with early text. The shards spoke of the salvation of souls, love, forgiveness, mercy, and of a blood offering from a savior named the Nazarene, who died for the sins of the whole world. Some writing on the shards brought Darius to shame. One ancient message was short. The written words confounded his tribe's belief system. *Nobody saves quite the way Jesus does.* In a moment of deep contemplation, he felt like a buffer between man and the world. Afterward, he quickly buried the box of relics inside a stone sarcophagus under a remote sidewalk courtyard. A hole was near a canal surrounded by huge blocks decorated in onyx, with images and hieroglyphs. Using water and raw talent, Darius managed to quarry the blocks. He decided that a rare find some time in the future might serve as the key to spiritual understanding, and begged God for divine intervention into his next phase into a new life in America.

The findings would make known a real reason to express the work of God's love and good news, but Darius did not have much to give God at this phase of his life. He felt unworthy, so he hurried with a state of emergency buried the elements, and desired to understand.

Before departing Darius turned around and stared back into the courtyard. He heard knocking from the *Box of Lux.* It was Lazarus. His voice was unspoiled, sweet like plum juice. "I am going to miss you, and will wait for you to return."

Darius answered, "Lazarus, some of us just know. I hear you in there, Mint of Zeb, shining still. The old feed store has passed, lifted, and shifted by men and women who believe in the creator of a high sky, full moon, and stars. I, like Pontius Pilot, washed my hands and closed my eyes, so the old feed store spreading peace across Mint of Zeb may rebuild again. The creation behind Mint of Zeb put gold on the stars. We are fortunate and were given means to leave the secret region. Tonight while passing the street vendors, I was compelled to think of a little idol made years ago. The points of stone horns revealed a day where I would want to leave this God- forsaken place but could not. I immediately crushed its head into pieces; the horns were sharp and practically cut through the sole of my heel. The other parts of the crushed sculpture I threw into the Nile. Your love for Devora compelled my feet to grind this beast into pieces. My memories of some pagan gods are timeworn, just like our ancient blood offerings and sacrifice. Our actions at this time in Egypt is a somber judge, and it has judged us harshly. Dark magic proved powerless. Wisdom and food offerings were splendid offerings for *Peppi*. He is our earth angel in spirit. While walking tonight, I remembered the spoken words of the eagle. The words are alive in me. Miraculous writings on sacred shards have increased my spiritual strength. A light upon my path holds authority, which I shall come to realize, yet do not completely understand.

Getting us safe to America is the objective. We have a quota gifted with the promises of Mint of Zeb and America. Our inheritance is vast, containing an alliance between foresight, private interest, nature, and art. Mint of Zeb's private ability and gold has created new entries. We shall retain the spiritual and physical doors leading to spacious light filled interiors. Your twins shall require plenty of room, a safe playground, and woods where wildflowers are. Before the ship's final stop, it is to pass through a ship graveyard where light wind shall clear the fog. Our overseas journey will take at least eight weeks. There was talk among the crew of food contamination, illnesses, and an overpowering stench. The Sa are heavily buying salt from tradespeople, only a few of them, the Yu, and the blue & black twins know why. Devora might remember. However, the seeds in her system are mimicking excitability. Unfortunately, I had to leave her alone to move you to the vessel. One thing I do know, salt is beyond the beauty secrets of the Sa, and we shall lift out of the salt and find a new life in the aftermath with those purest in faith. Then I shall ask the god of tradesmen is this resolution, free or fair?"

Lazarus answered, "I wish he were here."

Darius answered, "I think he is, and you will not miss me for long. A normally mixed society shall be in front of you. We shall always be together, someone has been to hell for our sake, and it is a Vampire's Kings never mind. I do not compromise with dog makers or slave masters."

Blue Dolphins

The following night the vessel left the port. It was carrying tons of salt, apparel, two hundred passengers, and blood trickling secrets. Throughout the journey, Devora spent most of her time sleeping in a bunk. Before their departure, Darius had convinced the Captain to prepare a blanket over straw for her mattress. Contemplating the majestic waves, sometimes standing erect and sleeping, Darius hoped for an answer regarding the priests' actions. His commanding inner voice might have an answer or even compel him to jump into the mouth of a whale. He had heard of suicides on the ship but was certain he would never take that route. Besides, an angel would have caught him.

Darius prayed, "Osiris in a blue whale I am stuck, pluck my thoughts wasting away. Awaken and place upon me a crown of wisdom and gold, otherwise disappear into, a wide open ocean of life in the spirit which was offered eternally."

Imagining a whale's wide hollow stomach, he grasped onto a side rail. Darius was angry that their journey was not yet a few miles beyond Memphis.

"The priests said we would have died to self if we knew what was going on in the temple." Darius began to struggle with the importance of choice.

"Did we have choices in the land of my ancestors? In the *Temple of Essen* which they created, seemingly Yu or Sa priests did not make room for a new age. They caught a glimpse of Devora and Lazarus's love, reacted with fear and banished all of us! Perhaps our temple and the land of our ancestors was made for us to leave, and our life plans have never been our own."

For days high seas tossed the craft under a blood red sky. Like a bleeding source seeking thirsty sinners, rough waters caused the bottom to clamor. The ship's crew guaranteed passengers it was food poisoning that killed half of them. Without going into much detail, the Captain said that the loud noises in the night were superior to a heartsick dare. Missing bodies forced many on the ship to contemplate passing trials with shadows. Darius supposed some men were knowingly going overboard and somebody better call the Captain. There is a time and a season for all services.

The ship arrived in Europe, but its stop was unexpected. With unflinching composure, the Captain made a brief announcement about the war. Throughout the journey, his cavalier attitude toward the passengers had been awkward. One minute it was love and the next hate. The Captain also asserted a minor leakage had occurred, but the problem could be much bigger. He was anxious because of breaking news that the Germans had surrendered to the Western Allies.

Afterward, conversations about the end of the war dominated most ears of the ship. In the mid-night hour, ten robust Germans left the vessel. Darius followed them. They were horsing around, on the seaport bouncing a tennis ball back and forth under the moonlight.

"Sounds like God, Heil!" One guy yelled. Darius observed their quick movements and thought, "I can make a ball bounce for myself."

They all read his thoughts. The youngest one responded, "The eagle like a ball is swift, come on join us!"

Darius waved politely as they confidently moved about with great agility. For weeks he had pondered their actions while on the ship. He imagined them to be natural born explorers. Most mornings he saw them roaming about toward the area where Lazarus and the three sarcophaguses were. Darius kept to himself, remaining watchful of their stern routines. Mostly, they towed the line and were looking to mop up any wrongdoing.

He refused to allow the Captain's announcement to cause further anxiety about the five-hour bad weather window. He remembered yesterday day's delight, the vastness of the sea, and a night encounter with wild things in 75-degree climate helped boost his shoulders back. The deep underwater canyon had gifted the crew with an explosion of krill fish. They also watched flying dolphins and humpbacks. For many days strong winds pushed up cold waters from the ocean's bottom. The deep-sea's appetizing gaze had pushed heavily from the bottom to the top.

The pluck of nature powered a sparkle of life in Devora, causing Darius to catch the wonder of her childlike significance. A sense of lightheartedness existed between them. In one wave and out the other dolphins were the highpoint of the journey. Their presence reminded Darius, we are all in school.

On course, the ship left Europe, it shifted through patches of light, darkness, and box jellyfish. Darius had discovered some things missing. It was five o'clock a.m. when he moved along a less obvious route toward the ships hold. It was hard to see, and careful repetition allowed him to go unnoticed. Immediately he detected two missing sarcophaguses. Devora quickly crossed his mind, "I want to be with her night and day, but I must keep a watchful eye on Lazarus," he whispered.

His eyes quickly scanned the cargo, "The sarcophaguses may have been stolen on our late night stop in England! These dolphins deserve two coffins? It's been weeks of sailing. I thought I heard mermaids calling my name. Very well, I will follow the call, but there will be much to be explained when the royal mummies awake."

Darius listened attentively. His foot tapped leisurely with the ocean's whisper to Norfolk Broads. The vessel passed a little port near a sandy beach. A foul odor began to consume the area. Darius plugged his nose wheezing for air, his mouth relented. The sarcophagus near Lazarus was intact. Darius softly knocked on the *Lux*. A loud, comforting growl followed.

The sound reminded him that all things work together for good. He refused to picture them separated. It may cause another onion field in his inner man.

Darius reached into an old cotton bag. It held large chunks of bread and wine. The elements had become the nerve center of their long voyage. He fed Lazarus nightly. A little lantern emitting a mint green glow helped achieve a cozy atmosphere. Lazarus pondered with the occasional silhouettes stretching across the sarcophagus. He thought, maybe it could be different if I could see your eyes, brother. As his grinding jaws mingled with a slob, intruding thoughts about Lazarus' condition yielded to contemplations about the living and the undead. Both had something in common, they were like old students.

As Lazarus ate, Darius considered faking his own death. He whispered, "I never wanted you to be something else, Lazarus. Perhaps I should take a ride with the call of a siren, or call to the fringes of outer space. Things might be different, purified into a place where souls go for refinement. Why did I listen to the selfish request? Devora is helpless without her total memory and believes she has immaculately conceived. If your condition as a dog remains, you will no longer walk with two legs, or even dance to a love song with your soul mate. Your own children will have no refuge in open arms. What have we done?"

Staring into the sea, he twitched the cotton bag from his hand. The past seemed tainted with vices, and with each breath, time moved slowly. It was in front of past challenges within sounds of rising and falling waves. The future was in so many ways unknown, and most days filled with Devora's hush;

She was no longer excitable. Silence had won her over with swelled billows on passing sea. Every handful to Lazarus' mouth made Darius focus on their future. Although blurred, there was one thing he had faith in, the spoken words of the eagle's promise.

Welcome To America

FOR THE LAST twenty-four hours, the tradesmen were talking about the port in Oakland California becoming a leading import- export gateway for worldwide containerships. As the ship moved toward the Oakland dock, Devora finally said something, "I'm hungry!"

Darius, responded, "Devora, we'll eat soon."

"Are we on the Mars yet? Give me that planet." She barked.

"I am no such fool, Devora! Puzzled, he scratched the top of his head. Was it the pleasure spirit or the seeds," Darius wondered.

"Welcome to America, Devora! The ship is preparing to dock."

"When will I see you again," she asked.

"Stay here, I need to get something," he said a husky voice and headed to the hold.

The *Lux* was wide open, and Lazarus was gone. It's nearby companion, a sarcophagus had also been disturbed. Darius would later return.

Angrily, he turned his head toward an echo someone was screaming, "What, motherfucker can't tell me nothing!"

"How could this be, miles across this damn sea? Poseidon, I do not understand. Where is Lazarus, Osiris?"

His tongue rolled, "Lazarus, Lazarus, Lazarus!"

Darius hurried to the dock, and roared into the open sky, "Dog, don't make me lose it. I will become a lion."

"What did you say?" An African American man asked. His manner emanated purpose. He was holding a stone box, not terribly large. A letter G engraved on top of it was shining brightly.

Lazarus stuck his head out from the west side of the dock.

"There you are!" Darius shouted.

Lazarus was hiding behind a wide basin. He panicked and plunged up to avoid the unexpected shots from a gun salute. His four paws hurried straight into town like he was throwing up war. The occasion for honors brought about more than eyes of chance.

Lazarus groaned, "The *Lux* never bled when I was inside of it, now I am outside of it, time may change me."

Standing in muddy water, Darius yelled, "No, Lazarus, don't run away, come with us!"

The young African American standing near a bicycle was wearing a rosary. His beads were lightly swinging over the stone box.

He said to Darius, "You may not believe this, but I was brought to this very circle to save your life. Hail Mary wants a rider!" His glow took Darius for a surprise.

Darius was unfamiliar with a Christian rosary, so he took it for an ankh.

"Young man, you look like a rider, do you own that bike?"

"Yes, Godspeed does not lack messengers or willing servants." He replied.

"You must be a brother with a purpose. Well, that dog of mine who just ran off, one day he will hope for change, and his transformation will happen in the land of the free. We have been at sea for eight long weeks. Although on this ship, in our time a mythic time, spells felt like eight years."

Darius took the young man by the shoulder, testing his wakefulness he patted his heart.

The young man answered, "Sounds like it was all a dream, if anything, I'll buy the sea. It's wide open! Look at it, my Egyptian brother, and have faith that your dog will find you! He shall mark his course clearly."

Suddenly, the young man blew into his stone box, laid it safely inside his basket and rode off. Darius composed himself. Visions of an American dream were replaced with panic. Darius quickly returned to the ship to get the Lux.

Devora had been alone much too long. The sight of her regal beauty and ladylike fingers cupping her pregnant belly helped him appreciate a very feminine profile. She was watching the port and a flock of seagulls. Her next motion was surprising. She untied her veil and threw it to the birds.

"Her gesture was ludicrous! Strange, I had a migraine, but the sight of her uncovered head and ringlets helped it to go away." Darius thought.

"Special lady, I must believe you are not for turning. Your action must be a sign of a newly expressed freedom!" His words were harsh but candid.

Suddenly, a slight breeze blew her veil toward an Asian teenager's lunch. The boy's sprint left Devora so amused that she thought her teeth would melt.

"Are you boys scared of ice grains?" She yelled below.

The teenager with a melancholy stare cried out to Devora, "I'll eat your ice cream if you eat my ice cream, but the most obvious challenge might come after having a mouth freeze!"

"Give me that ice cream," She said, thickly, holding out her hands in the distance.

A daring dockhand shouted loudly, "Shut your mouth! Hold up, chopsticks. Now she's got her nose up. Bet no one can do it like me! Now, welcome her to the neighborhood, biters."

A welcome committee on the dock of the bay locked arms beside the ship. They were dancing near a gutter shouting, "We're only dancing, and in dance, all people are not the same."

Others waved, and then there were the people who appeared each morning, waiting to sell ice cream, snickers bars, books, and flowers. It was a delicious sight.

A Trillion Things

AFTER THEIR ARRIVAL at the port twenty-five years ago, the family immediately took up residence in Oakland, California. Devora loved the new home. It was a mythical Queen Ann Victorian sitting on a cone-like hill. In the corner of the third story, there was a large bay window. Three windowpanes engaged a panoramic view of the settings in which they created their life. Darius renamed the estate Westside, never imagining the name would represent the entries of repentant souls. Darius had a big ego and did not need to be loved by anybody when it came to business. He was aware that a group of deceased religious people had once occupied the home.

It took seven days for the family to settle in. The *Lux* sat in the vestibule all seven days. Darius thought of Lazarus often as he passed it. On the eighth day, Devora hid it behind a door called *paramount*. The enchanted area was like threads entering a sewing needle.

Squinting into bright sunlight, Darius pondered the lives of the deceased religious people that had once lived there. He whispered, "How long will they mourn them? Nothing's up for discussion."

It was well over a hundred years ago when Count Shylock Gruden, a tight lip imposter, a striking laywoman, Nurse Birdie Collins, and six nuns ran a school at the Victorian. On July 16th, 1946, Darius decided he wasn't going to slip past an old glass jar any longer. It was tucked inside a stucco wall. Nothing there seemed neglected, except for this unforgettable glass jar that dominated his thoughts. The urge to open it swelled with sounds and the smells from the chimney. Preoccupation finally had its way. One casual morning in fall, he decided to pull it out. The jar felt cold, like a knife-sharp wind.

A presence behind him announced itself as *The Ghost of Westside*. Darius heard his introduction plainly. It was opposed to the calling of a champion.

"Don't do anything! What is inside the jar, is unseen because it is enclosed in darkness," the ghost said in a morose tone.

Darius went to his fireside chair and sat comfortably. Moving back his hips, he answered him in a strong tone while peeling off the cap, "It's cold as ice. I'd better be cautious."

His hands felt stuck before he moved them like his hip was a pencil.

"If I can't do anything, make it snow in this room. Then I'll sink my knees in the snow. I won't bind you by affection."

Darius was not a stranger to the supernatural, or its use of the dead, and their ability to speak in the spirit. Soon, light from a nearby window met a moldy cap between his very tight bite. His jaws used no restraint while picking through things carrying soot and dust. A light mystical smoke appeared over a folded newspaper article. The creased piece of newspaper was part of an enormous stash of color transparencies buried at the bottom of the jar.

"For Pharaoh sake, I can't lose these!" He sighed.

The very first transparency was a happy bride and groom on a ship. He fondly looked through all the transparencies, and carefully returned them to the bottom of the glass jar, and opened the newspaper article. A photograph inside the middle section of the article garnered his attention. Six individuals with their backs against a wall stood expressionless. Two stood like a familiar force. The title on the tabloid read, "The killer of Carondelet." It was dated 1890. Count Shylock Gruden, Nurse Birdie Collins, and six nuns had died from tuberculosis.

Fr. Louis Yafeu, Devora's spiritual mentor, advised Darius that only six deceased bodies were in cots, and then buried in the

Victorian's courtyard *Jacobs Garden*. One could see the tombstones at the crest of the hill from the upstairs windows. The graves were located in an old barn where old ship materials had been reconstructed with quality lumber. If one tilted their head and sized the crossbeams, the barn was the shape of a ship. Deeply etched on every single tombstone, was *Hoad Hellman*. Darius was shocked as hell and felt included in a proposed alliance.

He removed the jar cap from his jaws and muttered under his breath, "Will the world's ever learn? I don't need a first class clairvoyant. Aah eight people in this photograph. There are only six tombstones in the courtyard. I guess it was hard to kill on this block."

He twisted his goatee, and reached for his sweet Swisher, next to a cup of Swiss Miss hot cocoa.

"It's not snowing blood, and my shit is as smooth as a witness to pass a movement that passed. An Egyptian pact kept many off that heavenly stool. By good sense, temples were erected, and the builders did not get dropped into a blood- pot. In America I will do what I was created to do, to survive the rules of power without the blood! *God bless Jacobs Garden*, it shall always have the finest overseer, one that flawlessly follows up on things that remain to be seen."

An eerie haziness leaped into his stare, and the depth of his imagination and a practical world opened. He shifted his gaze back on the newspaper article, giving his attention to Count Shylock Gruden's front teeth. They were a little gapped; other teeth were unusually crooked and pointy. The Count was balding; some hair cropped to his skull draped from each side. Surrounding expressions of tolerant faced nuns wearing antique glasses looked frozen in time. They were standing close to a few rain boots lined up on the Victorian's porch. One nun had her mouth wide open as if she were shouting at someone. Something about Count Shylock and Birdie looked humorously astonished. This tic set them apart; they were marked. Darius immediately recognized the mark. It was time, and time changes everything.

It was right before five when Devora's cackle passed through the hallway. It sounded like a play to pay shrill down the backs of every ass born from a five-dimension spread. Darius gave another sharp look at the photo and then turned it around on its backside. Fading letters read, *I drink Jewish blood*, my soul craves salted almonds.

Darius could make heroes who could catch his handkerchief before it fell to earth. He turned toward the scales that only heaven could produce, folded the newspaper article and sighed, "Ghost, as soon as the undead find out I have published first, the living shall happily come see us. Do not try to overpower my family. We are more than clairvoyants, or building blocks within this mysterious process of understanding all things, including governing the living, dead, and undead."

The Ghost of Westside quickly trailed off with nothing human but his long shadowy nose. The transparencies in the glass jar began to glow. If the transparencies could talk, they might have said, "*The Ghost of Westside* had created hatred among them."

Darius sensed that any judgments left up to God, and his wedding guests were never lost, but always found in time through his discoveries.

He considered, "Vampires are here in the United States of America! I suppose it is not so simple to take a dead species and make enough of them, so they do not die of isolation. They will find an environment that is convenient enough, compared to that which they once wandered."

Darius bowed his head and brooded over an encounter which took place in being, and in time. All of the Mint of Zeb were aware of the event. Two-time travelers from Europe landed in a secret Egyptian underground cave called SOS. They had discovered a complex system of Yu and Sa priests. Also, alchemists lived among sixty-seven confined Vampires, BCE. The time travelers used the crypt as their next vortex for the living and the dead. They understood that succeeding in the cave was not enough. It was about how they succeeded, and how much they succeeded.

In the far reaches of the incredibly large dim cave, there was a tomb. In the past, it served as a link for cruel Vampiric experiments performed by selected priests of Yu and Sa tribes. For centuries rare forms of experimentations took place. There were no real winners in that area of the tomb. The underground conclave was sequestered. In a span of one thousand years, the conclave was extracted from being in ordinary time.

The surviving leaders would eventually tell the peoples of Mint of Zeb an extraordinary story of an extra-terrestrial appointment which produced massive, mysterious components. In one isolated moment, unusual elements caused an event that to this day offers more than feeding frenzies to beguile human minds. Eons ago, the tooth-rattling eruption released sixty-seven Vampires into an unexpected fate of coming carnage. The surge formed a swirling windstorm, producing an opening for a great escape. The Vampires, acting without a moment of hesitation, quickly settled in the caves catacombs near the eldest of its species. The catacombs were below a massive tomb.

After the eruption, a mushroom of cerulean smoke quickly summoned the time-travelers to hide under a blue velvet burial garment. Light and time moved fast within a mythical shield that no one before them had ever experienced. Then out of the smoke came vivid reflections of their past that began to mimic their present. The impressions inched closer and closer to the burial garment in which they were sheltered. A powerful optical bender inside the garment forced their reflections to face an unexplainable mystery above the cerulean smoke. It was the Mystery of *Those Who Must Be Kept* that pursed their lips and gobbled past reflections whole, causing an audible snap, hurling the time-travelers out of the cave into a 3 1/2 mile long tunnel sealed in granite blocks. It was about sixty feet above ground over hundreds of sarcophagi. The tunnel-guarded secrets that were made of nightmares that no one should experience. During their rapid walk through the tunnel, a race against centuries of time combing through mysteriously would soon propel them out of the tunnel. After landing safely, the time travelers came to their senses, one turned to the other then roared into the nervous sky, "As long as we are together the rest can go to Hades. We can never be apart, or lose each other for the wrong reasons, for we've been confronted by terrifying figures, and have escaped a horrifying death!"

More apprehension set in when they saw small holes forming inside their palms. The bleeding was from landing wounds. They wiped their wet cheeks and bloodied palms on the burial garment. When their palms touched the garment, their holes closed then quickly healed. Unbeknownst to the time travelers, the blue-velvet burial garment was holy cloth. Many Sa and Yu priests and alchemists were afraid to touch it, due to its extraordinary power. Customarily the burial garment remained untouched. Its physical might and extraordinary restorative powers frightened most in the conclave. It also terrified the time-travelers when they saw their wounds miraculously close and leave no hints of tissue scarring. With great uncertainty, they folded and left the blood covered garment in the tunnel. Following a long paved granite flooring, east, toward the rising sun, they finally found a safe shelter.

The travelers eventually landed back home in the Carpathian Mountains. Their desire to one day return to the cave and achieve profit from the perilous cosmic fallout was essential. They supposed the explosion had killed everything inside the cave. However, Vampires do not die, a few ugly priests lived, and the Yu and Sa priests would one day make many to understand why.

Oddly, the after effects of the explosion caused the confined plasma eaters in the cave to lose the desire for human blood. Many of the Yu and Sa priests and alchemists rejected burnt offerings. Other confined humans also declined sustenance. Nevertheless, the explosion produced a red mercury substance. Its canal was long. A small number of surviving wet-cheeked ugly priests emerged carrying more jerking bodies to confined Vampires. The ugly priests were disappointed at the Vampires rejection of human blood, and it left them with nothing to do. All the while, the alchemist encouraged the remaining Yu and Sa priests to consume what was available. It was hard to predict what the ugly priests would eat. It was like asking what would a chimp do in a library.

The red mercury creep was slow. Once it gained momentum, it spread rapidly. After seconds within its grip, the confined Vampires had already begun to melt from willful starvation. Together, the meltdown of fluid was enormous. When the liquid reached dead human bodies, many living humans were also soaking in the melt, and dying slowly. The combined remains and submerging parts of the earth with red mercury were fatal in and of itself. Within days it turned into a blood-orange marmalade and liquefied, creating a lush river where bats from the catacombs fed and grew strong.

    The time travelers did not belong to the Egyptian cave's thirst to caress or crush. At home in a district, east in the midst of the Carpathian Mountains was one of the wildest and least known areas in Europe. The tangled buried wilds of an ancient and unspoiled area were preserved in an arc of untamed wilderness. The labyrinth's eternal landscape and lively pale moons that had triggered the medieval times to yield had awakened. It was 1945 when the time-travelers landed back into the unchanged world of chasms and crypts of debt. After disappearing from the massive and mysterious cave in Egypt, they feverishly fed their domes with plausible answers concerning the horrible research and experiences in BCE. They agreed that some Yu and Sa priests were murderers and that the ugly priests were like apes in velvet, doomed to repeat their heinous acts of unspeakable alchemy. The time-travelers believed, later using a time machine, research, and intense study of ancient writings, they could calculate a successful plan and returned to Egypt to stop the horrible Vampire experiments. Unto the people of the Carpathians, they promised to one-day return, and bring them the best of the beginning and the end of which is to come.

    Upon their return to the underground cave, earth shaking as it was, neither the Yu nor Sa priests or alchemist had disposed of the leftover remains, leaving the travelers an unusual opportunity to observe the salt of the earth's intercession. As helium and other elements spouted from the travelers hovering machine, they watched new elements combine, erupt, and disappear.

    From their machine windows, the travelers pitched a special concoction of salt. The concoction combusted quickly, as if it was fire smoking gas and then busting. Soon Egyptian soil from the earth's muddy water combined with a special concoction made in Europe finalized the mysterious consumption. Minutes after the elemental breakdown in the underground cave, floating objects appeared out of the burst of energy. Dissipating vortices impelled them to commit and play the Vampires advocate. Like one kind of people, disbanding vortexes agreed that compassion drew the time-travelers to the cave. Traveling through the enormous cave inside their time machine, they eventually came upon many priests loaded to the teeth with weaponry. The priests were dazed, confused, and jealous when they saw the time-travelers hovering over their charms and advancements. While the machine traveled throughout, the ugly priests and alchemists attempted to block all innovative efforts to learn more about the vortices and Vampire species. After weeks of wandering through different areas of the cave, the travelers returned once again to the region of ugly priests who had disappeared without a logical explanation. Only a couple of visible Yu and Sa and a pair of alchemists had discontinued all inhumane testing. They speculated that if the ugly priests were just cloaked in darkness, like armored talking heads between galaxies and dark matter, two Sa and Yu priests were different from all of them. They were righteous in all their undertakings and walked humbly with God. Together with a few alchemists they collected and stored the remaining weaponry, and fearlessly began helping the time- travelers. All efforts to continue empathetic experiments with the red mercury river and remains carried on like tumbleweeds rolling past human resource struggles. They worked fanatically to bring an understanding of the condition of the species. The time travelers' unorthodox experimentations, grounded in their own magnetism, science, and other natural forces, went on for years. Their commitment to empirical exploration, esoteric technology, and insightful invention was a communal undertaking with the righteous Yu, and Sa priests and the last of their alchemists. The undertakings brought them all significantly closer to understanding the species condition. The eldest Vampires who were colder than the moon, living in hidden areas of the catacombs, were exceptionally intelligent. For a time, they could exist on exotic states of special material, matter, absorbing through slits in the catacombs, and the red mercury river. The original Vampire species agreed among each other not to destroy the time machine or kill the team of hard workers. Instead, the species observed their experiments in secret.

Through an unknown mystery, the Vampire species began to perceive human compassion and boldness. The eldest carved solar discs on the stone caves in some tombs. This was done for the honor and compassion of the ugly priests and alchemists, which they would one day consume out of necessity for what was done to their captured members. The eldest of the species did not understand forgiveness or mercy. It was not demonstrated when they had been confined. Yet, it was morning, and in the evening they would see a beautiful spectacle.

That fated night in the underground, out of fearlessness and dynamic elements, a Vampire named Julius The Handsome, was cast down by the time-travelers into the catacombs. For the first time in ordinary time, he placed his feet on solid ground. Rising from muddy waters, in a secret region of the *SOS* underground cave, the amazing beast, who thinks for himself slipped his chain, and soared. He was a remarkable thing, a redeemer of Vampires.

After the making of Julius, the eldest Vampires placed the spectacular golden torc around his nude waist and became psychic companions to him and the time-travelers. The species remained invisible but were satisfied with the methods the travelers used while creating their unburied treasure, Julius. He was free, separate, independent, powerfully intelligent, beautiful, oddly compassionate, but calculating. The status of human beauty and compassion the eldest Vampires would never possess nor desired to. Their beauty was unworldly, magical, and untouchable. It did not belong to the Julius. The time-travelers produced the air of an oracle which composed a spring of mystery inside of Julius. The travelers were the only ones who held the mysteries to further other secrecies which could enable the eldest Vampires to advance conditions beneficial to all on earth. In Julius, they were sure to find a cure to wane appetites for the blood thirst that they craved. After all, it was far better to breed and linger in the catacombs feeding off of exotic states of special matter, than to awaken wicked humans who once held them captive to cruel experiments inside a huge amount of gravity working to hold the thirst in place.

In the night where they first met Julius, they all gathered around him passing on survival knowledge. In time, the upgraded Julius would learn to see all things from the authority of eldest species and become all things to *Those Who Must Be Kept*. Far into the future,

Julius left the SOS underground screaming, "Where do I go, where do I go from here, makers of mine!"

The eldest remained, and to this day they are at peace, waiting to consume the greater beast of time, an illusion, that held them to the great lie of an ugly humanity. Any dead, cold, flat bloodsuckers surviving after the making of Julius, endeavoring to slay, or destroy him, might meet a time, a mythic time, where they all might die into the mystery of *Those Who Must Be Kept*. How to get back to the loving truth of what happened would take place in black print, through the wide-open fiery eyes of Julius. A light to their feet had always been the undercover daddy long leg to them all. His light did not make him feel like he was wasting space on the earth after all.

Only hours after Julius left the SOS, the time travelers hovered over an area in the cave and heard groaning coming through open slabs inside a tomb. A pair of surviving Sa priests isolated within cried out to the time travelers,

"Consume us from the inside out, and may darkness tremble inside the black hole within the catacombs! The experiments did not save us from the shapeless mass of melt or the remains seeping through our cell. There was a bucket of blood near, and at the sound of your coming we threw it over the spreading mass, it is now turning into black oi, which we shall consume within minutes."

With a crescent of moonlight slanting through the ancient slab, the two Sa priests drew their last human breath. Darkness was their canvas and a little light became an encounter to poison them in traps. The melt reached their bodies. Soon after, they awakened to a new prison, a subordinate form called *Fly by Nights*.

The time-travelers roared, "We have used the light sources! The essence of all good strategy is simplicity. Don't change the recipe of the very first recipe. The ugly priests were an abomination, the apes are dead, and a worthy language not translated into a machine from another language will survive."

They continued their travels inside the time machine with the loyal righteous Yu and Sa priests and the pair of alchemists. Later, they created a powerful society inside a single holy pyramid within the Egyptian cave. If anything decided to destroy the holy pyramid, it would be a death sentence and awaken killing squads. There the conclave continued to explore the mastery of their works and creative range. Their works produced another bell-shaped flying time machine. Everyone involved marveled at its ingenuity. In ordinary time, they could ascend from the pyramid into a hidden paradise above *SOS*, called *Labyrinth*. The *Labyrinth*, like a great flying bird of glowing material, was also a living organism floating inside and outside of cerulean skies. There, intangible energy was created and harnessed. A great conclave seeks immortals to live and work there. These bright Immortals have raw courage, enjoy their work, and have complete mastery over cerulean energy, which among other substantial things can be directed to manifest powerful forms of life and death on earth. Inside the *Labyrinth,* cerulean energy can be created, and even direct cerulean smoke before its advent in other spheres. The immortals out of cerulean skies are simply majestic and reveal understanding and light to those who choose to walk the dead and undead for purposes of getting and bringing understanding to humanity. The *Labyrinth* became a beautiful living paradise for the time-travelers, *Those Who Must Be Kept,* and a crew of immortals, who are the guardians of cerulean energy.

Later in time after gaining understanding, findings, and observations of good works, the Yu and Sa priests departed the *Labyrinth* in the bell time-machine, and fire descended from the sky. Their landing in the ancient region of Egypt was successful, and they began to develop the civilization from which the descendants of Darius and Devora lived and ruled, the Mint of Zeb. To this day, the bell secretly resides in the *Temple of Essen.*

The time travelers from Europe promised the loyal Sa and Yu priests that they too would one day visit a garden outside the SOS. In Egypt, nothing of a legalistic religious nature happened during BCE. Nevertheless, west of the SOS cave, something spiritual happened. In the magnificent bell- time machine, as promised, the Yu and Sa priests saw a large desert garden. 187 blood- bought royal Egyptians lived there and believed they were a part of a body, soul, and divinity that had not been born, only acknowledged as a gift to them. The spirit of the body was and is still in time, and would come from

Nazareth. When the time-travelers saw this miracle praised from their time machine they marveled, and understood that this God-man was Jesus Christ, the savior of the world from a time in which they lived, ate, and drank from in the Carpathian Mountains. Would those that came after understand? The travelers set their course before leaving with the intangible power source of faith traveling within and outside the *Labyrinth*. Later, they settled in Egypt to participate and help reveal sacred scripture. This word they knew existed, it fell like fire descending from the sky. The accounts were also revealed in the 187 blood-bought giants in BCE who proceeded the Nazareth. The time-travelers would one day offer the knowledge to further the spiritual developments in Mint of Zeb's vastly wealthy empire, and there would be a price, a need for those who were called to willingly suffer in Jesus Christ. Julius did not qualify, but once in a blue moon, he'd soon fight those who imposed unnecessary suffering.

 The aftermath of the explosion from the electro-fluid of cerulean energy was changing daily to red smoke. It lingered within the catacombs for some time. After the departure of both time machines, the red smoke began to rise out of the cave. It linked for a portion of time in the form of a cloud which hovered over the 187 ten feet tall, royal Egyptians. They gestured in unison at the process of liquidating the Vampiric species. It was so amazing how they naturally responded to wandering smoke that virtually spilled over them while fumes forced their nostrils to inhale slightly as if something foreign was sucking water out of their nasal tissues. It was not poisonous but was an assuring sign, taken as an indication that Vampiric bodies had vanished. Leftover golden ashes fell upon their faces, it became their glow of glory and their hearts filled with gladness. Clothed by golden halos from the spirit of Osiris, they walked toward the cave. However, the 187 blood-bought Egyptians never really knew if the Vampires from *SOS* disappeared. They only felt that if any Vampires or humans had vanished from the underground city, they were not dead, and a part of the undead. Centuries ago, tablets written in Cartouche said if the true sacrificial body which had not been born yet did not convert appointed energy, power might get misused. In other words, with no bodily form, Vampires or humans linked to the catacombs could potentially become a team with entities from the catacombs of understanding agreeing to work with them. Yet, the blood- bought Egyptians hope was in a Holy unborn merciful, forgiving, conditional body. The main condition was suffering. The moon nor the sun could not devour the heavenly body, and would later arrive to willingly die for their sins and the sins of the whole world. One Creator had put the beginning and the end in his being. The 187 giants lifted up their voices for all the glory because they had faith that he was worthy. The future world might obey his reason for coming or not. He was the godman to love, a savior of souls for those that believed, and he would come from Nazareth. Would those who came after understand why they praised the King of Jews? Other giants believed life on earth was a constant overcoming of suffering through the godman.

Suddenly smoke billowed from the photograph. While staring at Count Shylock's teeth, Darius' energy felt sapped a bit. The very sight of them appeared to boil down to a few words, his eternal power, and money. He broke his thoughts of his past in Egypt. Darius was a master at the discipline of exercising spiritual power. His ability to recuperate from supernatural attacks was unmatched. He permitted himself a sigh of relief and spat into his hanky. Finishing the waning sweet swisher, he noticed the fringes of his lamb's wool shawl starting to unravel, and used the cigar to cauterize the excess fabric. One last draw aroused his lips, to force the bunt to drop like ash. His brash cough overpowered the loud children splashing outside in soapsud puddles. When his dry throat settled, he raised from his chair, pulled back thick bone drapes and pondered. Vampiric entities are a strange element to be permitted by God in every time, but it is nothing that I am going to get hung up on. Countless of them have adapted like accident murderers, or organisms having miraculous capabilities resembling makeovers. For some, their flesh does not change when injured. Others come in sheep's clothes, wearing the guise of a mortal. However, they are not mortal. Certain ones are so advanced they lure humans like flies to toad tongues. These are the great pretenders, portraying to serve humanity, but their agenda is to consume like a market without mercy for its game. *Those Who Must Be Kept*, in the cerulean skies outside of time when awakened, do not oppose their champion. They give life or wipe it out. Sadly, the nuns were prey and vexed by dust that had not settled.

A Bible verse recited by Devora entered his thoughts, **"I am sending you out like sheep among wolves. Therefore, be as shrewd as snakes and as innocent as doves."**

The children's laughter faded. He continued to place mental stock in elusive moments. Closing the drapes, he shrank back into his chair and cuddled a wool Christmas blanket. The scatter of frolicking children calmed him. A long silence urged him to cross his bony arms, with two thumbs up and fifteen minutes behind, he tightened the newspaper under his armpit then scooted the rocking chair over to the front room window. The spirits of the transparencies whooshed out of the jar, then spoke in unison. "By reaching for God, the all-knowing, the nuns may have known something, even if their reach fell short. Sure, the flesh was destroyed, but not their souls. Like a huge centipede embarking on a nocturnal hunt, darkness outmaneuvered them, but evil destroyed the school. Fr. Louis and the church must not allow them to slip into purgatory. His priestly order is the last defense against malevolent forces. Darius, you are like a lion and a fox, just watch and see! There is no double reality bone inside your body."

Darius answered, "Sounds like a necessary recipe for happiness, go on!"

The spirits answered, "One day you shall be called to go to a secret area in the east, far side of Romania. Heed the call, for the view, is spectacular. You shall meet Julius' order, the Jesuits. They educate good students and are friends. In this secluded area, you shall find the good Queen of Gypsies. She sees the personal spirituality of all and takes advantage of the circumstances that the Sovereign God of the Carpathian Mountains offered. The Queen of Gypsies is in excellent physical shape and has infatuating bright eyes. She is also a prominent member of the ruling class. They shall treat you as one of their own. Her trusted Kingdom is never conquered. Neither is the Jesuit order which she has helped to flourish. The Kingdom reflects the *Queen of Song*. In return, the people of the mountain bless the order with treasures and music which they all hold as a symbol of their eternal way. The rhythm of the night, young and old contentedly covered in a bearskin, dance to share this eternal gift. A Sovereign God gave them this system. The night dance of their enemies willingly succumb to and obediently serve Romania's Kingdom in the afterlife. The enemies' wealth and power have always belonged to the Gypsy Queens ruling class. Actions of great men helped her acquire power in ways only known to those who like to work with examples inside the mountains surrounding comforts. Her teeth glisten beautifully, and power is the Queen of Gypsy's eternal friend. After enemies give beautiful things back to the Kingdom, she puts compassion back in. The Kingdom that has always been produces room for all that ever was; beauty, grace, and fulfillment. Listen attentively to the Queen of Gypsies, she knows and shall tell you stories of processions throughout the Mountain, and of a committee of the pious Jesuits of Rumania who have remained long by her side. These special Jesuits do not interfere with governmental affairs. Their role is to educate groups of poor people who come from caves to learn new ways. The poor tribe's radiant bright blue eyes can create light inside and outside the mountain. Like the polar night, this comforts *Those Who Must Be Kept* and the Queen of Gypsies. For centuries bright light has gladdened the hearts and shined on the committee of Jesuits. Pay attention, Darius, the Queen of Gypsies, must not slip into purgatory, and shall never enter hell. You both are earth and heaven bound to majestic threads of wisdom, understanding, trust, and eternal bounty. Your Kingdoms have always been on earth and in heaven. One in your glad clan will discover this secret and is to become heir to guardians who shall send her many wonderful things. Another in this glad clan belongs to somebody of flesh and blood and feelings, a marvelously prolific creature. Members that come after every generation shall discover the secret, and surround their life force around this exclusive way of a prosperous life. Once discovered, it is the discoverer's time to reap the fullness of all a Sovereign God offered. The sky is the limit. A sudden windfall cut off and silenced death gods nigh the sky, leaving behind shadows on a wall of one truth.

Darius ride with Romania's high-strung filly. Like lips around a cigar, a forked tongue parted the sea to explore. What is your price for not accepting the eternal ride? We shall tell you: fifty death gods, and they shall return to *Jacobs Garden* as givers of many precious metals to ensure a prosperous future for the glad one. Now, pull back the curtain and stand tall. Look at the gardens fullness. Like a court jester, the wall shall humor the glad clan. A secret constellation shall be the great inheritor of its pure majesty. For that reason, Julius shall defend it, until Christ the ruler returns. The secret constellation must never be harmed, suffer too long or be destroyed! A Sovereign God offered everlasting life and great treasures to this constellation. If deliberately harmed Jerusalem shall be consumed, and the earth will quickly starve until lavish means are returned to the constellation. A powerful Galaxy reemerges as the luckiest Galaxy in time. It was written Jerusalem is Holy. Chosen earthlings must help Holy Jerusalem from destruction. *Those Who Must Be Kept* and the constellation shall reap and govern a flourishing nation on a renewed land on the earth, under the sun near the thriving Galaxy. Darius, your clan, is untouchable, unsinkable, and uncrushable. Like a bear's bite with fruit between its teeth, Devora is to preserve and reap. If offerings and regalia in our Galaxy are stolen, or trampled by the odor of the thief, like the clearance of poetry the thief shall devour strange fruit. Royalty passed on stranger fruit and its blood pool, another cover it with patches for a sick bed that stole Christmas where no one sells souls because souls were already purchased."

The spirits could see Darius' brain working. He let out a soft breath, "I shall not doom myself and go after darkness or Vampire. My life, like sunshine, comes to me. The best recipe for happiness is a Sovereign God. I shall one day bless our secret constellation with wisdom and treasures. It shall be through our glad Clan. My feet walked in both worlds down the Victorian's hallway and even strolled the basement, which is another story as someone else holds that key. Now, I shall grow colder without Lazarus, as it was I who betrayed him."

Darius folded the Christmas blanket with the intentions of later burying it with a hope chest in *Jacobs Garden*.

He sat the article down on his thigh. More invisible eyes jolted from the jar. The spirits of the transparencies whooshed out the window and then back into the glass jar. Darius' eyes glared at Birdie Collins high boots in the photo. Count Shylock's ivory-tipped cane appeared to be plucking one boot tip like merchandise, trading starched collars for prison stripes. The Count looked like he just didn't know what to do. Between them was a Persian cat. The pussy's bone chilling stare seized Birdie's devilish wave, and its long tail pointed like a boss to trite religious lives. Later, Fr. Louis informed Darius that Birdie Collins high boot kissed more than Count Shylock Grudens' cane.

Fr. Louis Close Up

LOUIS YAFEU WAS born in West Africa. From the time he could stand, he was baptized in a world of spiritual warfare. He spent most of his youth and early adult life in Germany. His mother, Emelia Steiff, was born in Berlin. She was a German missionary, and while spreading the gospels in Yorubaland, she met and married Abiodun who was of West African and English descent.

Shortly after they were married, their son Louis was born, then Abiodun went missing. The tribes were told of a rumor that snails or cannibals had eaten him. On that ill-fated day, Emelia never saw any left- overs. She and her son settled in Heidelberg. Its reputation as a residence of intellect was on top of the world. Louis prided himself on its reflections and virtue. His mother had exposed him to Christian values and German folklore. She equally reminded him of legends surrounding his father's African ancestors.

One story he cherished was a legend about beautiful talking blue & black twin snail- like beings. Many members of Abiodun's tribe did not have faith in the legend and considered it heresy. Neighboring tribes said the legend caused mass hallucinations. Not until darkness weathered the glow of fire would night calls toward perfection awake believers who went one way, unbelievers went another.

The storytellers spoke of a race of intelligent influences descending out of the sky. Traveling at the speed of light to descend into stunning groundwater caves, the life forms fashioned crystal skulls and sculptures. Their unseen authorities mirror a vigorous planetary scene. Tall, beautiful blue & black twin beings levitate up during bursts of radiation from the sun. When the solar flares recede, time bends. The complex social organisms successfully travel into space through a golden disk, then back down to beautiful caves leaving behind thick unusual foaming waves. Radiation never affects the beings, the substance does not pass through their traveling vessel. Only on the occasion to make a deal with gods will they venture out of the cave from tombs of resurrections, and into cities. Much like bones meeting Mephistopheles at the crossroads, it's rare and special.

This legend was important to Emelia and Louis. As a hard working teacher, she strained over the circumstances of Abiodun's disappearance and decided never to tell Louis of the alleged cannibalism. She believed her husband's mission was to prove the existence of the blue & black twins and discover caves in subterranean portals which might link to a hidden world of crystal skulls and statues. Extraterrestrial exploration gave way to his departure. Ultimately, it made room for household rhymes, songs, and folktales to spread in Africa and at home. His parting also helped her to renew her faith in Jesus Christ and the belief of sons and daughters of God.

After living a refined life with Louis for many long years, on the eve of Christmas, Emilia's ageless body was taken up. He was twenty-one when her supernatural parting occurred.

He asked lovingly, "Mother, who knows how to make flowers stay? I saw you coming back to me. I found eternal life in all that you taught me. You, my hidden treasure, have become heaven's highest crystal jeweled angel, a friend to the Nazarene. Archangel Michael now holds another mighty amethyst military scepter, and walks and talks with you."

After her passing, Louis passionately searched for divine instruction and understanding. He attended a private religious university in Heidelberg, spoke German, English, and French. He was elegant, possessed a photographic memory, and was the tallest man at the University. Louis respected the intellectual side of things and had accomplishments in metaphysics, classical music, and hand-to-hand combat.

While World War II and profanity- peppered rants, hemmed the ears of those who peered close, he took a peculiar turn and accepted an internal discipline as a Jesuit priest. He had an uncanny ability to deflect scrutiny and decided to join the male religious order. He didn't have a problem with the forces of the Catholic order, and felt united there, in a time in history where everything appeared divided. At the time of Louis' ordination, the Nazi party had declared the Jesuit order public vermin. He was living in a time where the meaning of love was trying to be understood and decided not to allow public persecution to reduce his enthusiasm. A swastika above his church alter helped him to meditate more deeply while drinking in the purity of what was offered to him. The Catholic Church was most captivated with his ancestry, and his installation as a Jesuit afforded great opportunities as a world traveler and spiritual mentor.

Eventually, his vocation aligned him as the leading exorcist in San Francisco, California. However, his position was concealed due to the nature of a special kind of spiritual warfare.

Part of Fr. Louis' obligation was to look after the Victorian in Oakland, Ca. It was part of a large logistic operation within the Catholic Church. Much time had passed since the mansion had been occupied.

When he met Darius and Devora, he was sure that a rare opportunity to honor actions of greatness and mysteries were present. After only a few meetings with the couple, he shifted the Victorian into their care. The only condition that came with the Victorian was that Darius could not open one door inside of it, called the *paramount* unless Fr. Louis showed him the way and offered him the key. This door like a double reality was behind a wall that led to a private chamber. A magnetic force emanated from the wall. Fr. Louis gave Devora the key because he understood that she had already been called to a peculiar mystery. Indeed, she knew the way of the same spiritual ranking.

There were other doors in the Victorian, and Darius passed through those freely. However, the mystery of time was extraordinary as it powered through the *paramount* door. Former things that had expired were given and made new again, and the perfection of totality was there. It was also necessary for time to change, and for each one who entered or departed to receive what was their own, and everything enrolled in advance.

Wisdom urged Fr. Louis and Devora to move the box of Lux, beneath a blue velvet garment inside another miraculous door. The Lux behind the *paramount* door reflected many mysteries including time travel. Most significantly, souls were redeemed from the power of the grave by a redeemer who offered a little wonder, Holy blood.

Whenever the Lux bled, time altered and hidden dimensions transformed beyond metaphysical weight or measure. Its authority could return with another day for keepers of *Justice*. This was something beyond anything any mortal could ever fathom. The *Lux*, also like Mint of Zeb's ancient pyramids', resonated with many planets striking a cosmic navigational portrait of the past and present.

Flickering Against The Unknown

DEVORA'S FIRST FEW months in America could not compare to the ceremonials of her Egyptian past. Within six months, and only one month before giving birth, the Victorian's library took her for surprise reflections. The world of books helped her to adjust to a new life. It was remarkable how she assimilated and transformed the drafty Victorian into a great household. In just a short period she adapted to her new world in Oakland, California.

One early evening an unexpected hail began thrashing against the upstairs windows. The huge drops of hail did not distract Devora's interest in a book titled *Machiavelli Rage*. Like millions dreaming in the ceiling, the plot about hunting the wicked was very intriguing. Hour after hour, her focus deepened. A leftover smell of chimney smoke loomed. It spouted a long forgotten memory of a once enjoyable hash high. Devora, an observer of reality from a distance, was riddled with questions about the book. She rocked inside a fastened rocking chair. It was strange that the old rocker was bolted to the library's floor, and could rock. The chair was out of place, it even seemed out of ordinary time. Unable to break her attention from the book, she reached for a stuffed dumpling on a side table. It fell from her soft grasp. She whipped around long back and forth seconds picked up the dumpling from the floor and ate like an event that was close to time.

It did not take long before she heard a whisper, "We like to go slow." She turned the light toward her head. Makeup fell off her face.

Snubbing the voice, she answered, "Why would someone bolt a rocking chair to the floor, in front of this library?"

Hundreds of blood-curdling novels and pocketbooks were in front of her.

"I bet it was not to save the day like this fairytale novel at hand's reach," she exhaled and eyed a *Grimm's Fairy Tales* book. Grinning half-way, she sighed, "The fiery elements of *Machiavelli Rage*, will not prevent me from reading the whole book. The knowledge of good and evil must be examined! My God does not want us to give up our free will."

The whispering apparition had entered the library from behind the *paramount*. The presence had achieved admission inside ordinary time through her ancestral box of *Lux*. In a whisper, he introduced himself as "*The Ghost of Westside*."

His shadowy long nose glanced downward, he supposed the book was written for a shrewd generation, for those who were born not by usual means, nor by generational preference, nor by a man's decision. The fiend had gained days inside the city of Oakland. The box of *Lux* gave him free rein, and he was now ready to find anyone who was full of wonder, dread, and fascination.

At the sight of the moon, he peered in close sneering, "Hey, dumpling, you best appeal. This thing is bigger than a beatnik party. I am unable to take on the skin of men, but, years ago, my tush sat in your rocking chair. A Bishop buried my flesh in *Jacob's Garden*. Later he bolted the chair to the floor. Glad to see the bent oak rocker runners are still rocking!"

Devora groaned under her breath without looking up. She knew *Machiavelli Rage* was more than beatnik party. It was thoroughly fortified, a sure thing that paired *Justice* with a Holy Army. Devora was like its ring of host that desired to win *Justice* by signing on as a keeper. With her pledge, *The Ghost of Westside* projected a vision. He desired forgiveness through observation of the words in the book. He was once a Rabbi, famed for leaving traces of himself behind every corner of the world. He sold scroll cases containing esoteric wisdom and wrote pocketbooks of convoluted verses known for promoting psychological soil where trickery flourished. Some of his pocket books were still in the library. Years ago he was made a captive of the Victorian, tied to the rocking chair and left to die like a bent twig.

Peace, Truth, and *Justice* had always been her clan's mission. Might Devora now be a witness to a ghost's bloody revenge, right outside an American window? She trembled, deciding the mysteries of *Machiavelli Rage*, held divine instructions on how to stay alive in this land of vampirism, protect human innocence, and defeat evil aimed at her family. The cosmic horror book was a phenomenon. Every page oozed authority, and left her thinking out loud, "What is an American prayer? I am afraid of Americans, not hauntings, or ghosts with manageable information.

What's more, my clan does not desire submission from ghosts looking for absolution. *Die Nuss* is light years beyond every ancient method of spiritual protection. Even magical spells do not work against us."

Devora's ancient bloodline history understood the rising levels of her own rage-required acknowledgment. To change the present, by faith, she might use the necessary elements of any matter to supernaturally hurl righteous indignation into the future, and past. *Machiavelli Rage* like the present was alive and stirred guesswork with an aura of mystery of the forbidden. This wonder was one of the more intriguing leads to come out of the story's message, which resonated with her experience as a hunted sort in Egypt. However, above everything else she read in the book, she was joined by one powerful sentence, "You don't hunt something that you want to catch, you hunt to kill."

She understood *Justice* was in the book and sensations had choices, because everybody had choices, especially in America. Confident this statement was sustenance, she finished the novel with the belief that in America, hunting the wicked reaped something bigger than a beatnik party. In the land of runaway Pharaohs, hunting the wicked was treasured and rewarded, especially by the Sa. She stood up. Her breath hitched in her esophagus slowed. The shadowy hallway outside the library was untouched by fading chimney smoke. It was as if the invisible watcher had fueled his stench to withdraw into stolen drama.

The Ghost of Westside had caught her attention. He taunted, "Your clan can't even bear the idea of one less smile in the world."

She answered softly, "The Yu are peacemakers, not killers. We have always examined the stages of life with questions. Questions are inspiring, and much hinges on communicating with any enemy, including Vampires. *Ghost of Westside*, you, must submit to the blood of Christ who came into the world to forgive you. He is my defender, and he makes me want to shout, for all his glory. I can't just throw all that away."

His hair-raising answer was bloodcurdling "The forefather, ho hum! So, my dear gatekeeper joined at the hip to humans. If there is no change in humanity, then there is no doubt human ugliness will slop up at any hole in the wall. America shall witness a battery of running blood! It will become raw profit for assassins under duress perpetuating barbarism and human indecency. Rage rules and I am its prince. Vampires follow the smell of blood."

Devora answered, "My beautiful tribe, the Yu, are descendants of the royal bloodline. We have pursued *Justice* and peace. If I am to continue to pursue *Justice* which has been set up in advance and peace, there will come a time where I shall say America is not right all the time. What will become of my own generations, influenced by their horrors? I shall prepare my daughter. The Yu tribe has already prepared a name for her. It is Galaxy, and those that are loved by her are safe from predators. I shall likewise ensure her way into the *Paramount* by offering her the key. My daughter is destined to carry on in our old ways of spiritual battle. Our secret method of old will never be forgotten for we learned it by the ancient Yu and Sa priests, who established Mint of Zeb in Egypt. These priests were like tics, and we have the tics of all their courage. Indeed, we are the original and greatest Vampire slayers who ever lived."

The Ghost of Westside thought, "I am mildly awed by her hutspâ and shall watch over her!"

Beyond the walls, *The Ghost of Westside* sensed Fr. Louis approaching.

Devora's heart started beating rapidly against her chest. It felt like it was going to shatter when thinking of the world her daughter may need to prepare for. Suddenly, dripping from a leaky roof in the attic forced her to look up. The droplets fell on top of the book. Her bottomless brown eyes sealed off space above. Seconds later her attention landed on the page that held the flourishing Nile River from where divine power emerges. *The Ghost of Westside* peered back into his own discovery of the power she held, then disappeared.

A hard knock interrupted her thoughts. A sigh of relief followed. It was Fr. Louis.

"Come in Fr. Louis, I was just finishing a book about hunting the evil in fate, and those who create hatred among people." It was hidden like a precious jewel in between other great books.

"Ah, *Machiavelli Rage*, the sun of the creator comes. You have discovered something of immense value. This library once belonged to Count Shylock Gruden, and Nurse Birdie Collins, secular society."

"How did you know I was reading *Machiavelli Rage*?"

"There are many methods of deduction, methods of hunting, sort of like rumors. I am aware of every novel In that bookshelf, and the power of *Machiavelli Rage* triumphs."

"A triumphant story," she said.

"Indeed, a truth about a powerful mystery in the blood of Jesus Christ. The redeeming blood is present and offered. His blood conquered evil."

"So, tell me how do rumors get started?" She asked.

"What is hidden I will be happy to proclaim, for I am a priest who is to look after his flock. Rumors have circulated about Count Shylock Gruden, and Nurse Birdie Collins. They have employed Vampires. For over a century, theories mushroomed like errands. The Vampire species are their companion entities who occupy the famous Gosa Hotel located on a hill in the next city over. After Count Shylock and Birdie Collins had left the Victorian's school, they and several Vampires established themselves in the multitude of their own riches. In fact, a thirty-four-foot tall tower of books looms over mounds of starving worshipers at the Gosa's private chapel. They are all the rage. Assemblies of seventy Vampires and human slaves help each other every Friday night. Truth be told, Hotel Gosa houses Vampires. They have worked, drank, and fed on the inward parts of Count Shylock and Nurse Collins humanistic presentations and deviltry. Their rebellious teachings and opus of denominational discord produce power inside the Mephistopheles of cedar offices. Bloody feasts are like ugly 100 year turns, and abuses are mutual. Count Shylock and Nurse Collins skin have wildly benefited, they look young enough to devour. The universal church will send a true priest to redeem souls. He shall arrive with an axe and a solitary candle to destroy the cult, but first, *Those Who Must Be Kept* must freeze flames inside a hidden *Labyrinth*." These words prevail, "Destroy evil, O God, let them fall by their own counsel. Cast them out in the multitude of their transgressions for they have rebelled against you."

"Fr. Louis, shall you pass over with an axe from seventh heaven, silently like a blue bird armed before angels? Or zoom down the hungry hill like a hound dog summoned from hell. I sense Angels on the trail. If necessary, these messengers shall meet you at Hotel Majestic to plan a victory. You very well know the objectives of that hotel. It's in the neighborhood, and whispers crawl to the gods of the listening. Human bloodshed emptied by ill will may produce a lower level vampire species. I must point this out because it is the Yu's duty to protect and initiate goodwill. *Die Nuss* is necessary, and we enjoy the perfect presence. Our tribe can slide into the secret *Labyrinth* where confessions of new beginnings call us to serve our Maker. The winds and salty air there help preserve our body of truth. At times I have a recollection of a fabulous being named Lazarus. He has no mud on me! His final destination is in the flesh and spirit. We have always strived for the vitality that sheens like salt. Only if threatened with poverty or weapons of mass destruction shall cause the Yu to rise to the occasion to protect ourselves. We cannot and will not be defeated. As of now, there is no immediate threat."

"Please, do not contend against my message. Thank you, for your love and consideration. You are a living flower that never dies, we were the fathers before we were the sons, and the Nazarene is our unifying factor. Daughter of God, I have the position of authority from the rock of Peter to unite and to tear down strongholds. Inside Hotel Gosa is not a grand Hotel. It is composed of two old-fashioned brownstone front dwellings, welded into one. The brood born in the rubble of a district named *Lipar twelve* are not human. They are Vampire apparitions parading symptoms that no properly deceased person should display. Ugly turns drain flesh dry then re-grows insides, ripping and widening body parts. Some rise from the dead full of holes. Then the fleapits disappear, later. It is a sight to behold."

He reached into his pocket and handed Devora an un-opened bottle. "Here, smell this."

The bottle reeked heavily. It was Vampire blood from Hotel Gosa. One frightful night, Fr. Louis had drained the last of its transformations. He would have done the right thing to prevent the making of these things but was not expecting to hunt them down like jaguars that just let themselves out. His physical weapons were not at hand. Instead, with just moments to escape, he drained Vampire blood right before one turned, and fled. Devora kept her knowledge of Vampires in Egypt private. She handled the bottle carefully and knew the scent well.

"Fr. Louis, I guess that means you helped save me. I am not ready to meet my maker, for legions would have come back to earth through the Vampire ghosts of Westside. This must be prevented."

Beholden to her response, Fr. Louis pressed her hand. His grip left it white with a lingering imprint of his fingers. He gazed in awe wondering how she knew about the ghosts of Westside.

"I am protected. Heaven does not want me just yet. Hades is afraid that I may take over!" Fr. Louis assured her.

"That's the spirit, Fr. Louis, "You're on fire for God. I do not know how much I can take. The universal church and I have a double blessing, and that does not include suffering in vain. Many in the world are just young and have not come to a decision. Please fight for their humanity and souls."

Fr. Louis knew many of the slaves of this blood sucking civilization who say God does not see serve the bloodthirsty with their own humanity as a twenty-four-hour concierge, in unions, government, military, and the arts. Human slaves move their evil agenda all over the world, many are deadly powerful and terrifyingly dazzling.

"The slaves bring blood for Vampires that lust for it. You have a real message, even if it is in a bottle. In these times we know where mercy can be deposited." She stood up straight.

"Come closer, Fr. Louis, I am determined to psychically hear the private thoughts of Count Shylock Gruden."

"You desire to understand, my child?"

It took a moment for her concentration to adjust. Piercing into the atmosphere, she supernaturally perceived Count Shylock's voice. It was a surprise to Fr. Louis how much she wanted to hear his voice. Going deeper into a trance, Devora was undeniably successful. The Count said, "Thank God, my daughters and her troll tots have escaped, in evening clothes!"

"If I may cut to the chase, what arrogance, no grown man who fights with his teeth, has ever intimidated the Highest God," Fr. Louis groaned.

"While Count Shylock's pets consumed their bodies with his hunger sure, they will no longer enchant or array his skin. It was left preoccupied. The last layer of fear took with it a private, freewheeling, frontier whose spiritual power shall never succumb to it," said Devora.

Fr. Louis practically jerked his neck. "These self-indulgent words have frozen my heart. The Count was friends with the Bishop!"

Her eyes came into focus. "About a week ago, I saw this Bishop. He was in a straw hat, drinking beer in a bar downtown San Francisco."

Fr. Louis noticed her skin. It looked pale and was growing lighter as she grew more and more aware. Her hands were shaking. He put his arm around her and drew her up close.

"I must confess, within one hour after our first meeting, my connection with the Church as an institution of signs, behaviors, and works shed a task built on a surprising metamorphosis. In that hour of astonishment, the seal of gold above the front door birthed a living eagle, with a golden beak and golden wings. The temperature was 40 degrees marvelously amazing. The being surged straight into the sky and the creature shook like things that make us press on. Now, I must help free a lovesick parishioner named Mina. This parishioner was living on her nerves."

"It sounds like Mina, and the creature with golden wings are traveling living beings. Their actuality is part of great possibilities," Devora answered.

A flashback entered her thoughts, about the eagle appearing to Darius in Egypt.

"Yes, Devora, Mina has a name to live up to. I stroked her hair and felt like I was home again. The truth about it has a mighty lot of nerves, a delightful specimen of greatness was before me. My first thought was to throw the bird over my shoulder. Instead, the huge creature hovered awhile behind your head and then disappeared. It was a sight to behold. Our inheritance of goodness is full and beyond common understanding. It is time to reel it in from a sea of hearers, watchers, and the wise ones. Sit down over here, for home is truly where the heart is."

Fr. Louis positioned another seat with great care. Devora's thin body sank inside the comforts of burgundy leather.

"Devora, there is no need to fear the darkest hour, squalls wracked with unhelpfulness, or any inheritance of tragedy. Your voyage was long for an awesome purpose."

"Thank you, yet I am lovesick for my first love who shall attain fidelity with the highest word," Devora answered.

"Has your first love bid you adieu?" Asked Fr. Louis

"No, I am jeweled with fading recollections of my past life."

"Perhaps this is so, but today you have peered into the mind of Count Shylock Gruden, not your first love. Like Calliope, chief of all muses, your love shall rise and soar like an eagle. The Count's running shadows and textures have weighed on many failures. He proved himself unfaithful, and our spiritual solution must bring forces into equilibrium. Soon a secret cellar behind the *Paramount* will open. The bright light never blinds, and *Blind Justice* shall have one day. At times *Justice* exists inside a secret epistolary, and when it is visible, it is made public for one day. Many attempts at the epistolary destruction throughout the centuries have occurred. It has survived fire, water, tearing but immediately restores itself. Many throughout the ages threw it into the sea, yet the epistolary always returns to its true keepers. It is the same as our universal church. The rightful owner always returns it to those keepers who said, "I gave you Eden after the deluge."

"Who might these keepers be?" She asked.

"You may come to know them, but if the rightful owner did not return the epistolary to the keepers who once traveled across the wide sea, an eternal lovesick nation would reap its horror lessons from their embrace with unfaithful gods. *Justice* is not a liar. Even angels desire to look into those things sent down from heaven. Fidelity and faith in hearing the word have determined this according to the will of the rightful owner. *Justice* flies like the eagle and enables all-powerful living god's to soar. *Justice,* I say *Justice* not the false teachings at Hotel Gosa, or Vampires who feed on blood traps."

"Fr. Louis, I am aware of the eagle's presence. Let the epistolary speak for itself to those who are born to handle it. My clan and its mission are very different. I am prepared to throw the eagle over my shoulder, and then offer it with an ave of fig trees on a hill of faith. Like fruitless trees, fruitless unfaithful stewards' will be removed from my Creator's garden." Devora wiped her mouth.

"There is much to build on that hill. Its eyes are always searching to find faithful stewards."

Fr. Louis drew his hands behind his head locking his fingers together, his chin pointed upward.

Holding Darius' vision of the Eagle in her heart, she asked Louis in a low voice, "is it time for us to walk the dead, and undead. Shall we deposit them in the box of *Lux*?" She looked very eager and white.

Fr. Louis had aided her in hiding her ancestral box. He was also the only living man who knew of its place, and the first to proclaim its glad melody, floating clear and musical on the air, announcing the family's independence.

Fr. Louis looked straightforward. "*Those Who Must Be Kept* have never lost hope. Inside the *Labyrinth,* Galaxy holds music, intelligence, crystal kingdoms, enormous round portals of blue galaxies, magnificent towers. It is a beautiful paradise. No one is cold.

Everyone is full of love and looks to every living thing upon earth for petitions. Everybody is at peace, with one another for they survived someone and something on their own. Virtuous Spirits, eternal roses, midsummer parades, beautiful jeweled onyx, diamonds, and quartz of many colors, cover tunnels, big complexes, chambers, and corridors. Like one professional paint job, inside one song that becomes many in the earth musical vortexes and silence creates a soothing atmosphere sealed after their kind. A paradise inside a pyramid exists undisturbed until awakened by one heart which holds a unique key that unlocks the secret epistolary and dedicates it to one love. What works for us does not work for everybody. There is no fear of darkness, and many asked for and were given diamond eyes. When we were joined away, our light was lit for them. A mystery for something more majestically maintains itself, and *Justice* is above everything else.

She cries, "She made me, oh whoa, oh, in the name of goodness, and everything was done just for the Nazarene with arms wide open."

"Beneath a blood moon in the *Labyrinth,* a wine of river appears once a year between the pines where many are raised to eternal life.

One Sun is an open royal passage, and on one good foot fat vessels carries a book of misdeeds called *Come back because it's dark now.* One there never drinks wine, and the triumphs of his kind are the last of their kind on earth. A solitary candle produces a cosmic radiation providing light and beautiful harmony to a marvelous paradise where a twin named Future, the blue and black twins, angels, and messengers rule along the side of *Justice.* Beautiful light beings wait patiently listening to the sounds of *Justice,* who has a permanent presence and is not absent. She loves them, plays very fast and helps to reflect glory under the sun with an open sky that can create any color of the rainbow. Those who take the hand of *Justice* shall be spared from earthbound cages of captivity. Once someone on earth forgives any being in the *Labyrinth,* one must not reheat sins for breakfast because like a cathedral of meat pies there is always a great way to deal with pest. Everyone there has an ultimate destination, heaven, where everybody knows the Nazarene, who anticipated their coming. When humans who love the *Labyrinth* get together on earth and say a little prayer, many get knocked back up happily singing, please don't cry for us. Our ambitious fingers are happily in your meat pies, and our finest cuts are always shared with those that we love, not through meekness but with grand and powerful delight."

When Fr. Louis was a child, the fortnight of freedom came as an archangel. He escorted him into the *Labyrinth*. His mother, Emelia, also told and explored many of its mysteries. Yet, it took him several minutes before realizing something was not right. The *Labyrinth* was a place where relics and purification stay, until the final call.

These are lovely statues, but they have nothing to do with reality. Those brought to the *Labyrinth* are waiting to ascend. Together, they lovingly wait for a final graduation and ascension to heaven. Our prayers, songs and good works on earth are good for them.

Devora replied, "I have learned from a private source that most relics of *Those Who Must Be Kept*, are not behind the *Paramount* or the *Labyrinth*. Many relics have been removed and hidden in a Center which shall one day rise up to heaven."

Fr. Louis replied, "You did not think the dead would wait for you? Unto a living hope by the resurrection of Christ from the dead, we one day ascend to heaven. Those relics do not have a life touch or the secret epistolary. I have brought some ashes and many Holy Relics from the road of plenty. The mystery of the Magdalene, a relic of scalable size surviving behind mosaic tiles behind the *Paramount* shall be considered, for we are living, hopeful, and faithful for things that sometimes we cannot see."

"Magdalene, who is she?" Devora asked.

"Magdalene was an ancient human, ringing practical counsel for modern-day humans. She is one body inside *Those Who Must Be Kept*, but cut off from pure understanding in the *Labyrinth*. Among the landmarks, her causes are still in time and space. We cannot ignore the mysteries of her torn garment made for *Justice*. The effects stay where power shares itself with the power of an Egyptian desert that landed into open parts of wide-open living theaters of cosmos. One hammer and many bricks built with water and her brokenness held together to bring a message of hope. We went to a garden in the rain where showers of bread released her from the hold of the distinguished thing and costumes that bind. Your twins have a hidden assignment. Like neighbors just a stone's throw from green pastures, they are spirit, and they are life, magnets for seeking souls. I recognized their mission in the womb. A vision materialized the hour I met you. The revelation nearly seared my pupils; an audible message accompanied by blood, my blood! The agony felt like scissors cutting through bone and skin. I quickly hid my bleeding palms, knowing in that hour I was confounded to reflect a spiritual condition. It is true, a new relationship with the sacrificial blood of Jesus Christ had emerged. I confess this because in my passages I experience the true nature of the blood of Jesus in its real presence, as truly present. Ever since that unique hour, when my tongue joins communion, the Savior is within me. So let us thank God for mercy. It is what Christ was made to offer humanity."

"For women like myself who look to the horizon, *Mercy* and *Justice* may both be wrapped around the belt of my expecting."

"Long live the belt of *Justice!* I will point to the works of Birdie Collins and Count Shylock. It was many years ago when I found a journal of admission. Birdie Collins and Count Shylock used instruments of wire coiled around their twisting hands, ripping the passages of innocent ghetto girls. That evil hatched in this very mansion while vampire eyes offered payoffs. Together they fed them body parts, finishing off thousands of undeveloped thumbs, and snipped necks of fetuses. Sadly, the bloodshed of hunted fetuses continues to this day."

"Killing the unborn shall improve with time. Where there is an error we may bring truth," Devora softly answered.

Fr. Louis let out a moan and looked like he'd swallowed a bunch of wasps.

"Here is the truth. My awareness of these practices and schemes surfaced quickly. It was the first Monday after Epiphany on a cold January afternoon. Shortly after accepting a teaching assignment in this Victorian, I observed a despondent Puerto Rican girl with beautiful red hair wandering towards the downstairs cellar. Her footsteps were unsure. I followed her and hid behind certain things, hoping she would not perceive me as a predator rustling with ghost and wind. I leaned towards two wide sheets hanging between me and a cement door. The beautiful girl did not close the door, or draw the sheets completely together. A tiny slit allowed me to peer inside. A great evil was behind the sheets. Minutes before another killing, I saw unborn hacked fetuses lying on the cement. Hundreds of shelves were inside old walls detained with jars stacked intelligently like a warehouse of squared debates on morality. Seven wrought iron beds sat heavily on the dark colored basement cement. Two beds were occupied, and I refuse to tell you by what. I quickly positioned my head out of view. My tongue locked. I tipped away from the crisscrossed sheets, and like a master switchblade muffling a generation's demise, my tongue leaped. This can't be tolerated, *Justice*, I say, *Justice*!"

On my aching feet, I removed my shoes. Questions immediately surfaced. Is it illegal to destroy this house of pain? The door of trading sin had opened! I shuffled upstairs. The left sole of my foot was pricked by something causing me to slip, the pain disappeared fast. I gathered myself and stood to attention.

Devora flushed with focus, frowned. "Fr. Louis, have you been worshiping at a different sanctuary? You did nothing bad. Let's have a time or a pie. Stress can't exist in the presence of a fine meat pie."

He continued, "Devora, please we must not think of our appetites; anyhow, hanging around after midnight, I found something in the corner." Suddenly, the phone rang.

"Come on come on! I whispered; please pick up the phone. Someone finally did. I found a journal. The name Mina boldly printed on its spine intrigued me. I felt better just having it nearby and opened it. Inside the pages were two chains. One chain had a pink heart on it. The other chain had five little diamond karats with two gold letter. The journal had several entries. I flipped through each page; a little memo fell out. It was signed by Count Shylock Gruden and Nurse Birdie Collins, 1925."

"What did the memo say?"

"Clear instructions by the Rabbi, outlining abortion preparations written and approved by the clicking of Count Shylock's teeth."

"The Rabbi was *The Ghost of Westside* famed for leaving traces of himself behind every corner of the world." Devora privately thought.

Fr. Louis continued, "What I read was unfit for any beating heart. I seriously felt like I was holding my own. Mina, just a girl, was a part of a platform of quiet killing, used to aid a criminal system. The entities involved were of an altered kind, who belonged to a structure that made an agreement with hell."

Looking very sternly she asked, "Don't tell me the destroyer and thief had come among them smiling as an audience to destroy the perceptions and distinctions of right and wrong?"

He answered, "They must be accountable. In the name of greed, a covenant of death thrived in the basement of this religious school. After a time, actions would give way to organized structures, priding themselves in the slaughter and wholesale of unborn fetuses. Humming away their shame, groups would later twist consideration from the right meaning into the wrong meaning, For this reason, *Justice* must act on behalf of barrels of bygone flesh. These murderers shall inherit a promise, and a choice tune, unlike anything they have ever heard."

"Answer me, Fr. Louis is it the judgment of death on them? The Yu have told ourselves uplifting life promising stories. We sing about virtue's triumph, and extended our hands of friendship to the life of wisdom."

"Devora my brave one, I am hard pressed to describe a wretched condition about the wicked killing the innocent for revenue. Who has caught a grenade for Mina's pain and others subjected to brutal pressure? I say the time is at hand to make a stand. We must hear the choice tune of a whistle and take, its arm as well as its affection and thank God for righteous judgment. My soul is sore, but Christ shall heal it, for I have not created my own unique brand of *Justice*. *Justice* is blindfolded, not prejudice, she does not care who you are and shall break the teeth of brutal deliberate ungodly profit acquired from little body parts.

"Oh, the monster of death! Fr. Louis, you do not need my permission. Those who are out of their wits, and those in the wrong, time will show. It sounds like you're waiting for your time to uphold no system as that. Will you be making a trip to the Hotel Majestic today? I can hear the blood of the aborted, it knocks like a pulse from two chains," Devora sighed.

"Yes, child, there is not much controversy with people in the know. Our time on earth shall respond with righteous judgment. My actions are similar to the coats you have knitted for your unborn. For a time, rare wool and animal fur will protect your children from tough winters. So, it applies to some forms of vampirism, if worn for many an inordinate length of time. Eventually, some kinds of human beings will be on their way to extinction."

"Fr. Louis it's dead simple. Hell has no fury like *Die Nuss*. Vampires hate it, especially under the burning sun. An old friend of my Great Grandfather, one of the best Vampire commissions in the world transcribed writings from a book called *Star*. The commissioner's name is Van Helsing. Yu and Sa Priests gave him access to our ancient reserve in Egypt. He is a friend from their earliest libraries and a friend to Mint of Zeb. Van Helsing, the merciful Vampire-Hunter, predicted that someday in the far away future I would conceive twins through the Holy Spirit. Your perceptions hold truth. The twins I carry are destined to use and know the secret of *Die Nuss*. The girl I keep within me carries a name. It is Galaxy, and she has already mastered its power in the womb. The method shall push humanity to seek her help in her twin, Future. So breathe in and out to bless the skyline, Fr. Sunshine, our Louis, the teacher of souls." Devora grinned half way.

"If they are immaculately conceived, then your womb was without the human intervention of a father, but that is a virgin birth. I have not been called Louis for many, many years. Most call me Fr. Louis. Please continue to do so my child. Your Egyptian past is indeed a mighty past. Be blessed with healthy children, prepare them for the salvation of souls, lives of unity, greatness, and wisdom. God planned goodness for your children in every generation, because of the will of God and love."

Darius shared with Fr. Louis the real details of what occurred to them in Egypt. He was aware of Devora's state of mind. Still, her mind, body, and spirit were so rigorous and perceptive. Sometimes, glimpses of her past life were remembered. Fr. Louis remained silent about the statement of her immaculate conception. Besides, he did not trust Van Helsing prediction.

"I am aware of the black holes in the atmosphere when *Die Nuss* is in effect. In the night of *Die Nuss,* its smoky metropolis portals to Mars and the stars reflect understanding within the essence of these twins you carry. They shall do no evil, as they have my blessings to an untroubled heart and sound teaching from the Word of God," said Fr. Louis.

"Fr. Louis, I threw the secret *Die Nuss*. I go numb and only care about what is real. Extend time. You say the word of and sound teaching is the absolute key. To catch a Vampire, you must understand the Vampire within yourself." She stretched out her legs. Fr. Louis peered into her stomach.

He answered with a smile, "Close to the time of giving life, you shall bleed the moon like armor. Claim it, when enemies become the family's footstool *Justice* shall be served meat pie, potatoes, and herring pies. An audience shall eat every bite of it, my child?"

"You appear to be very aware of the ancient *Die Nuss*. It always eats!" She composed herself.

"And never dies, its basic task unleashes clouds of rare sediment. The dark forces that can ordinarily do evil, well they swiftly become visible. That primary source is obliged to face a dominant yolk, and like top scoring laundry detergent, the success rate of the mysteries of Die *Nuss,* is100%. Evil forces submit to it, or turn to ash."

Holding her belly, she gently flung herself against the library shelves. It was a secret area hiding the front of the *Paramount* door.

"Devora, time shall bend in this Victorian behind the *Paramount* door. Alas, many years have passed since those atrocities, yet the deeds of the basement continue all over the world. It is true, downstairs is clean and swept, and sure the present has invited your family as living custodians. Your family is blessed. The delicacies of crust, are both carried and preserved by tasty filling. Consider yourselves blessed. But the time given to cease aborting babies and profiting has not ended. It has only gotten worse. I like to work with examples. Here, I shall repeat and give you an example; nothing human, but their faces profits from aborted fetuses and then eats its remains."

Frowning, she answered, "Play time is over, we shall shave their time. What a den of subhuman monsters! The ultimate price was the death of many little people in the city, and beyond it. You prepared big people to think of their souls regarding the lurking truth of survival without morality.?"

After a long silence, Fr. Louis went on.

"I preach and teach the gospel. Although, in a thousand years I may not make Vampires, only warn humanity, and preach on forgiveness, mercy, and a Just, God. The condition to feed on blood is in the nature of Vampires. One condition of a loving God is forgiveness of errors. If one seeks forgiveness, it is there according to the Gospels of Jesus Christ."

"While we have you, what year and time were you in when you started protecting yourself and forgiving, Vampire Hunter?"

"Does the year matter? In the confessional, time is at one hand, the belt of truth wrapped snug in Jesus Christ. I am not Jesus, perhaps more like Moses. It has been put in my heart to seek, and to lead people out of ignorance. As a man, Moses sought to lead his people out of Egypt and was permitted. My response to hearing many young girl's confessions eventually drove me to contact the Bishop, because the Count had impregnated daughters given to Christ."

"Perish the thought, a grown man who fights with his penis is in a hidden passage. He is the hole in the deep hole!" Devora sneered.

"He isn't here. An action plan gave a rebuke it plunged Count Shylock into the hands of a devourer where blood runs cold. Damsels in distress, lovely brunettes, little redheads, beautiful blonds, and daughters of wooly locks abandoned, asking, "Where are you, Papa?" Fr. Louis appeared frustrated.

"Sounds like everything did not go according to the Count's plans. The action man of counsel and scold gave way and tried to do the right thing," answered Devora.

"You speak of the Bishop, and your comments stand more than merely revealing. But Count Shylock had plucked the positions of many girls suffering in misery, with promises of some goodly gift, scarf, or ring, fraught with danger and spoiled in the crafty tenderness of their sweet innocence. From the realm of reckless profit and twisted sensual appetites, he had tricked and used them all for his own pony drive."

"And so, the Bishop, what did he say?" asked Devora.

"The Bishop's response stuck to me like a botched execution, aghast; I yelled, monstrosity! His reaction to the activities in the basement was stern. Leaving us with the obligation to seek *Justice* within a paradise where nature rises from the dead: There we have learned that the Bishop's name took on another meaning."

"Go on please, I shall survive the winds and flames."

"Before dismissing me with a blunt reproof, the Bishop asked.

"Fr. Louis when will they slay us?"

"I will not let you go to the unknown alone Bishop. Vampires exist, one may have the strength of thirty people. I am sworn to protect you."

The Bishop sighed, "Now I must confess to you, Fr. Louis. Tend to your own ditches with an everlasting shovel."

"After our discussion, I worried and wondered for days about his comment. About a month later the Victorian closed."

"What happens to everyone?" Devora asked.

"I assume Count Shylock and Nurse Birdie Collins slumber, encompassed in soil beneath a subterranean paradise; forgotten ditches weighed down with compromise. Its weight lures some to remember the deeds of the basement of nobodies."

Devora dropped her head.

Fr. Louis continued, "I cannot forget their doings. Months later, looking out my back door, I had another vision it accosted me like my bleeding palms. It was an Amazon with blood frothing from her mouth. Unremorseful collective kills and a decline of many innocent unborn lives gave me something to strive for. I permitted my mother's blood to speak. So, as good as they come in that business, the bloodthirsty condemned the Amazon to a done deal."

The star spangled song began to bleed through the *Paramount*. Devora struggled to reverse her role, just as Fr. Louis reversed his.

Combination Of The Empire Beyond

ALL IN THE Westside awakened to a thunderous noise. It was pure energy from the birth of twins. Lazarus and Devora's son, Future, was born with royal blue- skin, oceanic eyes, and a patch of silky white hair. His face was that of a royal prince. Galaxy, his twin sister, had ivory fair skin, root beer calf eyes, and tiny blue veins down her temples. Her veins moved like clear water, running through the darkness. Their beauty mirrored the heavens, showing earth what blended powers had achieved. Heavenly hosts rejoiced over the new champions and called them beautiful.

Darius smiled wide in amazement, and whispered toward the East, "Devora is a very special lady. Lazarus, I wish you were here. Your twins have left her womb, a prized palace for a new spiritual race from the future. And what grateful eyes your twins have. Look they both have high arching brows and deep round eyes."

With this hearty announcement, everyone stared into holy cuteness. An old, well-maintained Raggedy Ann doll sat on a nearby bed. With it was the love and happiness that many who once lived in the Victorian, had given to it and other red yarn penny dolls. Hands of tension soon closed around quiet moments. Before long the midnight air oozed a sweetness. The scent was rather comforting, enhancing everyone's impression of closeness. Galaxy hummed and then vomited. In the future, nothing would make her vomit again.

A fountain of sweet water spouted into the atmosphere. Minutes before their birth, Fr. Louis had supernaturally observed a cosmic condition participate in life and death. The umbilical cord had wrapped itself around Future's neck. Gazing at Devora's belly, Fr. Louis witnessed power move into distinct dimensions. Future's heartbeat was visible, and faint light fed a phenomenon. Its uncontaminated energy nearly blinded everyone. More light pushed upward, its vigor manifested a mushroom hue of brightness, and the power impacted the whole room. Little by little, it grew upward, flying Eastern as it approached the windows, then blasted outward into the neighborhood. For reasons of a Future, that was never his, a hue of blue-black light exuded from the infant's palms. This intense light poured into Galaxy's hands; her spine moved like a vision spreading its wings of power. One last push stimulated infinite authority. She cried as they took on life and death. Devora whispered to the beautiful light, "Swish." There was a pause, "Swish," and then there was peace of the God of Future.

Future rolled over but was afraid that he would choke in inches of shallow water. Formed, filled, and made on pieces of a prince's primer, fear of flesh intruded, and his short life became spirit. He was free, like the angel of death exchanging breath from the gods of creation.

The midwife studied the twins for a few moments and greeted them with a smile. "I am sworn to protect the twins. They both have salvation. I deem the boy dead, only in body. He is as prominent as a single stain glass window in an unseen world, and he shall return to the earth as a Sovereign, handsome, dynamic ruler. At that juncture, Future, the King shall be born.

He shall be a popular ruler throughout his reign and shall be blessed with long life in a prosperous vigorous kingdom."

Fr. Louis sprinkled the twins with a little holy water. "The blood of Jesus protects and saves. I cannot wait to show you our kingdom!" He insisted.

She sighed, "Just for a second I thought I remembered you. Shall we all be in heaven together, or someplace where our demons hide? My name is Daciana. I was a Pharaoh's wife with lots of land and sheep. I have never baptized or been baptized."

Daciana was a private person and wouldn't taunt from a door like isolation. Devora told Fr. Louis that she was from Egypt, and sailed on the same vessel with the family. Fr. Louis thought she looked Egyptian, but her strong Romanian accent told another story.

Darius read Fr. Louis' eyes and thought that pretty woman could be anything she wants. Her artistic temperament was monopolized at my birth. She is a genius.

"Fr. Louis, do not get too close unless you can show us how to enter your kingdom. The twins are precious, take good care of them." The midwife insisted.

A loud knock at the door nearly left everyone speechless. It was *The Ghost of Westside* bleeding through the door as solid as someone concerned for his safety. The midwife's hair rose on her head when she perceived his presence.

"Making for us chambers, I don't think so. I am a force with a duty to maintain spirit, flash of no muscle." The midwife said with a smile.

Darius moved close to Devora and the twins. Both experienced in paranormal encounters were stunned. Amazed they listened to the ghost shriek.

"No will high enough was compelled to open the door, so I used my ghostly crew's strength to bleed through. I cannot trust myself to any of your hands, for one of you might snatch me. According to legend, one of you has been visited by the wraith of Vlad the Impaler. The Mighty Ladylove will visit another."

Daciana quipped, "Ghosts cannot set a passage to the sprinkling of blood and water. The hands of Fr. Louis are flesh and blood. He has thick skin and is doing a great job. But, you are a phantom."

Fr. Louis interrupted and then opened a well-designed musical box sitting on a French antique marble hutch.

He rebuked the Ghost, 'The Bishop buried you in *Jacobs Garden*. Long ago you died like a bent twig because you gave out instructions showing members of a religious community how to abort innocent babies. Death caught up with you. Why do you return, Rabbi? The old practices of this Victorian have not caused you to forget its irksome world and turmoil?"

The Ghost of Westside soared hysterically through the room and stood nose to nose with Fr. Louis.

Fr. Louis continued, "Future bounced back like a palm tree surviving the storm. The boy died free in the spirit to create spiritual conditions. One last epic trip swung into motion a resurrected spiritual relationship with his twin. *Ghost of Westside*, you are an enemy. So, leave because you cannot sneeze! Messengers in heaven arise, to bless and protect Galaxy. The boy's spirit departed in a celestial mystery."

The Ghost of Westside screeched, "Doodley Doo, Galaxy has a flare for the dramatic. I dare not meddle with such high matters, just hope the messengers support her."

His long shadowy nose turned to Daciana.

"Whom have you lost, Daciana? If you don't count, it may be too late." At footpace, he trailed off.

Daciana whispered, whom have you lost? When I count, it is never too late."

Darius was suspicious of the phantom and disbelieved that it had an interest in their lives.

"That is *The* Ghost of Westside. He will be back. He is seeking forgiveness." Devora insisted.

Daciana allowed a few seconds of silence. Time halted, and tensions rose. Her loyal round eyes could populate a regal empire. From a concealed perch of celestial bodies, one might have believed human time stopped for the purpose to seek lost royal subjects.

She asked, "Has the Phantom and his league of legends harmed you, Fr. Louis?" Her tone was detached.

"A woman is often used as a means for those who live the family life." He whispered.

"Future was the last great thrust of former might. Let us all have a hug and permit me to take the flesh. His spirit is our paradise; I must get back there. It is like time marching on to enjoy the sunlight as if awakening from a dream on a glorious moonlit hillside, shoulder to shoulder with those that we love."

Devora sighed long and gently laid her hand over the twins. She picked up Future as if one would pick up a lost precious gold coin. Handing him to the midwife, she sighed, "He counts and received all of Christ's glory. I shall cherish his all too short life. A life who searches through a changing sky as if many awakened into the magnificence's of a surprise where one's birthright is never sold, stolen, and only cherished."

This gesture spoke a thousand goodbyes. The family understood what appeared as a loss was a plus in cosmic origin. Their upset was one of the highest soul searching victories on earth. A mystery inside and outside of time would empower Future's spirit to sprout resurrection seeds inside Galaxy and the whole world. Fr. Louis understood that these gifts were for supernatural combat and only attainable by way of Vampire killers, or soul deliverers.

Regrettably, most of the humanity had turned away from spiritual warfare and understanding, creating breathtaking roles for their family, the greatest Vampire slayers of the 20^{tht} Century.

T and One Tough Moon Bite

TESSIE MAYBACH LIVED eight miles from the Victorian. Galaxy was two years old when Tessie accepted a position as her au pair. The family called her Sister. Four times a week she read stories and aired Galaxy's clothes by the inglenook. Mostly, she enjoyed Tessie's humor and wisdom talks during cold winters when tiny flickers of sunlight poured in on hardwood walls. At times bright light highlighted the faces of penny dolls. Seven lifelike dolls sitting on a handmade bench stared back at hundreds of toys in a huge dollhouse. The toys were from every part of the world and looked as if they were living in a live hotel.

The Ghost of Westside, too dead to die, sometimes stood quietly around them, unseen. He was dreaming his own nightmare of Galaxy. It took two to wake up Dolly Daydreams. Anytime Tessie and Galaxy did the twist and blew dream bubbles; it was in the name of when two or more are gathered. This special dance left *The Ghost of Westside* feeling double-crossed. There were consequences to this game. Tessie could see the dead, which also included his ghostly crew. She called their coming together, "The Setup." Sometimes the sight of the dead was a blessing but many times, "The Setup" was a hardship forced to turn into blessings. For the most part of her life, the very sight of the ghostly crew drove her to a neighborhood church. Most Sunday's, members flung themselves against pews, shifted in their seats, or fell and tossed about on the floor. Praying that the others would not eat you took up half their time. The pastor was a part of "The Setup."

He was a spiritual traitor and practiced a dark form of Voodoo. After dismissing church members on Sundays, he gathered another group. They performed rituals guaranteeing *The Ghost of Westside* and his supernatural crew spiritual submission from the pastor's members. The unseen crew was spectacular to catastrophe, and in exchange for psychic submission, the pastor received financial control of his member's finances. He also summoned an Incubus to shadow many of the vulgarly rich female members.

The fiend watched and followed poor Tessie around like a pet. She fought it with the very things received from the pastor, the word of God, gospel music, and prayer. Her faith in Jesus Christ and the power of song broke all shackles of any supernatural falsehood that endeavored to advance her in its deception or passions.

Tessie delighted in telling those who walked in darkness to pray with their eyes open or closed. She was a willing model of servitude to Jesus Christ. Her spiritual fate was in the deeper parts of her heart, mind, body, and spirit. These hidden treasures also reflected upon one of the most powerful Vampires of Egypt, Julius The Handsome prince of all Vampires, who had so much success because of those who never gave up. The Handsome did much for himself and held millenniums instead of centennials. He sailed across oceans with Darius and a pregnant Devora.

Tessie was eighteen years old when her relationship with that family began. She kept membership with the neighborhood church much of her adult life and was so plain that neither of them thought of her as anything but sincere.

One night before bed, when Galaxy was about seventeen years old, she asked Tessie, "What happens in churches, the zoos, circuses, and dog pounds when everybody goes home? You seem to know everything!"

"It's a secret, but here is a hint. It is a place where wolves forget to die to avoid a certain kind of future, and against all the odds we are to survive in body, soul, and Spirit; and you are to prosper so that we all can prosper through you."

Galaxy sighed, "Wherever this secret or signal is, I shall ride on a sure-footed Yak. The beast will carry out our bags, keeping its pace with harmony. Am I a welcomed daughter in a kingdom of the daughters of Eve, or a lion among wolves?"

"Good night, Galaxy, look to the bright stars in the night sky under a waxing moon just as your blood relations did from Mint of Zeb. Remember, I only want to see you loving what God created you to do. Leave the herald of cosmos to heaven and nature. God's messengers shall visit and prepare you and those that you love to blossom like royalty. At the sight of your togetherness, a King will smile and then go his way. He will return to prepare you for a beautiful conception marked in mystery. A Kingdom that stooped down was given to a constellation of wisdom, its splendor is not set to fall, but to shine as a Sovereign Prince."

Galaxy asked, "Where is your scepter, shall you slaughter ruthlessness with your breath? Will you quickly shatter our enemies from Mint of Zeb, my parent's region, and prepare a way for our secret to flourish and rise to great heights because of a promise made at midnight in a high castle. Will those enemies be born to serve as subjects to my twin, Future?" Galaxy raised her forefinger to her lips.

Tessie sighed, "A most welcomed mystery."

The next day Tessie walked into the local pound. Lazarus had succeeded in getting her exactly where she was supposed to be. She did not have much money in her pocket, but somehow his dog eyes persuaded her that he was the one. One eye round and dark with interest appeared to have a thorn. It looked like a road on a clear day.

"Have a seat, brown sugar. The wait is at least an hour," a pegged-leg pound worker growled. Her nametag read Lucy.

Lucy shook her cane. The foot of her shadow appeared as if movement deferred. Lazarus began barking at the shadow, then launched towards Tessie.

"Stop that dog! Where is that Pound Master when you need him?" She pointed the cane towards Lazarus' hind legs.

Tessie looked like she had just swallowed canary seed. "This is not the Social Security office. Why should I wait?"

Lazarus fell to Tessie's feet.

Lucy adjusted her bum leg and spat into her hanky.

"Excuse me, Miss, no little fire here! I'm on a sentimental journey. So reach back with a spoonful. All animals must be on a leash. The rules are in English on wall one, wall two and three, same rules apply in Spanish and Chinese."

Tessie answered dramatically, "Well, for the second time, this is not the Social Security office. I'll sit down and take a number there. Whenever asked, what do you want? I said everything, everything, everything. Do you want your Social Security?"

Snow cone Lucy hesitated and thought of the man who never returned with anything. Now it is rather complicated. He can't give everything away, nor is he in the mood to bleed blue or play tug of war.

"I want four thousand a month." She quipped.

Two knuckleheads headed out the door.

Lucy blurted, "It ain't funny that the pooch might get put to sleep if he stays around here. Oh well, finality just missed an opportunity. I do it for the dogs. Free of charge! I see and do not see. Take your words of everything, and the dog and get."

"Don't mind if I do! Long walks and fresh air will sort things out. Bow bow bow yippy yay! Come on dog, and thanks a million, Madame."

Tessie looked into her new dog's eyes, "We are in this world together friend!"

Lucy had learned something and it kind of rattles.

That day Tessie named Lazarus Chew, no other name than Chew fit the black and white canine.

His tail brushed against her ankle. "You can call me Chew, but I am never going to give up my real name. I have roamed alone now for eighteen years. So, why not, let's be friends."

The long walk home was as personal as a view of unavoidable poverty. The scene of cracked pavement sprinkled with smashed liquor bottles, cigarette butts, and beer caps fell to loose shadows.

Two audible sounds were Rusty Wagner, and Lazarus' paws serenading chow time.

Rusty liked moving about on the corner of West and Realm Street. Many called him a shaking giant. Even the neighborhood ghosts had a hard time with his monstrous self-image. It could make elephants kneel, and body- bags vanish. Others in the neighborhood said he was a Hail Mary prayer rolling through like rosary beads. He was the kind of guy who just refused to be contained. Rusty was an intelligent, hard navy man, saved by Jesus Christ. He believed and accepted him as a friend and savior but never asked his mediator for help to practice his God- given authority to stop drinking.

Drug dealers idolized a bleached white towel flopping about his light-brown baldhead. They said it absorbed street stories of Purgatory under the dark side of the moon hollering for another thug's soul. The miracle towel wasn't screwed to his head; it was loose to wipe bits of sweat. This particular summer was hot as hell. He wore his sweaty bare chest proudly. It complimented his favorite black and orange sweatpants. He'd often adjust an embroidered "Bride" & "Groom" handkerchief hanging from his back pocket, half wrapped around a silver canister filled with his favorite alcohol beverage. Most in the neighborhood believed that he was different. He often used his voice to create long pauses, then periodically took his handkerchief to blow his nose. Another man's spirit shared Rusty's body. The Spirit's name was Cut Drink. Cut once had the freedom to explore his old city with cobblestone streets, quaint shops, and historic buildings in a nearby mountainous region. One might say their paranormal arrangement was environmentally sound. Like a room without a single window to the outside world, Rusty's love for alcohol opened a window for Cut to enter. If he had allowed the Holy Spirit to enter his body instead of bourbon, scotch, and beer, life might have been poles apart.

Cut Drink's story began in nineteen forty -five, after the war in England, near an open space of a city for the dead. The weather was below zero that day. Icy- water helped the ground to hold dead bodies longer than expected. Burial rituals on this mountainous region made it quite clear that when one body goes to the ground, another gets turned up. The people that lived in the mountainous regions had been genuine in having an end to violence during the war; even if they had to implore witchcraft. When Cut Drink sliced broken glass across his wrist, he bled out near a hidden channel. The Nomad laid six inches under water on top of waist high grass. After seven days, an iridescent soldier boy and his Chesapeake discovered Cut perfectly preserved on the floor of the channel. The winds icy water and salt air helped to preserve his body. He was wearing a frock coat and a top hat. It stuck to his bloated head like glue.

With every third step, the iridescent soldier boy looked around thanked and praised God. He had only been in the military for three days but had great wisdom. He decided to dig a grave and bury Cut Drink. As a token of respect, he laid his hat over the grave. Cut's spirit saw the soldier boy's good deed, and it compelled his spirit – man, to rise out of his body. He whispered, as his spirit lifted, "God grants every life."

Cut hovered for a while over the area and observed a small boy who was near a cluster of rocks. One huge stone hid his frame from the iridescent soldier boy. The small boy was sitting and carving something. The soldier boy walked near the rocks and was startled. Noticing a few wooden horses erect on some smaller stones, he said, "That is the best wooden wild horse collection that I have ever seen."

The young boy smiled and gave one wooden horse to him. Before running off, he yelled, "You shall return it to me later. I shall ride you like a beast on earth that runs freely enjoying the blessings of God! If my gift is not nurtured and pleasing, to vital energy, my God shall swallow you up, and spit you out to the future, which you will serve happily and dutifully. This is our future, living wisely on the great land with bright stars and fertile soil. God never fails because of vital energies, trust, faith, in Sovereignty. Now come back."

"No, promises," the soldier boy said and thanked the young one for the gift.

"Then I shall be your authority, and our vital energy will make sure of that! God speed," and the little one departed from the dead like a wind at double speed.

For many years Cut, the nomad's spirit, roamed the earth like wild horses, until the day he signed as an agent to dwell within Rusty Wagner's body. Custody of his body began on opening day of Renesmee Liquors, 1965. Rusty was like a ritual that everyone wanted to take part. One night shortly after the store opening, a friendly foreigner invited Rusty to a secret subterranean tunnel. The channels were quiet and beautiful. Many there knew how to make music that clings to hope, and brilliant light that could put anyone into a state of hibernation. Occasional sounds of water droplets echoing throughout the stone chamber over ancient arches and unsolved mysteries drove those that dwelled there to survive. The rain and city water fed the pockets of vegetation and patches of moss inside the tunnels. Five giants, men but not men, sat on majestic Jasper stone seats, they governed those that lived there. Very few living outside the long tunnels knew the mysterious culture existed. The underground tunnels extended for miles and miles. Those who were aware of the location and purpose kept it hidden. From time to time the Giants would agree to seek new blood. Like the outstretched arms of a little boy lost and a cavalier, their methods opened an opportunity of dreams to reality. The passageways have existed for many centuries. In no other way like any other collection of vast systems prepared to sustain are they commonplace. The place grows stronger and more inviting. It has seen many conquerors over generations, is as solid as the day it appeared and maintained by mysteries that drive many forward. Rusty plowed the resources of the tunnels back to his neighborhood, in Oakland California. His methods were like poetry, fitting into a good pastime at perfect pitch. Music among other things dedicated to the subterranean channels was necessary. The view was a rare one. As such a view, or trove, will never again offer the triumphs and challenges of the overhead footsteps of passerby's, to walk this way.

Fr. Louis had a proper discernment of most spiritual things. The moment he gave Darius and Devora the keys to the crystal-ball like Victorian on top of the subterranean world, he understood they were to inherit more than smiles that showed too many teeth. Rusty had a bright one. Cut, would eventually do most of the talking.

Fr. Louis, clearly saw the family would come to tell him of an offer with a *Nameless Builder* who was a secret spirit associate of Cut's. The Church had paid for the Victorian in full. Fr. Louis, the guardian, was destined to offer it to Darius and family, who renamed it *Westside*. Ever since the exchange of key holders, West and Realm Street has in so many words towered over the 1906 Victorian. For many years, Tessie had decorated the broken down community sidewalk with her scuffs. On her 37th birthday, she decided to add a march and pen a happy birthday to you in chalk. An unpainted storefront would celebrate its final building phases, with, "It's your birthday song."

It was breezy that day in October of 1964 when the *Nameless Builder* persuaded Darius to invest in Renesmee Liquor Store. When Darius accepted the bid, he supposed a new storefront would keep him busy. Furthermore, it could place plenty of stakes in the neighborhood's enterprise. The store would face the Victorian, enabling him to keep a close eye on his family and new business. Regardless of circumstances, the neighborhood married a myriad of tricky fanatics, creating a world's stage designed to turn vinegar into honey for what Fr. Louis called, *Sinners Hood*.

"The neighborhood looks mummified!" The *Nameless Builder* said.

"Or more like its supremacy is endangered," Darius answered.

"Exactly! A man of your resources, with his right hand free, can truly make a difference. You realize as well as I do that hope does not put food on the table or improve sidewalk cracks."

He watched Darius clinch a shisha pipe with his left hand, then offered him some orange juice, a pen, and encouraged him to take notes.

"In Egypt, a wise man that uses his left hand also relies on his right. Thank you, don't mind if I do take notes."

"One condition," the builder insisted. "Let me build Renesmee Liquor Store."

"Not so fast. Wait a minute," Darius' good judgment told him. "I do not even know this man's name."

Reading Darius' mind, the *Nameless Builder* responded, "A name is just a legion."

"A Legion?"

"A great number of breeding's from earth, things or multitudes, seen or unseen. Everything has a beginning. The beginning of a story, the beginning of life, good, evil, love-hate," said the builder.

"In my world, it is not how you begin, it is how you end. In Egypt, we call this life force." Darius answered.

"I am sorry I brought it up. It's not as I am teaching on morality, but here in America this is what we do, build legions. Most grow on life force regardless of the circumstances," answered the *Nameless Builder*.

Darius continued to deliberate, "I have a good sense that is what America seems to be all about, the never ending task of relationship building and negotiating. I'd like to change America for the better. Galaxy is nineteen years old. All her life she had three birthday parties, and before long she shall be graduating and I will gift her with my old Mercedes. Soon, she will move on with all of the best of things; now it's a perfect time to get it started. Although, before perfecting our union with a handshake, I will insist that one side of the storefront is assembled in brick and the other side in stone.

"Let the games begin, answered the *Nameless Builder*."

"Humph, games I thought we were building," Darius said.

"We are, it's called the game of a prosperous life!"

"Oh, the magic of believing," Darius thought.

Caught up in 20th -century reflections, Darius accepted the builder's dream bid. While a thousand stars twinkled under the black sky and over brick and stone, the *Nameless Builder's* own circumstances elevated. In the course of construction, Darius learned that the builder was a master sorcerer, and could scoop up individual stones and then render himself invisible to profit unwisely. He also learned that the *Nameless Builder* was a head slave to a coven of glamorous male *Flyby Nights*. He was lying about his real intentions for the neighborhood.

For centuries his methods left the eldest Vampires repulsed. *Flyby Nights* crush bones and leave them on floors as decorative signs.

The blood of needy families pleased them. They'd amuse and then finish off whole families beneath the California moon.

While the *Nameless Builder* continued to build, a few submissive human slaves of *Flyby Nights* laid in wait and snooped. They watched him sing a daily chant, "profits before principles, desert before blood." Many ferocious plans were in place. Vampire societies living in the city on the hill were unaware that the *Nameless Builder* and slaves of *Flyby Nights*, anticipated the soul of the neighborhood. Monsters from the no- fly zone, a section area inside Hotel Gosa, only wanted blood without leaving proof that they exist. So, when the plans of the *Nameless Builder* came to light, it infuriated powerful Vampire societies. The plot might bring unnecessary attention to their underworld, and doom the most magnificent Vampires living in the city on the hill inside Hotel Gosa.

By any means necessary Devora's bloodline and gold, assets were to be protected. She elected to destroy those within the subterranean hideout. The underground channels have seen many conquerors over generations and will remain as solid as the day it appeared, always maintaining mysteries that drive many headfirst. When her *Die Nuss* was required to engage, its might was supreme, and could potentially force the other Vampire societies into battle. All of Julius' creations were created to surrender to *Die Nuss*. Julius taught, "Fool them because gold, precious jewels, and cash money were at stake." These resources to any Vampire taking on human ways were as vital as human blood.

At times such as these, subordinate *Flyby Nights*, and their slaves would dare to test the shrouded mystery of *Die Nuss*, putting all of earth at risk, even pushing very, very powerful Vampire covens into their crypts for thousands of years.

Die Nuss launched with nine hidden disks, two- time machines, and the ability to bounce through water and fire. Out of water, fire, and other elements discovered by the time-travelers in the SOS underground cave a surprise was born in the wake of an underground dig, Julius. When they made Julius, the time-travelers began to understand and appreciate the importance of a source of combat that they created and named *Die Nuss*. In the beginning, Vampires were created for the method's reasons. Dig first, money later. Only the foolish elected their own destruction.

The eldest Vampires created by Julius were over a thousand years old. Originally they were unbelievably magnificent, wore helmets and fanciful hats, rode the finest thoroughbred horses, drank pure blood from chalices, and kept many favorite concealed pasttimes. They were not like the *Flyby Nights*, who enjoyed trickery and raw despicable bites to human flesh. Throughout the centuries they'd gathered at *Twin Towers* located in the soul of Carpathian Mountains. Julius permitted the eldest to breed at this particular location for centuries. During these times the *Flyby Nights* abstained from breeding and feeding. When Julius 'eldest bred, their union intended to create the purest Vampires through systematized intercourse. The practice occurred in a few different ways and finalized by them. Very few of these Vampire societies exist in America. Some have departed Egypt and Europe to occupy remote regions in America. These families are very mysterious. Many are hermits, collector of things, some have odd names, but they are not oddballs and are stronger than the eldest *Flyby Nights*, and slaves combined.

For reasons only known to the time travelers who created him, Julius never listened to hermits. He frequently looked to human slaves controlled by Vampires and *Flyby Nights*. Many of them were wealthy bankers and accountants. Inside of Julius' purest conception, one of his friends listened to a hermit, Devora's midwife, Daciana. The hermits took small bites of willing virtuous humans who respected their history. The hermits helped and protected them from untold dangers and secrets veiled behind the mysteries of Vampirism and extreme cruelty and brutality.

Devora's ancient bloodline linking arms in Egypt with settled governments during the making of Mint of Zeb enabled *Die Nuss* to flourish to the degree undreamt of the by the Sa and all of Egypt. The royal residence of the Yu and their descendants also preserved the life source and method in the afterlife. It was a divine gift given to Devora and her offspring. In the fullness of its own power and mysteries, they knew *Die Nuss* from their umbilical cords. Darius was born Sa. He gained some ability through loyalty and association, but he was mostly skilled in Egyptian mysticism. Out of Devora's need to survive in a new land, she shared some of the secret methods with Darius. The Sa had very little exposure to its full power and secrecies. Even to this day, their tribe is unaware of the capacity of *Die Nuss*. Like the best of what reincarnation can provide it only gets stronger after death.

Devora and Darius had no other choice but to protect their family from the *Nameless Builder*'s potions, phantoms, and *Flyby Nights* covens. Unseen rays had swiftly taken effect on Darius. Minutes after watching the builder lay the final bricks before the completion of a small tower above the store, Darius' vision was attacked. A force like a gun that didn't jam tore into his left eye, making it useless. He immediately sought Devora's help. Her *Die Nuss* quickly sealed the destiny of the nameless fury. Vital threads hemmed in the pursuits of completion invoked a million sound soldiers with aims of supernatural phenomenon, and it was victorious. Remarkably, one effect of the method stimulated perfect vision in his right eye. Darius had multi-colored eyes which could change when he was speaking. An increase from fifty percent capacity, three seconds before the loss of power occurring in his left blue eye, relocated to his right green eye. The extraordinary transference of power was entirely beyond explanation. Tables of mysterious components of eye fractions called by Devora's *Die Nuss* defended and shielded him from further injury. Darius's eyes restored like flesh seasoned for little wonders would share a thousand noondays setting before earth.

Meanwhile, Tessie and Fr. Louis believed it took a village to raise everything all together. From the beginning, they had been aware of the *Nameless Builders*' evil intentions. Their involvement of faith facilitated in completely crushing every single associated curse of the building blocks, its nameless fury, and the crew of *Flyby Nights* attempting to control, destroy, and kill the soul of their neighborhood.

On the eve of that terrible battle, one thousand *Flyby Nights* formed weapons against Darius and his family. By not honoring ancient Vampire treaties one thousand of the purest Vampires were laid to waste in one night. Ten thousand *Flyby Nights* and their slaves from the underground tunnels gave power to Galaxy's *Die Nuss*.

"Oh, might she turn into the monster they all loved but feared. Do you know who she is?" Darius asked the *Nameless Builder*.

"I got a girl at our store gate who does not know who she is," the *Nameless Builder* answered, sarcastically.

"Oh she is beautiful, and what a lovely day it is for the power of ten thousand consumed by her *Die Nuss* appearing on behalf of *Justice*. Oh, death to *Flyby Nights*, and Vampire's if treaties are broken, for Galaxy may awaken *Those who must be kept*! The love and loyalty between Future and Galaxy are beyond the power of *Die Nuss*." Darius shuttered.

The purest living Vampires on earth in ten thousand five hundred BC would consume her enemies if any enemy breached treaties in a mystery shrouded in this ancient system where blood was channeled into the core of the highest mystery. What's more, those one thousand laid to waste in the afterworld are subjects to her twin's authority to honor him. For it was written in their ancient reserve called Star that it is good to give their one living Creator eternal thanks from the bottom up within a virtuous circle. As one hundred thousand feel his men.

The *Flyby Nights* assembly, *Ran Mac ally, that silent killer goes on looting treasure,* living in the city on the hill were alert. They flew low. It was in their best interest to cooperate in the world of swells which Devora called Watchtower. With that virtuous wings did not burn. And the eternal *Die Nuss* guarded its method, like those who are called in the argot, to safeguard its rewards. Indeed, *Die Nuss* governed and exceeded the knocks of minions, holding the franchise of hate, greed, and eager set-ups for blood menus in their neighborhood. Leaving the method intact for one secret member to get the mums, for your *Justice,* and still, some ask if *Justice* is blind and all tied up? Indeed, *Blind Justice* promises to wake the others. It is a slam-dunk when the innocent say's delicious, and seas the day.

West & Realm & 8 Mile Journey & A Golf Course

ONE NOVEMBER AFTERNOON a few weeks before a terrible battle, Tessie, and black and white dotted paws walked side-by-side all the way down West and Realm Street. Tessie claimed that God had empowered her with a supernatural strength that allowed her to walk eight miles. It wasn't even a working day. She had spent most of the day visualizing plans for retirement. Her soothing voice and a distinctive spiritual veil within Lazarus' pupil encouraged him to continue with her. With faraway eyes inside a peculiarity, he happily followed. During the long walk recollections of his beloved Devora grew. Every day has a genesis, and clusters of nations likened to the first fruits of the Valley of the King offered them love songs. He did not know that the love of his life was just a bus ride away.

Like someone's hard knock life, somebody could be anybody. Tessie sang and tapped along the pavement where the store was in construction, then pointed to the *Nameless Builder* who was assembling bricks.

"Chew he is not the one, we'll tackle it together!" She quietly whispered.

"Name your song, Renesmee! Wasteland gives prospect!" He cried out loud.

"That *Nameless Builder* is not the one, but you already knew that. He would kill a greyhound, after running it to death, and may even have employed killing squads. The wolves in the neighborhood are never overwhelmed. Many are like lion's carrying heavy loads and shall triumph. Some in the neighborhood have more pleats than a Catholic girl has in her skirt. Listening to music shall straighten those out. It is a strange time for him to be wearing undergarments with dancing skeletons and assembling bricks." She muttered under her breath.

"Wherever there is a carcass there is a buzzard somewhere." Lazarus reflected.

"We'll need the spirit of Rottweiler by our bed. My character is alive and well, and I'll get you some treats later!" She assured Lazarus, who was hungry for dog biscuits.

"And stop playing with the mail!" She yelled out to the builder.

Days before, the builder was following a thug near some community mailboxes.

"Put it in a song! Call it Renesmee Liquors!" He shouted out again and continued working.

"I know what he is up to; I am not stupid. My neighborhood protects the same ole song! I know a sad song when I hear it and all points in between. The neighborhood must stop the bloodthirsty conflict. It's like the beginning of a history of the first humans, beginning with Cain the Fratricide." She thought to herself.

She quickly scanned the sidewalk for some rubber bands and decided in all her getting, get understanding.

"He is not going to pigeon hole us! A pocket full of bands could make a dog dance, but this builder might put a rubber band man to shame."

With a few bands in view, bob and weave Tessie tap, and one wag Chew was at attention. A few days later on the final day of the building's construction, *Justice* forced the builder to take off his undergarment.

He bellowed to *Justice*, "So why don't you kill me? And who let the dogs out?"

She shouted back, "You best watch what you say before you crumble like pastry! You were given the opportunity to build and enhance the neighborhood. Instead, you built with the intentions of harming folks. When the appetite for alcohol dries up, the store has to go! Hide those godforsaken death shorts, and disappear!"

Suddenly, *The Nameless Builder* threw some bricks at the brick wall. Turning to the other side, to face the Stonewall after nearly perforating it with an angry punch, his five knuckles shrank leaving behind a visible print. An intense rain began to pour. The wind and impact forced *The Nameless Builder* threads of bones to ascend into the galaxies.

"Bye, bye, and bye, I am programmed to receive the truth, and it shall set me free!" Tessie sang as she marched down West Street, as the *Nameless Builder* floated up and on. Her final words sent him, and his undergarments back into a camouflaged space rock amidst other crooked footprints with mustaches in the mountains.

After the storefront had been completed Cut introduced Darius and Devora to a peculiar street artist. At first glance one may have taken him for a poor bum. His shiny metallic black sweater and black hat were made from a different cloth. He was dark skinned with thin lips, high cheekbones, and of an indefinite age. Most of all his mind's eye stretched authority with a promise. This being was exceptional.

In a monotone voice, he spoke, "Let me refinish and paint the stone wall. I'm different, yes I'm different! The mural will be beautiful and bear gifts for ear hustlers who understand what's going on. I am like a statue of the West Coast of responsibility, my parliaments do not burn, and tonight we can be as one. When you and Devora wake from dream time we can take exceptional decisions and even play golf together."

Darius did not play golf, Devora did, but they both believed and accepted the dream invitation. Tessie was faithful that his magnetic genetic paintbrushes would help to perform like a truck Turner mission. The street artist pledged not to disturb the memories on West Street, especially since time and fading memories can be humanities' worst enemy. He counted his work as joy, adorning the stonewall with a gathering of men who were designed to create a condition.

The street artist named the wall "Stacking Cheese," and believed all the people illustrated on the stone side were painted in peace with those who made peace, for California dreaming.

Acts of divine providence compelled his set of paintbrushes to participate with the past, present, and future. In time it helped shape countless living conditions.

Homestead & Heaven

To protect the street painter from any possible attacks, Tessie prayerfully petitioned God for security. She appealed for a greater purpose beyond anything imagined to take place on the Stonewall. A merging of like-minded souls due to prolonged contact filled them up with uninterrupted joy for seven days. From the Victorian window, she yelled something positive to the artist all seven days.

"I've got a crush on you, timer tall! You're heaven sent. Remember, trust the one you're with, your paint brush!"

On the last day, he replied. "Pleased to meet you, such things you say. Do you know what the red stripes represent?"

She responded, "Is faith still relevant; I got more than good music inside me?"

Using his right index finger, the artist pointed to the last stripe on the American flag.

Suddenly, Tessie noticed his thumbs were missing.

"He paints with such ease," she thought.

Although he was flesh and blood, he was not human. One elongated forefinger dripped red onto his brush. "A gift for you, Tessie," he said.

The painted wall scenes absorbed the neighborhood's heartbeats. One scene produced a genetic blend between a young black boy and white girl near a blood red door. The American flag was between them.

"Brown sugar, the boy, and girl require more authority and were not made to suffer. Don't act like I never told you." He continued.

The painter used substances mixed with hydrogen peroxide to paint the girl and boy's skin, allowing for the absorption of mysterious nutrients enabling him to take life force which might seal someone's fate.

Tessie replied, "Thank you, I love the scene, but you lack the courage of your conviction. Sir, I have come to answer just your imagination, a choice to become what you became. I was given authority." She sang,

"Hit it, fork!
Holy warrior one head.
Red stripes bloodshed.
Bold raid for the dead
Blessed by homestead."

The painter turned to the setting sun. "I am a being of taste and melody. There is still life in these painted scenes."

He poured an unknown blood red liquid substance into his palm. Like flowing fluid it ascended and descended into the atmosphere. The unearthly color in his palms made Tessie think of a very important crusade. She sighed, "Don't make me look any longer, I heard a sound wave, alright."

King Me

It was the last month of Tessie's employment with the family. For weeks she was spellbound by the various scenes painted on the store's stonewall. The depictions gave way to contemplations about talents that she would never possess. *Renessmee Liquors* was finally stuffed full and ready for business. The day before the opening she spied from the window and saw a falling box cough out Paraphernalia. Bits and pieces of broken glass pipes fell, scattering like marbles toward the store's front door.

"*Renessmee Liquors*, can't be undone, it is locked in something that had always been," she whispered and quickly closed the window curtain.

That same evening, during a brisk walk to the bus station, Tessie was sure that she heard a voice crying, "When you're in the window you can do everything. Let me out, let the right one out!" The orders were the craziest thing in the world, and it was coming from the store's mural.

"Something might read my thoughts," she pondered. Traveling at sunset was risky when a Vampire loves a woman. After turning the corner, a very thick mist came over a shoebox of a church named *Brotherhood Presbyterian*. Oddly, other parts of the area were clear. The large parking lot on an open dirt field facing the church and some modest homes looked as if not just the dead would make the menu.

There was a distinct whisper, "Tessie, thank the heavens you're back. Only you can leave me without a place to rest."

She hid her thoughts. It was Julius. He was sitting on the church rooftop seeking a window into Tessie's mind. She did not give him an inch into her thoughts.

"My dear, the night before the Liquor Store's opening, you dare to sterilize your thoughts with holy water. You are no plaster saint, Tessie."

He quickly vanished.

Looking in the distance, she saw a Rottweiler walking towards the church.

Its piercing blue eyes carried a silent reserve. Wonder filled the air as she watched the hound stroll into the evening field. His walk toward the church appeared calculated, like some cosmic manifestation. Its black coat mingled with the coming darkness. She wondered who owned the dog. Was it Cut's, or did it belong to the *Nameless Builder*? Perhaps the dog was there to guard both men like a force demanding corner rights.

The Rottweiler took an alternate route into the Victorian's courtyard. He stared at Rusty who was perched on a nearby fire hydrate around the corner from Renesmee Liquors. He was watching a few rats gnawing on some poison that the *Nameless Builder* had flung down from the scaffolding. In the meantime, Tessie remembered the Rottweiler's solemn eyes. His stare conveyed a message of paternal concern, "better go home before you catch a deadly cold or even death."

Her blood ran cold.

"I am more into the heat then the cold, and must deploy like a fleet of submarines." She picked up her pace.

Tessie believed the dog's ominous stare was a warning to prepare, watch, and listen. His piercing stare reminded her of a song she once heard, *Nobody Lives Here Anymore*. She determined the hound was God's Rottweiler with a message. His sharp eyes were ready to strike intelligently and reflected the coming of rusty nails, broken boards, and the strangulation of spirits threatening to claim many lives. With this warning in mind, a strong understanding came over her. It was honest and employed a menu of simplicity. With every step, she prayed, "If God can save me, he can save anybody."

A friend in an old International truck saw Tessie walking and offered her a ride. She kindly accepted, they talked and rode for a short while. Tessie said it was ok, to get dropped off a few blocks from her home.

"Thanks, friend," she jumped out the truck and waived.

In the distance, she saw Lazarus. His slow trudge up the street and clickety-clacks of the distant train tracks encouraged her to pick up speed. She was sweating a little from the humidity. Suddenly, the Rottweiler came to mind.

She wondered if the dog had prolonged contact with them, might he consume Chew?

On the other hand, Chew might consume him. One thing was as sure as the final ride of a north conductor; both dogs were created with strong appetites.

"To eat or to be eaten that is the question." She contemplated.

"You've got a friend in me, dogs. Hope the sidewalk feels cool. Chew, the dark side of the moon will swallow the heat soon, I promise."

One would have thought an angel threw cold water on Lazarus paws.

Bang, bang, bang!

The sound of flying bullets struck the atmosphere. Tessie took cover. Lazarus followed. Skrrr skrr skrr… The sound of the moving car was loud.

The ever-present street man, Rusty, must have always been right behind her because when she looked up, he was face down on the sidewalk on the other side of the road. He had dodged bullets, broken glass, and escaped death itself. The shots flat out missed him. A big window behind a large porch collapsed into seven lungs.

He quickly rose from the pavement, ran across the middle of the road towards Tessie, fell on the lawn and cried out, "I am a mighty man, girl!" Then his spirit man shifted into the grass like a bat swirling into a cave returning gorged with food before dawn. When Cut's spirit left, Rusty's body rolled a little bit closer to Tessie. She had jumped on a small patch of green grass. He tried to grab her by the hand, but she did not permit him to. Tessie ran over to the sidewalk checking it for blood and did not see any.

"You can't touch this in the heavens, hell, or on earth. The blood of Jesus was not a flash in the pan; it was drawn and shed. Go home, boys! There are levels to this, and it is by my faith in Jesus that Cut is protected," she shouted to the speeding thugs!

The boys yelled back, "ding a ling, ding a ling, spreading like jelly!"

She studied the Chevy as the Busters sped off into the slipping sun. The taint devoured the highway to hell, and then without warning, bad boys no older than peach fuzz tossed a wire. Above the rim spat fire with back-to-back caps dashing into balling tires, a pigeon laid crushed under its fury.

November rain began raging, in weird blazing heat. Such a shooting was also unheard of in Tessie's part of the neighborhood. Road youngsters, a blizzard of bullets, she pinched her shoulder and recalled Cut slipping through the cracks of the concrete coded ABC. The rain had washed the letters away. Rusty, wearing a white muddied T and blue jeans with rubber bands tied to the bottom, picked up his limp body, slapped her little palm then ran off.

An hour later, undercover workforces freckled the streets. Their movements resembled a reptilian fleet. Ordinarily, it took 15 minutes for an emergency response team to arrive for routine matters. Is this the new normal? She wondered.

A disappearing sun slipped off the rain. Soon nightfall met a dance. Some youth were playing double Dutch in the rain. While hammering footfalls broke up wet soil, it nudged blood relations to offer heaven, Spirit.

She whispered, "Standing by and doing nothing would be like a rose in the desert unable to proclaim its reason for beauty."

As one teardrop fell in a circus of hungry death squads and phantom suspects, Tessie prayed. "Beauty is what beauty does. I shall call forth stronger arms, messengers, and kneel as Lions kneel in the survival dens of fiery hoops."

She did not own a gun, but in time guns and fiery hoops became maneuvers, paralleling successful ricochets with youth hollering, "Free lunch!"

Tessie snatched two chains. Dangling from her neck was a little locket. Pills hit the ground like influence feeding ground in a war with her psychiatrist whom she named the *devil's mistress*.

Tessie was born with excessive fluid on the brain. A shunt implanted to relieve her brain pressure helped. As she matured, medical doctors acknowledged psychiatric issues, which led to excessive treatments causing more harm than good. It was determined that she would not live more than twelve years. Tessie defied all odds. As years went on, like an epic escape, she left science astonished. Their treatments led to more prescriptions of pills, eventually causing cancer and the need for a part-time caregiver named Brünnhilde. In odd ways Tessie's spiritual strength grew extraordinarily, demonstrating to so many people at the Center, that faith is still relevant.

Racing on with Jesus Christ, and taking an aim by crushing unnecessary pills beneath her heel, she prayed daily to humiliate her medical doctors.

"No pills! Cool breeze, ain't taken em again. I'll do the right thing, and un-cuff this mistress." She made the sign of the cross, thanked God for grace, and then attached two chains to her neck.

It was Brünnhilde's job to see to it that Tessie took her pills. She swallowed them sometimes. Other times she hid them under her tongue, spit them out and would curl up in her bed like a potato bug.

Waiting to exhale she sighed, "A match made in heaven for the hearts of many." Continuing to deliberate, she asked, "Is prayer more powerful than pills or flying bullets? Are the shots in the neighborhood a sign that something has failed to deliver on aspirations?"

Eventually, fierceness would get the world's attention, but only when other children from radically wealthy areas began turning their guns on each other shouting, "God isn't going to fix this!" Even now wires placed around the hearts of many would reveal who would betray whom first.

"Woof, woof, woof!"

"I bless the fool who has to listen to you bark. Sit, Chew, sit!"

He obediently fell to her feet.

While an early evening cloud draped over them, Lazarus had a flashback to his last days in Egypt. He expressed remorse with a long whine. He remembered the rebels before leaving Egypt. A long piece of spit fell from his tongue like the used condom he was sitting on.

"Get up, let's go home. This place is unclean! It's unbelievable!" Tessie said.

From that time on, Lazarus was more aware than worldwide knocks on a hull trading wickedness for relief. Homeward bound they went.

Blind Street A House That Telegraph Built

Tessie resided on a cul de sack named "Blind Street." Its long narrow lane curved like a peaceful nap extended into West Street. West and Realm was an 8-mile ride down Telegraph.

Seventeen homes bordered the narrow street. Each dwelling comforted the other like men in mirrors facing a legacy of burning bushes. An old wives' tale passed down for generations said one song in a dwelling, and well beyond the gold shaft of sunlight from an angel's room shall eternally sing, *Dear Mama*. Its might, a tower of strength, also reflected the cul de sac to preserve a lullaby for those who wish upon a star. The people loved the song and gave it the best of care.

Tessie's prayers in the quiet parts of her soul valued the people in her community. Dead right she controlled them. In all her life not once had there been a home burglary, termites, or mold. The hoggone- wild gangsters nibbling from the bait of salvation knew not to rob her, or any of the homes on Blind Street. That area just refused to experience the nightmares of thefts. Black cars on the side of two narrow lanes and steely poles along its aisles were as unsearchable as a king's heart for the poor.

A few blocks down was *Shields Grocery Store*. Before reaching home, she stopped inside to buy dog food and a coconut.

Lazarus had been slobbering about all day. He was either perfectly happy or hungry.

"Wait here, and I'll get those biscuits I promised you."

He waited near a thin pole and recalled days in Egypt when servants stirred pots and filled bowls. As the liquid part of blood coursed through his veins, he remembered the statue, Alia.

Memories bloomed from past nights when unceasing streams of sapphire coursed through the statue's veins. The memory felt like a first meal and triggered more than a mood. He longed for real freedom and liberty. As a result, love pled his case before his Creator.

"Shut your eyes, and you will not notice me, Alia. Time feels like feet dragging with limestone rock carved out a thousand years ago! The old reduced to scorch and ash like an untouched snack bar, my appetite wanes. My search for Devora bears a resemblance to illuminating shards of what was written. Time isn't the most valuable thing. Undeniably it has produced more thirst for love than *Justice*. Is it not a matter of hope, or only a matter of time when we will meet, again? But who will wake-up your body? In a very short while, this woman Tessie has prompted a personal faith within me. And I do not entirely understand her particular faith.

It reminds me of sacrifice and the peace I briefly felt on the day I choose to flee the ship. A man near his bike sighed Hail, Mary wants a rider.

His words enveloped my heart, but I panicked and ran from Darius and my beloved. May I walk this way on mosaic tiles in Egypt? Our footsteps once swayed to mortal bliss.

Where is Devora? Darius spoke about a promise. It has not transformed my form. Should I call to Morpheus the god of dreams, a plea that shall certainly stir the pot? Alia, your veins are burning. I sense it, but might not return to tear my jaws into them. Have you become a mirror, and I a diamond in the rough? Shall I scratch you to prove that I am real? Remnants of my past were in a mirror touched by the love of healthy hearts. Must I leave you then shoot through glass to uncover the truth? I am indeed tempted; however, the sight of broken glass kills you quietly. Alia, you must help find my love, my brother, and my children. Do the hidden details of your actual manifestations always have to play the happy harlot?"

A long sigh sounded like a wave of unanswered questions. Darius settled on not merging with the statue's spiritual identity just yet. However, its mission for blood was indeed on the brink of exploding. The food of hope, love, and truth would abide for now. Though, if his joining with Devora stayed veiled, it was only a matter of time before the statue would wake. Its identity was only sleeping and has since 14 BCE.

Schmuck & The Don

TESSIE HURRIED DOWN the aisles at *Shields Grocery Store* and caught the scent of death. The smell of rats had become a pawn in a bigger game.

"Junk Food!" She cried, tracked back and checked the shelves for dog food.

"No dog food! Somebody is going to have to explain why there is no Gravy Train."

Tessie grabbed some dog crackers, milk, Kilpatrick's bread, a small bear-shaped bottle filled with honey, and a coconut. There were a few customers meandering about when a short, stout man wearing a black hat, suit, and bifocal glasses forced Tessie to protect the meek possessions wrapped within her arms.

Let me find out, she wondered.

"Hey mister, can you spare a dime?"

His spit flung and split into thin air, "No! You poor make do with public service!"

His front teeth hinged outward. He was holding an old music book and some Wonder Bread. Without any regard, he pushed a cart into her rib. She flinched, tucked her chin and privately thought, he dead, yep he dead.

His nauseating odor soaked in the only shield between them, the shopping cart. It belonged to a big man who was wearing a black cap.

The big man gently squeezed in between them and the cart. He was holding a pack of ice. "Sir, I can't figure it out! That impulsive push took only one step for you, but for the lady and me it was a giant leap to rise above pettiness."

Tessie barked, "Disrespectful parasite just tried to crack the wrong dozen."

The short man was visibly shaken. He squinted his eyes lifted his glasses but kept his composure.

"Who did you expect to see? Why, between the pigs and the bureaucrats, I have to escape the pen, and y'alls taunts of goofs and mouths of isolation." He began whistling.

"Hey, schmuck, this is a line. I pay taxes just like you do." The big man raised his voice.

"Time to pray," Tessie whispered.

"Stands your ground, just like the rest of us! You talk like you're our prisoner, so present your ID to Jesus. He is the one that deserves your vote!" She bellowed.

Her glare could have domesticated a viper burning for a lesson in obedience.

"The big man interrupted. That's right Tall T. The very small man casts a very tricky scene."

The big man paid for his groceries and then gave Tessie a dozen eggs.

"Thank you very much, their hatching major!"

"My pleasure ghetto saint, I see you on the corner every day faithfully standing and holding the paper made of rags."

Tessie sighed tenderly.

"Would you like a bag, lady?" asked the cashier.

"Of course I'd like a bag!"

The big man swiped his knuckles turned around and stared deeply into the short man's eyes; without any change in tone, he said, "If you touch her again I am going to break your fucking neck. Keep your head up for brown sugar smalls. I am not mad at you, but if you whistle cloud nine, you'll get hotter than an eight eye's range cooking a turkey for an all-night party. The land that party pecks belong to us, and from the land comes everything, including meals on wheels."

He chuckled, and then flashed a button. It read, "You can't scare me I am a social worker."

It's Shady, Bam Was His Name-O

TESSIE AND LAZARUS had a good view of what was happening on the other side of the fence. She opened it. "Hey, pencil thin."

"Mind your business, it's in the bag." Her nostrils flared.

Cousin George O was as gay as a two-dollar bill. He was the kind of guy who ate the understory in a jungle, and minced rice with homemade chopsticks that he made himself. And they were rather beautiful.

Her fixed voice went right through him, "Jumbo Jaws you're always smacking at the sight of foodstuff!"

"I am worried. Where did you get that dog?" He asked

"Where was your ass at when Julius took cosmic manifestations, sucker?"

"I have a problem with the force of order, a weak, aging regime. It's sad. Ya know you can't afford to keep the dog. Looks like you want big dog status, and fleas, a huge one is in the house, yours truly Julius. He's inside waiting for you."

"We are united there since everything between you and I is divided." She smiled.

"Now come give me a hug. You have it easy. You're not the police officer of the world!" He grinned back.

Lazarus sat swollen like a packed keeper on a cradle of ribs.

"Get your happy skinny butt off my porch and go home. Where's my fifty- cents?" Her thoughts drifted back.

"Where did you pull that value out of, a bag of weed?"

"You owe me, money remember Georgie?"

"Be nice T."

"Cuz, you have plenty of souls to eat on the street, my pit is definitely off limits. He is a part of a fragile empire. Let's say, like souls that continue to transfer power because they have it. That is why he has jaws that lock, like the rolling stones if need be. Now gets, I want cash money."

"Be obliged! Nobody better snatch that kind of power. You're something else girl, I'll be back later on with fifty cents, to pay the bump." He said with a throaty crackle.

"Now see, I smell catfish and sardine fish pie, and I'm not smoking on no gas. All I need is what's next, and it takes two, so get to bumping!" Tessie wiggled a little bit.

The Ghost of Westside was spying. He wagged his ghostly nose and then disappeared.

While walking off, George farted. Its bark was in sync with the nearby construction team.

"Gas and loud two of a kind! Now drive off fumes and get to busting!"

"Indeed, Cuz. I smell channel number 5 from my rooftop, short whiffs. But, count my money, don't dress it up short, pay me bigly!"

"Sounds like suitable apparel for the holidays."

Their stares locked, as royal fingers woven through leather clutches do.

Meek Is What Meek Does

REAL DOGS SEE everything in black and white. For the last eighteen years, Lazarus' human vision focused on one mission, to find Devora. His love for her held full color. He scanned Tessie's front room. A Lazy Boy couch wrapped in plastic was the room's centerpiece. Its low back nudged against a bone colored wall that faced two horsehair love seats. They stared back like shielded places that never stray. The front room was simply clean. The kind of clean where mites in corners crowd on top of dust and crave to cling to bleach rags fixed for everyday clearance.

Pictures of Tessie's loved ones propped up on a Victorian mantel below an electric heater pulled off crooked smiles. Their beautifully wide grins were ready to love and accept anyone who shined just right.

Tessie hit the front room light switch. Suddenly, a louder noise high-jacked her eardrums. Lazarus' ears stood erect.

She sighed, "That's right the drippy underground maze of channels, drip, drip, drip. Follow me, Chew."

She got a large pot and filled it with milk and dog crackers. "Now, you ain't in everything, so eat, and stays in this bathroom until I return with ears on an angel."

The loudness increased as a thin smoke filled a dimly lit hallway. Tessie crept towards her bedroom door. It was slightly cracked.

"Shut the door." Julius' voice was music on the battlefield with time. Humming Tessie obeyed like any meek hostess would.

Julius was alone in a dark corner. A small wall light cracked down on his wool chauffer's cap. His distinct voice was low, it stomped her pink bedroom walls to hold a blow with cancer. While three high walls listened to everything watching monsters tear down other monsters, his voice deprived them all for Tessie's body and soul.

"T, the pipes need limits. The noise isn't necessary."

"What is necessary, my humming, the machine, or the mystery?" She asked.

"Your humming soothes purgatory. I envy it. The machine makes me hungry for the God of Abraham, but like a plumber when I desire either they are not with me. They are with you. The mystery is a mystery, and impossible to understand like the supply of unlimited grace."

"I smell a fragrant cologne. You do not want me to fall again do you?"

"The energy company is here. No, I do not want you to slip or fall. You do not belong on the ground. Your flesh has mingled with water and has bled plenty." He answered.

Suddenly the outside noise stopped.

"Who let you in?" Tessie asked with one raised eyebrow.

"The U.S.A, have you heard!" He clowned.

"I am chuckling, but it is not funny. Who let you in, Joker?"

"I have a light footstep."

"You should cross land or sea to do my bidding," Tessie whispered.

"My dear Tessie, if you'd known what I did in the past, you would have been blacked out! I have the ability to flow into what frightens you. Be still and listen."

His tone was hypnotic, Julius moved in closer then sat on Tessie's bed and began combing through her wooly hair with his fingernails.

"After rebels removed two ancient concrete slabs during a dig in Egypt, four mystic crystal statues thrown into the Nile surfaced. The crystal statues should have remained in the *Temple of Essen*, not thrown into the sea like fish food. Our hidden sea world will not stand for nonsense. Later, a righteous Sa priest discovered three royal mummies missing from the temple. *Those Who Must Be Kept* consider the crystal Vampire crypts, and royal mummies sacred."

"Who are *Those Who Must Be Kept*?" She asked.

"A powerful established spiritual army of Nazarene. They merit powerful influences of trails and influences over many spheres including their favorite, a sphere in terrestrial music."

"The royal mummies?"

"These three royal mummies were descendants from a conquering race. They are more powerful in the spirit realm than earth's oldest relics. Each nature remains true and has since the beginning. Neither side blinks. The royal mummies and *Those Who Must Be Kept* had given their life without knowing how to die. If you want to hear them speak, it shall only be through me and one other secret person of vital energy, who made a dead man come."

"Please, tell me more."

"After leaving Mint of Zeb, it was just after midnight when our ship departed Egypt to sail overseas with salt, three limestone sarcophagi, apparel, five hundred passengers, and other sacred items including my crypt. The sarcophagi sailed for weeks without a single window to the day world. A secret council protected us, and our treasury. A real captain never abandons hordes of treasure and tablets with cartouche and epithets of Aten. Otherwise, his whole crew might have been killed. Our secret council did their jobs well, after dark I did it better. Still, some on the ship began getting suspicious about many things. Like masked intentions mysteries remain best when they are indecipherable. After sailing and feeding very little, the ship arrived in Europe. We discarded a few heavily drained bodies by throwing them overboard to an assembly of Vampire sea creatures. In return, the bloodiest vertebrates' on the planet came out of the sea. We fed on hagfish-like humans feed on lifesaving rolls. There wasn't a lack of blood on the ship. I was selective, and precise about choosing the terms not during but after we arrived in the new land. Devora and the twins she carried would have annihilated our species with her killing method, *Die Nuss,* another incomprehensible mystery.

The ship managed to land safely at every port, until our final destination. No authority defeated our species, nor the moving vessel. Indeed we did not bet on it or follow it. *Die Nuss* is incompressible, like Devora's Messiah."

Tessie stared long and did not reveal any information about Devora or the family. She tried her best to block her thoughts, insisting for Julius to proceed,

"Please go on, my interest is genuine."

"Two human bodies decomposing near a crypt of *Those Who Must Be Kept* later formed new flesh. When the smell of decomposing flesh was detected, a mystery inside one-stone crypt caused the pair to open their *Flyby Nights* eyes. They were born out of a mystery and their own decomposing flesh. We refused to experience a deadly standoff with the unknown. *Those Who Must Be Kept*, would have destroyed us. Much of the time we remained inconspicuous. In England, neither Vampire nor *Flyby Nights* drank the blood of royals. The Royals happily entertained me with things that the Vatican hated. Do you know what sounds better than bloodsuckers Tessie?

"What?"

"What is better than a bloodsucking race is faith and belief in the power of the blood of Jesus, the Messiah, who gifted eternal life to those who believe."

"It makes you cringe and less powerful." She replied.

"With His name, everything might be done to protect Holy churches. Faith in the blood of Jesus deters Vampires. It deterred us from remaining in England. Some people and Vampires that left the ship returned within twenty-four hours after surveying, frolicking, dancing, and feeding wildly. Much of England has transmogrified. Even to this day, most Vampires say there is no England anymore. I crave a different kind of blood, that of the upper class, but I have abstained for many centuries.

"How bloody predictable." She answered.

"Only the eldest and advanced understand the meaning of this. We had gone back through time traveling to feed where masses were heavy. We owned our own currency and feasted all night in salons and barracks with lying eyes. When our sarcophagi arrived in 20th

century America, we were carefully carried off to a building. My dear Tessie, I am the first purest ancient Vampire to enter the new world. Now, I and the sarcophagi from the ship rest safely under a building. Our resting place was undisclosed then and still remains undisclosed. It is a kingdom shrouded in blood secrets and wealth."

"Hmmm, the building, of course, must be the Center."

"No, Tessie, it's a looney bin. And no one leaves with I would of, I should of, or I could of."

"It sounds like you are in the middle of a worsening epidemic. The way your eyes have looked at me in the dark for years, one might think you're here to finish me off tonight." Tessie pushed out both cheeks.

"You are very perceptive my dear. However, there are many Centers. I was most glad to be welcomed to the First. I can hear your heartbeat. Just a few more minutes, that's all I need."

Julius moved closer to Tessie and pressed his forefinger against her lips.

"Now pay attention, *Those Who Must Be Kept* have promised me that you and yours will not be turned or be killed.

"My family does not visit the Center. Only on one occasion, some have visited the looney bin. What is that aroma? I smell cologne, might this be emanating from the *Labyrinth*?"

"Delectable you are, the scent of cologne bleeds through the *Labyrinth*, but you won't be bitten! Your faith in the blood of Jesus Christ protects you. *Those Who Must Be Kept* believe a mysterious merging shall happen through you, as faith in the blood has promises that are desirable to them. They are pure energy, but hold power to transform the thirstiest Vampires of humanities' darkest times."

She wailed, "The fragrant Cologne is getting strong. What promises are there in the *Labyrinth*?" Suddenly Julius swooped her up. She felt carried through the air. They landed in one part of the *Labyrinth*. An assortment of things hurried out to him.

"You have died, and come back. You just showed me how space-time affects energy, and gravity, Tessie."

The fog in her head cleared. Smiling long, she sat cross-legged on an ice floor of the *Labyrinth*. Men are such fools, such absolute fools!"

"Would you like to spend an hour right in the heart of the inner sanctum laughing! Long live the Holy Labyrinth," replied Julius.

"All things are possible as long as I believe?" She asked in amazement.

"Yes, yelled Julius, let me tell the reason I have not chosen to feed."

He began flying throughout some areas within the *Labyrinth*.

"Tell it like it is, Julius,"

"The new world, with its ignorance and pride sickens me. My palate rejects their new normal, it's deadly! *Flyby Nights* consume without mercy. You carry an unusual gene which supernaturally connects you to the *Labyrinth*, our species, and *Those Who Must Be Kept*. Your love for your Creator is sincere. Since I have been a guest in the new world, critters, blood pudding from small mammals, and the blood banks have sustained me. The rash of lost faith in a living God has caused the subordinate *Flyby Nights* to spread and feed indiscriminately. Their slaves, haters, and doubters have stronger appetites and are willing to drain the human's mouth dry with dread even prolonging the passing over progress. I am the first purest of the original race of Vampires, responsible for watching over the crypts and three royal mummies of *Those Who Must Be Kept*. A crystal statue named Alia is the youngest of their kind. They have chosen to keep her. Four eldest who have their roots in the history of Vampirism are very powerful in all dimensions. Their bodies are hibernating in Romania and must not be awakened until their time. Until then, it is in my nature to inspire the lowest level *Flyby Nights* with a reflection, and encourage them not to feed as often as they so indescribably do. They have no reflection and are empty like identifiable mechanical creations. *Flyby Nights* are becoming too thirsty. If they continue their course, *Those Who Must Be Kept* shall wake the sealed tombs of a thousand years in Egypt. The fabulous crystal crypts of Rumania and America will also vacate their statues and become flesh."

"Outnumbered by things unseen, chatter, chatter, chatter I have never heard so much chatter. Right now I want the Pope, and I am not even Catholic!"

Julius licked his hand then wiped his thigh. "If you call me, I will send you on a mission with the flesh eaters of faith. In days past, the universal church prevented *Those Who Must Be Kept* from bleeding out everything but the last days. There is an additional threat. The *Flyby Nights* who stand defiant before law and spirit can now turn the animals."

"Humans are the lord of the animals," Tessie replied.

"If more do not come into the faith that a living God gave as a gift, *Those Who Must Be Kept* will permit the full awakening of the fabulous four and America will cease to exist as the world knows her, and history shall be made. Your Dog Chew is not who you think he is. His name is Lazarus, and his mission is instrumental in an extraordinary advancement which may or may not happen. Thus, history was made. He traveled with our sarcophagi. Two were believed to have been stolen; they were not only moved to a different place of the ship.

Hear this with your angel ears. Human faith in the living God must outweigh the *Flyby Nights*, or *Those Who Must Be Kept*, will permit the awakening."

"Why are you telling me this?" She was ill at ease and started shivering.

"No satisfaction, real food will not be available. Faith in the blood of Jesus Christ and the belief in my word is nourishing for humanity.

It is a type of food which prevents *Those Who Must Be Kept* from completely ruling over humanity."

"I am just a woman at fault, and yes, there is a substitute for me!" said Tessie.

"I am the champion of a species that is maligned. Knowing that our enemies cease to exist is comforting to me. Indeed, it is in my nature to feed, yet there is something about you, that I aim to please." Julius kissed her forehead.

"What do you take me for?" Tessie asked

"Sustenance, but humans like you keep me from eating most off planet earth."

"Aaah, then you have put some humans in the position to protect themselves when necessary. Some will desire sweet revenge, others shall take the liberty, get the best of Vampires, and wear Vampire skin coats. I will let it alone. The meek part of the cloak of Jesus shall be my armor and angels my warriors. The fickle finger of fate is powerless to bite my finger off. Julius, you sound like ole sloo foot."

Julius laughed. "Your finger is off limits."

She wagged her forefinger, "Welcome to the limit, I call on the blood of Jesus, and it is open to all. The Gospel says there is no place like it because it redeems. I can't be totally free within these gates of ice," Tessie felt like she on the razor edge of chance. Julius' body crept closer to Tessie, then he swept her up. There was the wind, and round and round went the *Labyrinth*.

"One more word from you, and I shall turn the lights off," began Julius inside the frozen fog.

Hundreds of butterflies swooped into a vanishing Julius. In moments Tessie was back in her room comfortably with the light on.

"He makes earth sound like a museum of corruption. I have been out on the streets serving everybody. Whatever was done that led him to tell of a world controlled by bloodsuckers? America is becoming a country of moral cannibalism. A wretched being, she has become. He may be right, as a hopeful human contender I must tell all to pray. I'll reel the flock in daily on the corner block in my imagination on seven bridges row. There are grass patches. I shall stand in the sun and rain. The federal head is not fake costumes of laws or bloody Vampire allegiances. Dear God, it's me, standing in need of prayer. I am thankful that you saved me according to the blood offering of Jesus on the cross," she thought.

There was a quiet knock. It was Brünnhilde, Tessie's caregiver. After standing silently for a few seconds longer, she knocked harder.

"All of this for Julius The Handsome, aka Dracula, Blackula, roll right. How will we ever measure his effect if human bloodshed blemishes the snow?" Brünnhilde could smell Julius. His smell to her was heavenly, like love in September.

Julius hovered behind her and whispered into her ear, "Took a train and flew 500 hundred miles for you, Brünnhilde! Tessie must be a special lady, I traveled a thousand, for her."

Brünnhilde could not see him but recognized his smell. It was similar to the smell of her homemade Christmas blood pudding.

She whispered back, "Indeed, Tessie's angels represent virtues which increase in quality, as she progresses."

Julius vanished.

"Are you alright, T?" Brünnhilde asked.

"I am alright."

"There seems to be a lot going on. Your humming could fully convince the dead to come back. Didn't see or hear anyone leave, not that I would with all the drilling going on. I hear a dog whining in the bathroom. I won't ask. May I come in, and see you?"

Lazarus was scratching at the door.

"Please come back tomorrow. I am alright Brünnhilde, just drowsy."

"Ok then, off to the Center. I left a basket of stuff on the kitchen table for you. See ya tomorrow sweetie pie," Brünnhilde gathered her things and left.

Do Not Bite The Hand That Feeds You

IT WAS LAZARUS' spirit and his quiet whine that woke up Tessie. The sound came from a traveling riddle, gifting her with a melody in the moonlight. Before long, that long-term friend, pain, showed up. It was knocking on heaven's door crying, wake me up when the nightmare is over. She was cross with the worldly lie, of "not the right fit," a crew of ghosts, medical appointments, and pills tumbling down from the self-hating hollow square. Her neurons began dividing inside a cry in the wilderness. "Forget it, wake up! It's a beautiful day." She said to herself.

Tessie raised her body a little, but before reaching for a bedside marker, she rubbed her lids and looked to the stars. One was falling out of the sky. The whining stopped. Impressed, Tessie began highlighting her own words. It might have been the color yellow quickening one love for the color purple.

"Oh that's right, the beautiful beast needs to pee, and I am sure he is hungry for more food!"

It had only been a few hours, but Lazarus was certain his waiting had a higher purpose. His hunger for Devora and the royal tribe was so powerful that it oddly stained the glass window. In full swing golden showers mirrored four corners while a moan to the rhythm of a magic carpet ride glided with a stream of royal purple light. Tessie hurried to the rest-room and opened the door. With amazement, she watched the beast soar through the stained glass. Inside a mystery, the tip of his tail disappeared into the night.

Staring as long as a quiet game of solitary, she imagined splitting his heart into pieces like it was hyphenated.

"Lazarus," she whispered, "I want to be with you where you are, yet I am the head and not the tail! I'll rest my head for now, and you will return because of love and honor."

Tessie left a little note on the windowsill. It read, "Are you listening, dog? Goodness and mercy follow me. Surely, that's good company."

Brünnhilde & Hiii Power

BRÜNNHILDE WAS ALSO the night nurse at the Center's blood bank. *Knott Pete Bunker* was in a slim but shady part of the Center. It was undisclosed to everyone except a few handpicked helpers. A train station intended to pick up helpers was located a few miles from the Center. It tucked along a nearby estuary near an old bench and newspaper stand. Passengers supernaturally summoned Brünnhilde through the twilight to lead them out of the station. A Lincoln town car arrived within 45 minutes and then off to *Knott Pete Bunker*. The dead of night turns through the corridors toward the Center were like making one's way through a thicket of ghostly legs. The blood bank was hard to find and was a fresh surprise for those who knew about it.

When early morning sunlight entered through a narrow space, it descended on a shut door behind two old stairs. An odd shadow cascaded over a faded bronze bell above the blood bank's doorknob. At an appointed time brightness quickly passed as it was keen on an upward soar into the heavens. Like angels excommunicated from a golden generation, the odd shadow would adjust and then trickle down into the keyhole, which surprisingly gave access to another side, the *Labyrinth*. Like a beautiful wall painting, there was a sense of mystery for the shadow. Like a veiled city of possibilities, other shadows did not lack assurance to participate and pardon. Nobody veiled in gloom chose to remove clerical clothing to honor flesh. This bright phenomenon has been mysterious and shall stay hidden until exposed. Then its perfect light will pour over those who are to receive perfect light. Those who were chosen to enter the *Labyrinth* wail as they feel carried through the air, and then are set down in something secretly wonderful. In one part of the *Labyrinth*, the sight of a thousand beheaded talking snakes from the synagogue of Satan wish for transformation into something better. After the righteous choose to return, some safely plunge near a staircase, next to a translucent door to the main Center.

On another door wraps red, black, white, and green tassels. Some tassels braid around the doorknob, other threads swing like a metabolism that delights its favorites with fortune. The truth among those who enter that door is never abandoned.

Brünnhilde came to manage the Center years before Tessie signed on as an outpatient. Tessie was acquainted with her heavy footsteps both at home and inside the Center. Her footsteps reverberated and knocked with trust, respect, and heart-wrenching truth amongst the fabulous four and their undisturbed crypts in a secret location below the earth. Brünnhilde's taps also competed with the sounds of the nearby train station. On occasions, her heavy steps could lure Vampires into hideous layers of a nasty nightmare. Like dragon breath or open seed, her throne of the inferno was prepared to burn kingdoms and broken Vampire treaties for the sake of the Center's well-being and success.

Her preferred whispering when passing *Knott Pete's* door was, "Pleased to meet you, remember, the devil was an angel too. He is a mystery that can appear out of nowhere by unusual discreet methods."

Brünnhilde was one of the 20th century's Machiavellian's. She savored the scent of a meal to come but refused to follow wicked trails of blood. She believed the Nazarene was the real food of the oracles of God, sometimes whispering to cheer the air, "The corridors are dark but don't be afraid, I am with you."

Knott Pete's blood bank showed itself not to be as it really was and appeared in a way that a very few could see it. To the great it was great. To the small it was small. To the human it was human, to the innocent it was innocent, and to the Vampire it was Vampire. Ms. Brünnhilde's help enabled Tessie and others to benefit from its resources which subsidized their care. After work, Tessie took pleasure from the art and music programs given upstairs.

One day, like a saint from good times, Tessie appeared at the door of the downstairs bunker. She did not enter, only stood there. As soon as her presence was felt the thing behind the door of the blood bank required truth to arrive in types. Suddenly, dark powers began to minister to Brünnhilde about itchy-skinned organizations taking advantage of the Center's weak and vulnerable patients. These powers believed they were serving Brünnhilde; however, they were actually working for Tessie and the infirm. Her great faith in God revealed a little favor to them. In every place Brünnhilde gathered, she united perfect light and truth. Only a few saw it. Tessie was one of the few and loved her so, but she also feared her because Brünnhilde believed God was a man-eater. For the account of this, Tessie believed that she would one day lay her own life down so that she could say, "Quiet yourself, you who have united with the perfect light, have united the mission bell and the Center's angels with us. You are the one to watch over. Our prisoners have rewarded us with extraordinary eloquence."

Tessie watched over Brünnhilde. Even though in a corporate sense, it was Brünnhilde's fire which watched over darkness, one day thwarting it from metamorphosing many at the Center into slaves of *Flyby Nights*.

The time was ripe for a day when an earth angel could pluck a mystery brand from one of the fires of Purgatory, gifting the chosen, with an opportunity to help the Center's tender condition. The brand would help shape the Center inside perfect light, sound teachings, and virtues. These spiritual assets were dedicated to Brünnhilde and the *Labyrinth*, a living organism floating inside and outside of cerulean skies, with the aim to help Earth become a better place.

The blood bank was the only one of its kind in the county. Many of the regulars relied on cash aid in exchange for blood. A bitter existence was there, a never-ending dietary necessity. This was the cost to give the great deceptive blood bank what it needed.

BRÜNNHILDE & HIII POWER

Some declared, "Ain't nothing going on but our rent," so of course, it attracted many poor people who donated and sold blood.

A few musicians performed on Friday and Saturday nights inside an area called the Hiii Power Brownstone section. Once a year, there was a trade- union dance, where leaders and politicians assembled. Sometimes some regulars and housewives who relied on blood for cash would spit on them when they left the trade-center dance. Beforehand the drummers had warmed their animal-skinned drums near a large area facing a registration desk and 50 seats. On weekends, members and visitors entertained with ambrosial nourishment. It was as though immortal spies had transplanted a classroom of unadulterated sound, and it pleased a little more than a musical drama for the Center's conductor bureau. Black horse, a massive desk sat over a flat stone patch with 165 mosaic circles, each within 125 pyramids. One unique pyramid inside a circle had a little line which beautifully extended itself outward. Like a field hospital for a sin-sick world, it was there, but faint. Most were ignorant of its existence until the time came for an earth angel to assist the limb. Its strength was weakening as others ignored and trodden over it, causing it to grow faint. But then the day arrived when its powerful reality appeared with the angel at hand. For years Brünnhilde had sensed its ineffable mystery, and to her, it appeared as a planetary limb of truth with a message. So far, the planetary limb was silently interweaving itself like a poetic reality, reminding God of souls who never forget. However, the best way to forget is to find something you want to remember. Musicians and poets were welcomed to produce a condition of free thought, death, and enjoyment inside of the limb. The earth angel and the limb would harvest time for the Center's truth, for as long as the people in the Center wanted. *Those Who Must Be Kept,* the crystal crypts, and royal mummies relished in it.

Recently, newcomers freckled the Center. Brünnhilde began to notice visitors were now occupying a once blighted section of the Center's basement, named, *Eight.* One hundred stairs spiraled from the blood bank to the basement. A glass door collecting dust was on the opposite side of the section. Dusty glass-saw its way into the eyes of every visitor, and any time Brünnhilde saw the door she sighed,

"Glass is glass if you think it's about something else you are going to get cut like a bullet to the brain or a hog on our menu."

She was not concerned for her safety or for the safety of the other live-in inhabitants. She supposed that it was the music and the words of the poets which attracted the late night newcomers. She learned that a few offensively dressed strangers actually lived in Section *Eight* of the basement. She never officially met them. From time to time she'd glanced up, and quickly dismissed the thought of them. As an ice sheet, they too were cold and distant. She sensed it was best to stay away from what was behind the glass door, noticing it was beginning to develop cracks.

She sighed, "This place is a hospital for everyone, but there is only so much that I can do!"

She toiled up and down the Center's hallway in her powdered blue suit with a silver sixpence in her vintage oxford shoe. She listened to her intuitive senses choosing not to cross over the threshold of the glass door in the basement. This way suited Brünnhilde.

Some nights, while attending to the Center's patients, she observed what she believed to be a traveling man coming out of the glass door. Later, she would come to know him and took solace that she could not bring herself to believe the worst about the beloved Julius the handsome. Sometimes she'd sigh,

"Julius, you are gentle on my mind. Why would I ever throw a brick into your ancient kingdom?"

He'd whisper, "Copper protects the dusty glass, Brünnhilde."

Every evening after sunset he opened the custom door made of thick beveled glass. Some nights his whispers to Brünnhilde traveled throughout the halls echoing, "Are you ready for the Center, and are you ready for me?"

There were seven copper rods, sturdily engraved in front of the glass door. Still, what was behind the door was even heavier, and squirmed at the prospect of Julius knowing Brünnhilde. In time their relationship was inevitable and simply dictated what potential might come out of the basement. Like an extended limb outside the mosaic circle, it was not up for destruction, could not be diminished or prevented from participating in the democracy within the Center. If destroyed by whatever means the ramifications of its enemy's annihilation was stronger than the rise and fatal draw of the last man standing near a wreath of poppies in the mighty halls of Valhalla.

It all started like a copying and pasting time shift fluttering along, never standing still for a moment. Then in the fullness of time, during Brünnhilde's night shift, Julius appeared out of nowhere; although, it was positively somewhere because the enemy of light bloomed when night fell, and the waiting was the hardest part. Julius, who had been staring steadily without her knowledge for many years turned and said, "Hi there."

His first introduction was strong, like a machine ousted by the height of something bigger than the two of them. Brünnhilde quickly learned he was swollen with tales, had a lean stature, the skin of an albino that could change at will, and a, go it alone approach. His tidy long white locks were unbelievable. They were multilayered and merged for various reasons with the unknown.

An ancient pendant, of the eye of Horus, clamped tightly to his purple necktie gazed at Brünnhilde like a door curtain. His presence was a perfect storm for a menu of bits associated with the future requirements of the Center.

Julius claimed to be the titleholder and sole inheritor of billions in gold- coins, and millions in gold bars. His inheritance enabled the Center to provide free care to the physically and mentally challenged for the last 100 years. When he invited Brünnhilde to manage the Center, she gladly accepted his offer and sighed, "The Lord forgives those who invent what they need on Brünnhilde's floor."

With bold confidence, her profession became more than just favorite moments.

Who Knows Why The Geese Go Barefoot

IT WAS ON Spy Wednesday. Julius cast a penetrating stare into Brünnhilde's being. It revealed neither triumph nor defeat. She was finishing her evening shift and appeared beaten with more than work. Her mischievous eyes fixed on an ominous wall painting. The timeworn illustration on the Center's main hallway wall told a tale of greed and lust. Brünnhilde's body was so close to the image that from afar it looked as if she was joined to a space inches away from a lovely veiled Virgin in an intolerable crisis. Incubus, a flesh fiend, was loosely clutching the Virgin's purple and yellow garment. It was the same monster Tessie's pastor summoned. The Virgin's raiment was more than a wrap filled with influences of gifts, false promises, and days of future past. Decorated with the garment's background were five red and brown manuscripts of world maps. Each superbly painted with a portrayal of mouths so wide, you might almost have fallen into one of them. There was a place in paradise, earnings, an interview, and food. A coat of smoke over the Virgin desired access to Brünnhilde's members. The Virgin's glory was stretched on a wooden blue and gold bench, with a mouth as wide as an open paper coffee filter, that gave way to Brünnhilde's imagination. The portrait's panels behind the Virgin presented untold powers. Brünnhilde's shaking foot paved away for the stormiest of all angels. Before long the pits of anger silenced her members.

Julius was near, "One of my best members smokes. Come within reach of me," she instructed him.

His footsteps were light as he moved toward her. "Your hair shines like my gold investments."

"I am an unnatural redhead, today silver hair is a weapon to carry on my name." She answered.

"You see Brünnhilde, unveiled on the inside of this Center's east wall breathes a series of panels heaved out of five set apart mouths. One mouth vomited out the colorful Incubus. It gives favor to the Virgin that has not encountered strands of bleach or color. Another mouth's morality tale warns humans of today's emptiness of lust and greed and shall go to great lengths to protect the Virgin's innocence. Other panels on the wall tell of discrimination, crimes against humanity, corruption, and war. The tale of lust and greed has angered you. In time hissing snakes will pound at a gate warning purgatory that greed and lust must be shamed, not rewarded or given glory to seeking eyes in the Center."

Pushed to tears she answered, "Julius, may I fade into the background on a watchful perch? My fighting spirit lives in more grave forms of battle."

"Brünnhilde, the word grave is perfect for our champions, *Those Who Must Be Kept*. They have always endured serious trials and courageous spiritual warfare."

"Let them come well within reach! Kindly open the door so we may witness the head of snakes crushed below my feet." She answered.

"You're a country girl with ideas at heart. Your words are like ghosts, they pass through life. The poet's verses for a woman such as you has a place on a hill with the sound of many waters and no worries. Assembled soldiers have managed to tickle your throat, so blow fire. Collect what is scattered into pieces in various dwellings in a place only known to your God. Only then I may know what truly lives behind your living God's promises. The Gospel wrote of a time when some at the Center might be saved from intelligence that connects them to the sum of the hound of flesh and its temptations.

It was, for this reason, I am a given message by *Those Who Must Be Kept*, for you.

"We were the mothers before we were the daughters. The Nazarene is the unifying factor." She sighed.

"Early in the morning, before the sunrise, a dog will sit at your feet. Thrones of understanding not subject to time and space endowed with wings of cranes shall be there. The dog shall reach its head up toward the heavens. He shall find corroding dark influences and pieces to his past and future. Like the oracles of past centuries, the voices that carry are as alive today as days of old. Let the garment of grace cover him. It is a sanctuary for the hound of heaven. The substance of what drives the dog does not change. It is faith, and his name is Lazarus.

There is a secret area in the Center. Pendulum swings in the right direction. It swings inside a glass case that plans to join him to the pure of heart. Tessie took Lazarus into her dwelling place. In total his mission brings hope. His real body walks by the grace of God and holds within it a total journey involving the gift of love, hope, faith, and truth. Ancient laws, disobedience, and a priestly magic spell on an ancient sarcophagus lid once recited tore Lazarus away from his soulmate. Their union contains within itself the greater mystery, divine love and transforming power.

When the dog speaks, do not run toward the glass door or open it. I assure you the tombs behind the seven rods are in their proper place. Truly, the persons chosen for honors only know the time. Three say no one knows the hour. Therefore, *Those Who Must Be Kept* will rest with the house of bread, who says miracles far out do tragedies. The authority of royal blood and truth proclaimed it is within this Center. *Those Who Must Be Kept* cannot deny this. Long ago they handed themselves over to death to deliver their fellow citizens. This was finished with no regrets to avoid creating further corruption, and more mobs on a sword's edge. Surely, some humans shall wait for God's answer to who was the greatest miracle of all. Was it the Nazarene or *Those Who Must Be Kept?*"

"Julius, I have forgiven those who handed themselves over to death, which I also call *Those Who Must Be Kept*. On first Fridays,

I often weep with tears of rain. My own mistakes lead me to the Nazarene's life-giving gift of forgiveness."

He answered, "I weep blood. Step aside and welcome me, it's Saturday and weep no longer. The fabulous four remain sealed, and my existence is minimum in its capacity until a flash of mystery hits, causing my tears to pour like a gentle slap inside their chosen hour of awakening.

Brünnhilde, you have forgiven what many have not, the unforgivable. Some say that they will cut their own teeth before giving up on what many will not forgive. Others will not apologize. Still, while most took in views of cities that I have tasted, the mobs of dinosaurs had the biggest appetites, and are the biggest bodies on any block."

"Again you speak using allegory? Julius, you must realize that I am learning twenty-four hours a day. I believe this Creator is Holy and no one can approach another than by faith in what the blood of the Nazarene has already accomplished for those who believe. Nevertheless, I am a simple woman burning with rage because of this wall painting. The wall painting is to sway the fragile and harden the experienced. Honestly, I carry forgiveness for *Those Who Must Be Kept*. However, I also sense the pulse of fury. Might this rage belong to them? Is it a symptom of hell or heaven?"

"Bravo, you have inquired fittingly, the range of *Those Who Must Be Kept* never slept. The protection of innocence and the family as the building brick of life was their root. You are their revelation put on a pedestal."

"Then surely I would never give that up." She answered.

"What blooms is carried by the winds. It is just a matter of time before a tongue like a lizard pursues silence. The pod of hush shall put an end to the ugly tongue, seeking to consume your desire for defense. The tongue's reign shall end as it sought to connect to seconds that would have meant your death," said Julius.

Suddenly a crackling sound poured from the painting. She pointed at the wall, "Memories are on the wall! Listen the panels cry step inside our vacation, its intention aims to attack innocence. Someday many thrones with lost eyeballs or hands will crave to pull out any appearance they choose. Well then, my startled gold leaf treasure, this night I choose to pick out the innocent, here!"

She pointed to the veiled Virgin's garment. Inside was someone small wearing a coat of a thousand colorful threads.

"This coat, like the beech tree, will pass on our memories!" She said.

Speaking in his softly spoken English, Julius voice never above a murmur sighed, "Startled treasure, hmm you have spunk. Will a tall paint- brush tell the story of a thousand colorful threads, making your little ones in the Center seem less powerful?"

"No, the father of lies was not permitted to enter, rob, or steal the Virgin's garment from any innocent being in our Center. We buckled our armor tight."

"By whose power did you declare this?"

"Courage, my Creator is simply irresistible, and my God's will was done! A woman of faith has arrived. I am horrified and must call on my Creator to protect our Center. The enemy is like a weasel who preys on the small and is too close to our doorstep, yet it has not chipped away our high ground."

"Dear one, when it bleeds it leads, the deadliest catch is an old enemy full of tricks. Its strength may be one of the lopsided matches of cast-iron certainty."

She sighed, "It was written, Behold, I am sending you out as sheep in the midst of wolves, so be wise as serpents and innocent as doves."

"Dear Brünnhilde, with the face haloed by a cloud of hair, the big view of the flesh fiend and the small view of your God cannot be measured in the Center. Nevertheless, opportunities to show swarms of miracles appear to be your purpose. May I ask what your battle will produce in this Spirit of age? You have lasted longer than most on their journey to confessions of new beginnings."

"Julius, God the Father made Incubus the flesh fiend, and it is said all battles have already been won through Jesus. My faith in God's Word is that the spirit of the Nazarene will tell the stories."

With raised eyebrows, her sigh stirred a groan.

"Nobody is screaming around here. However, the night is still young, and there may be plenty of time to warn the field of dozens before the champion of temptations feasts like wildfire. The Father of demand may surge this very hour, however, the coming dog backed by faith might help many to declare, I have gotten my faith back." Julius replied

Peering inside the coat of a thousand colorful threads she sighed, "We must watch with eyes which circle the sun like a star, and see that what is declared is honored. The Godzilla of Earths might be a crucible for the development of what I know as a time for mercy."

She clutched her bosom with the tenderness of a gathered mass of baby's breath.

"The Godzilla of Earths is a new planet. This battle might punch through and become a place for our fearsome creatures shaped by the nightmares of Vampires to land."

Julius balled his fist and gestured toward the painting, "Ahh, drawn out as a cage, surrounded by fans in the constellation Draco," he whispered.

"Julius, this very hour a champion of temptation may profit with death and feast with hellfire!"

"Talk about on a stump, are you eager to send Incubus off the wall and back to hell?" He asked.

"The power of the Holy Spirit prepared the sinkhole. Incubus the flesh fiend intentions shall fade under the night of a chosen hour. On the other hand, what about this dog that you speak of? Will his loyalty frighten people away? Here in the Center, we're made true. Many count their money on the train and watch magnificent views from hillsides. Is Lazarus a friend arriving at the Center to tell of liberty? I overheard you telling Tessie that the *Flyby Nights* come and go like darts or transient heartless heist, looking for a way out. I may have even witnessed these creatures flee from a door in the basement that keeps them shut in during day hours. Surely it must be for one reason to run and hide in dark uncluttered spaces then drain the carcass dry which makes you drool near the train tracks."

"My dear, while I sometimes feel as though my drool is situated in one of the lower levels of Dante's Inferno, it is actually just behind the custom door made of glass. You, on the other hand, have got to make it more livable."

"Why?" She asked.

"I can't tell you why, but I can show you how. You must surrender, but don't give yourself away," said Julius.

"Oh no, I won't do that! Immortals cannot be defeated. We are blessed and enjoy our blessings." She replied.

"Brünnhilde, think of it this way as you crack the code on your late night train to Georgia. Cells and sarcophagi get very lonely for light. Life after death may be possible on your floor, and my train," Julius insisted.

"You speak mysteries. You are the undead, Julius. It is best that we carry on separately. I've opened just one window in the basement, but never the glass door." She turned to a small aged mirror hanging on the other side of the wall.

"I look like hell," she sighed.

The wall painting echoed with laughter.

"Don't you worry, you will always look like an angel to me. If your eyes have merely looked through this one window you may take more time," said Julius.

"In your eyes, I see a hundred churches." She quipped

"This mystery stays beautifully preserved like beloved traditions passed from father to a son, or mother to a daughter. And what did you see when you opened the one window?" He asked.

"Two dogs barking as if to say, "It is not like we did not warn them. My immortal fist shook, like a trained leopard on a leash of a golden mortal in a golden age. The greatest lessons always come from one master. I believe in a resurrected life form. For now, my place is here among the living."

She caught her breath.

"Brünnhilde, you sound like you got it all. What is it all for? Is it possible that the magnificent unspoiled nature of the resurrected one will order a defender, a reliable friend of the poor in spirit, to extend something to me? Is it possible that my desire for your God might boost like property in a narrow little alley with a beautiful half-timber building in sunlight, and enter paradise?" Julius asked.

"Julius, you are a long time dead. Ages ago blood for sinners like me was offered. The blood of Nazarene reconciles, redeems, and forgives. Perhaps, God, the Father has saved you for His purposes, on earth."

"I regret the fatal clash between humanity and myself. Indeed I am the undead, and fasting does not allow me to devour you! On a diet of worms, blood banks, and critters, I remain to tell. If you don't have a time machine, you can travel with me into the painting. We can experience centuries of lights within a distance from the earth to the sun, in all its long-running reasons amidst the roaring furnaces and towering pyramids on a hill across a blue lake. Powdered face, you are immortal, but still a man-eater, and I am a….."

She glared at him, dropped her shoulders, and interrupted. "I shall always have comfortable shelter, in many forms. Last night I stayed comfortably at the Hotel Novena, fifty miles from the Center. Do you have an idea where you would like to go next on your journey Julius? The Cult of Reason has faded away."

He stepped forward, "When the lights go out promise me you will serve or write about me. I always have an idea going."

"Write? What is this ruckus, you are here flesh and blood, but not human. The *Flyby Nights* return like pets and repeat their comings and goings out of the narrow little corridor near the glass door. I overserved! I am going to the bank," said Brünnhilde.

"I'll follow you, and yes that is correct, *Flyby Nights do* not dwell in one area for very long. The hunger forces them to flee the Center out of necessity. They rarely eat their victims in the Center. This could bring unwanted attention. Their appetites for corrupt bankers is another story. Appetites for corruption is growing fiercer. *Those Who Must Be Kept*, have an ancient system in place. When one of the eldest awakes, 2 sleep. Alia shall wake soon, as *Flyby Nights* appetites are out of balance. It is my eternal obligation to protect and serve *Those Who Must Be Kept*. Blood will send for me as their eternal Judge."

"Julius, you talk as if you are their great Lord! *Flyby Nights* and their slaves mirror vile reflections of things that drip like spit from the Incubus's mouth!"

She pointed to the suspended creature's sharp-tipped teeth hovering over the Virgin.

"Are you the Lord of its world? She asked"

"Brünnhilde, Incubus is the Lord of its own world. It includes keepers that lack virility or true power. The beast flatters and slowly bleeds out what is dear to its prey. We see how its long teeth hover over the Virgin."

"Like a needful thing," she replied.

"*Flyby Nights* take or use lures to get blood. Incubus, the flesh fiend, has a story. Would you prefer that I trace the hints?" Julius moved in close. She backed away, "The hints are traceable, and the wall painting is alive. Vampires produce their enemies, *Flyby Nights*! Their slaves are vile, gathering in large numbers for false promises. Many might even be keepers of Incubus, the flesh fiend. Some in the Center may say or act like it does not matter where they come from. Well, it matters, and it matters what they do. Their vile acts will be proven since *Flyby Nights* slaves are degenerate humans with blood lust and bad blood."

"Brünnhilde, *Flyby Night's* slaves have free will and are drunk with the blood of things that exploit. They are addicted to false power and temptations. It is like *Flyby Nights* to feed on blood. Though they are a lower level species, darkness has grown in the wake of the open rebellion. Need I ask, what will you do?"

"The grand undertaking which spews from this wall- painting has become an epidemic, and the barrel of foul drool may attempt to shake the foundation of this Center. This cannot be permitted, I shall get an understanding with arms to battle in the spirit of the Nazarene." She answered.

"Spirit, that mighty name never gives up. Blood on the cross open to the world is not a secret. May I ask, where will you send the Incubus, will you banish it? What of *Flyby Nights*, and their slaves, it may be that their legacy shall impart understanding." Julius said.

Understanding, she turned her blue eyes away and dusted off her lime green suit.

"Your words are merciful, Vampire! It is not difficult to discern the existence beyond the glass door. The seven rods that cleave to it keep me safe from the tombs that we keep in peace under the earth. As Abe Lincoln once said, "If I had six hours to chop down a tree, I'd spend the first hour sharpening the axe.'

"I am not a slayer, but do not push me south of heaven," She continued.

"Your faith reminds me of Tessie's. Will the sparks twist into the northern lights? And might its power take on a dragon king?" Julius adjusted his tie.

"Incubus was created to show that there is a God who wanted to show us the ugliness of sin. Its presence strengthened me in my own weakness. My resistance to its charisma made more sense. As a result, I cried out to our Center, the Nazarene took up the armor and was victorious."

"The appetites of *Flyby Nights* will still uncoil from their secret places. They are unperfected. Unlike the eldest Vampires' these low-level entities drain blood dry, twist the heads of their victims, and leave crushed bones as decorative signs. Despite the melt of ice-cold origins, they are incurable aggressors like a land grabbing nation of thieves on the prowl for the defenseless. Their blood thirst never ends."

"My Creator knows what has been shown. I shall safeguard what has been gifted to me with one mighty name, and the earth angel of death shall help," she answered.

"Have a long look at the painting. But before you lift the veil behind what happened, remember, you will survive."

"Julius, I am the sight of those who dwell in sleep, who fought the good fight, and played dead to survive."

She waved her hand over the west area of the painting. "Straighten up! Boom, boom, I shouted out around the world. I will survive; but, not by the verve of *Flyby Nights* or their slaves. It's the one that you cannot forget," she answered.

"Are you bloodthirsty?" Julius asked.

"I have room for my blessings. My soul worships and has not been laid to waste. I am not drunk with the blood of the innocent. I rode on a seat of praise and worship. My lips did not push bloodshed to the limit, into a loud din of horns and execute without remorse. I am a new creature, blessed by God's promises and faith in a door that offered golden letters. My God gave living water through golden letters to the ones I love. My spirit sought, and it is thirsty for believers. Can you picture it? I have a field of angels because I am a landowner who left bits in the corner to the unpretentious in spirit. I harvested the field in this Center to the T, laughter ascended into heaven, never melting into the rugged wilderness for something evil would have fed on us like a vulture on a corpse."

With authority, she pointed at the Incubus within the painting. Behind the monster was a notebook under the moon entitled, *Sorcerer in the Moonlight*.

"Look at its widening view. Lying in wait, thick pages that go boo in the night inside a jungle of carnal deceit. This notebook gives its keepers an ache, and Incubus, the flesh fiend evil untold powers. Is it a necessary evil, Julius?"

"Not at all Brünnhilde, the keeper's book, is out of the bag! Look closer at the wall painting. Do you see the stone cat on the other side of Incubus? The cat's original cap, defiled by the cruelest most grotesque magic, can only take place one time on earth. On this very day, your awareness casts a *greater* light over magic. Now the Incubus may no longer hide. Unknowingly, the cat's original cap once helped Incubus to hide, but now truth and light shall work with *Justice*, who is your eternal friend. *Justice* has merged light and truth into your heart and hands. One act hard to follow shall carry out the work of *Justice* with a future marked to protect young blood."

"What is coming is so great it cannot even be spoken of!" He answered.

"The mysteries of rage will begin. I trust *Justice* in her greater understanding," she replied.

"And so did those in the beautiful, invincible halls of *Those Who Must Be Kept*!" Julius answered.

"Julius, last night, I saw something that can't be accounted for by the laws of nature. Its face was pressing against a dying patient's window. The nose was flat like a crossbreed, half human, half teddy bear, I was frightened but completed my assignment and contemplated its cause."

"Did you contemplate its course to help you to survive and not bleed you dry, that night?"

"Have some compassion!"

"The *Flyby Night* fled, correct?" Julius asked.

"Oh, a *Flyby Night*, this species as you call it may be a masked hero and not an enemy of humanities future which eventually becomes somebody's past?" She questioned with hesitation.

"If you agree to hunt humans like cattle because that is what will happen if left to *Flyby Nights*," he answered.

With great conviction, she uttered, "I will come to know the whole truth in time. I have not witnessed the works of *Flyby Nights*. Incubus, the flesh fiend, is most visible in the wall painting and outside the Center! Are *Flyby Nights* Incubus allies?"

"*Flyby Nights* lay traps for all that is seen and unseen. They are well educated at trapping and extinguishing prey!"

"Julius, you must not forget, the Center is akin to many guided missiles, those who are destined to reign with us shall be kept, and will use all that they have to get the rebellious hips of Incubus out of our ring of fire. Indeed, the ash of lust gives access to places most can't go, but only the Nazarene offers deliverance. Today the ash is our beauty and our weapon. In this Center, collective lust will be intercepted. We caught the thing while it sleeps."

"Do tell!"

"At night Incubus the flesh fiend escapes from the wall painting, but always returns by morning to sleep. I am the sight of those who dwell in sleep. As long as that thing is sleeping inside the wall painting, it can do no harm. You must understand that our members are masters at teamwork. You are aware of our artisans who work day and night in the Hiii power brownstone section. They also have lots of tools in their arsenal, and the ball of victory stays in our court. Together, we give the order to the moon, while destroying vile lust in our Center. In the future, if need be we shall live, occupy, and flourish on the moon, and might watch Homo sapiens perish on Earth in their unwillingness to change their brutal ways."

"Visit Jupiter where rulers and kings champion knowledge and *Justice*," Julius insisted.

"Angels who sing by night have not come for me or instructed me to throw a ball of fire on earth. At this time, I am echoing and constantly learning."

"More than a ball of fire is in this Center's court. Many here have studied a thousand lessons, fear God, and many have studied themselves," Julius replied.

"When the bell of the Galaxies hum, I hear the whistle of the wind in total space. When ripe I hear omniscience preached, and wait until what I hear is done right. When our team in the Center acts together, we rule. The power of lust shall never destroy our innocent in body or soul. The guilty begs for our forgiveness to serve what is wise and true. The collective appetite of the house of Incubus has crossed the threshold of the high walls outside this Center. Indeed, civilizations are at stake! I am sorry my friend, war has begun. We didn't fade and refuse to be stumbling blocks. We are a small and vulnerable Center. It is too close to our transformations. We shall wait on God, for you are not the source of knowledge, Julius."

"Brünnhilde, I do not know God, or the Devil you speak of; but your response is not calculated. You say you broke those things of lust through spiritual petitions, and teamwork. One extraordinary eye of light traveled into the clouds, crossed the bridge of excess, the heavens crushed the once dominant enemies' yolk? The eye of light exposed the high walls of vile lust. Yet, one is waiting to seize your throne in the Center. I have overheard *The Ghost of Westside*. He thinks that you're a heretic!"

Brünnhilde responded, "This ghost may make someone an acquaintance. The Center shall consume him. No friend of mine will weep before me. My religion is a private matter. My God listens because the enemy's response was calculated. It went against the grain of what it wanted and what it thought it had, hissing through theaters of fighting forces, with the aims to consume beauty and innocence. Unlike other foes on the wall, this enemy was bold. Its outgoing transparency of burning appetites desired to destroy the simple, and perpetuate lust. For a very long time, it was able to alter its appearance. Many of its victims were brought to their knees singing fire! I prayed to be free, and through faith was delivered from its warpath."

"Without your knowledge, I watched. The final scream was released in a time lapse, into a bitter passion, and reflected in Venus."

"Friend, a kiss was blown before Holy Blood consumed lust. In a split second, I won over Venus, and then returned to the bosom of divine mercy."

"Well then, Brünnhilde, let's get it started. A crazy long time ago, what was corrupting the youth?" he asked.

"Come again?"

"From your heart to my head, what corrupts the youth?"

"That thing! Look at Incubus, the flesh fiend its back again in the painting, with rebellious eyes faceted onto the Virgin's purple and yellow garment. As of tonight, its stare shall no longer pervert what is pure and sacred. A holy God never stood for it. The painted Virgin is hallowed. What is Holy must not be mocked. The Holy eye burned the filth out of what is before us for the sake of this Center's youth!"

"At the sound of your petition, the blood moon speaks! My evil eye has submitted before. The fire of perception is yours, we don't need to discuss much."

"Well then Julius, I shall find my rhythm and certainly get myself free. Truly this Incubus shall leave this painting tomorrow, and you are going to hear a roar, but it won't be from my mouth. Like a spy using the method going grey, time shall allow me to stand on the shoulders of ancient giants. I shall stand out to blend into an accomplished background, and become a credible back-story. The moon in the wall painting shall swallow Incubus."

"We do not need anyone?" Julius scoffed

"You may not need anyone apart from me."

A roar was heard, and designated ones in the Center destroyed fleshly corruption in every place wickedness laid its seed. Where there was an error, they brought correction and truth. The innocent at the Center kept on moving and pointing like thistles expressing the desire to see blessings spread as an open-air picnic, in a spiritual place of knowledge, that shall be passed down to the best.

"Could we have imagined it?" Julius cracked a smile.

"Speed is of the essence! I am not a plaything of destiny. A message has been revealed, and decadence that threatened us all in the Center was exposed," she replied.

"A few miles from here, I know of a girl, a special friend of Tessie's. She wears her faith on her sleeves and reflects your message. She has gifts and weapons of mystical lineage. Reality lags behind her consciousness. She is skilled with insight, building territory, and accessing all areas, even our Vampire territory. These skills are inspiring and can be used for the betterment of humanity," said Julius

Brünnhilde answered, "Many humans are left with questions that most prefer to dodge. In time, is this girl willing to join us to live inside a memorable full moon? Our special forces are recruiting."

"*Those Who Must Be Kept* and our eldest Vampire families shall protect her from the attraction of corruption. She is sober and prospers mightily on earth. Every time she returns to earth, she returns stronger more prosperous, and her precious memories linger."

"I sense someone's soul within an eternal history. What is the good of knowing her if you don't tell me her name?" Brünnhilde asked.

"Galaxy, *Those Who Must Be Kept* call her the naked tar girl. They hold within them her twin brother Future and do not need power for doing anything. Something beyond their capacity always gets things done. The season of plenty rests within them. Galaxy always gets truth and understanding, mirroring their throne of hearts. This I know because I was ordered here to watch you, her, and Tessie."

"I am acquainted with Tessie and learning daily about myself and my role in the world by reconstructing the cosmos. Is Galaxy a god, or a spy? " Brünnhilde inquired.

"She is a god, her talents are from God, and are used to destroy wickedness on earth. She was born to uncover the handiwork of her Creator. The written word is eternal and has already preserved the regalia of royalty and her future life and bloodline as an elite superpower that has successfully dominated all kingdoms on earth for thousands of years. This knowledge has been sealed. She and her descendants are nobility, endued with extraordinary beauty, wisdom, grace, and understanding. In her future a magnificent loyal

King rules by her side within a powerful military and elite kingdom. Their loving union shall produce extraordinary beings who shall rule highly advanced civilizations. Neither she nor her descendants must be enslaved, or slew by human hands, or killed by Vampire no matter how long faces grow. She is the direct descendant of the originator of heavens and earth. If human hands destroy her, the earth shall crumble. After Earth is rebuilt, she shall return stronger with loyal subjects to help her reign a vast Kingdom.

In the 21st Century, her mission is similar to yours and Tessie Maybach. Their gifts are offered back to one God. Galaxy builds up several levels of heaven, one soul at a time beginning with the discourse of greatness. Oh, what is it that the world does to them. Yet, the world shall not break upon her years, or take of her physical or inner beauty. Before the throne of three, she and *Those Who Must Be Kept*, are destined to win souls in odd ways. A priest named Fr. Louis helps her. He is a Vampire hunter and has desired to kill me since I arrived in America. He shall never succeed. My death does not belong to him. On the other side of death qualifies her for total Victory. Galaxy was summoned, to stand for a God anointed living cause, the expression of a victorious realm which includes Vampires.

"Fr. Louis, I know him. He is from the church triumphant. The Nazarene must be Galaxy's author," Brünnhilde insisted.

"They were delivered out of dark forces, snatched out of the hands of confusion, in the name of Jesus Christ whom you call the Nazarene. She and her twin brother are parallel to a collector of wonder for miracle making. The wealth that they bring to the world cannot be compared to the Yu tribe. Fr. Louis came to the world reading the minds of their advisors, and Vampires. The very sight of blood could not set aside his realm. Like a magnificent holy ship carried by grateful servants and joyful forces, on earth, they are mystically majestic.

Julius pointed to a hog painted on the wall panel. "Look closely, Brünnhilde. Modie Fab & the X sheep was written beneath the sheep in cursive. This signature leads to a secret vortex in the wall painting. Have you ever seen the Cathedral of Antwerp?" He asked.

Silence cuddled seconds.

Julius continued, "A spy aims to protect secret information. An assassin aims to kill. My Makers, born from a secret Egyptian Cave, created my thirst for blood. It is a part of being a Vampire. You are food, which makes humans our meal. Some, including myself, have chosen not to feed on innocent humans, I tolerate many humans, feeding mostly on animals. Like a mole, I have passed over secrets to you, a natural born enemy. Like an ear, I listened to Fr. Louis. As a double agent, I work for humanity, but I am loyal to *Those Who Must Be Kept*. I was created by two time-travelers who designed 100% pure vampire veins. The first-born inside the catacombs of the Carpathian Mountains permit me to receive one of the greatest powers on earth. Have you ever seen The Cathedral of Antwerp?"

Brünnhilde was lost for words.

"Near the Cathedral is instant Calvary under cerulean skies. Willing humans are kept in a coma while my firstborn aristocrats feed for spiritual advancement. They do not hunt for food. Willing bodies, comfortably suspended in midair, guarded behind glass containers eagerly wait for the greatest of my creations to feed. Human blood is reserved out of devotion to a special system. Special cloths are prepared to soak and then to strip their willing bodies of necessary plasma.

Those who bless my Vampire cult are blessed by it. This ensures a balanced process in the universe or many Vampires and people will starve. Silence shields this secret underworld."

"Gather them into the firepot. What is made of fabric or the eternal life of a Vampire is not fit for everyone. Sounds like the cult of hell! Other than food why would you stalk me? It's a bit annoying as fresh air on the mountaintop is good for me, and my body parts are not average within the complexities of the Center," she countered.

"The time is close, hold your tongue! You must recover what Vampires took, and do what the teacher tells you. The Cathedral of Antwerp is in a secret vortex." Julius insisted.

"A secret vortex? So are the anthills under my heels as I am willing to go around those to get understanding."

"Let me show you. Who needs stairs or flying wheels, when I can spit weapons from my own flesh? Our journey through time is fast, take my hand, and you shall see." Julius reached for her hand.

Her grasp brought more than an embrace.

"Morning is upon us, yet night awaits. Both need something in return," she whispered.

"Are we negotiating?" Julius asked.

"Some things should not come down to luck. Consider my perceptions a parting gift. We have to be quick. It's almost morning."

He continued, "The burning light, the hungry night, we cannot have one without the other. Look closely, do you see the hog and the sheep inside the vortex? The hog's name is *Modie Fab*. The X sheep have been divided into areas within the West of the Cathedral."

Suddenly, Brünnhilde was observing a private area in the Cathedral. She witnessed the sheep and the hogs fall into the mud. The hogs were devouring flesh.

"Now what?" Julius asked.

"I suppose the pig belongs in it, but the sheep do not." She came to herself, and quickly released her hand from Julius' grip replying,

"I have not tasted flesh or blood, only solitude. This Cathedral has never been completed, although, in all its completeness, it is completely immovable and completely beautiful."

"You are aware." He said.

"Julius, you are the hunter they all fear. What is beautiful is that some humans believe God's saving grace is for its own purposes. I am having a light bulb moment. Vampires and the *Flyby Nights* believe it is through me, that they shall all one-day walk during the day, and not just under moonlight sway." Brünnhilde smiled big, reached into her pocket, pulled her cotton white gloves out and put them on.

"Cheerio, I am going to the bank now. Bunching together in large numbers provides a level of protection against being eaten."

"Indeed, we are happy in your blue heaven." Julius bowed his knee.

The Obvious Is Only Obvious 2 Him 2 Who It Is Obvious

LAZARUS ROAMED MOST of the night through alleyways and deserted boulevards. Loud echoes thumping in the dead of night from the train station pointed him toward the mouth of the estuary. Within minutes he had reached the Center.

A strange hum emanating through a cozy relationship with the train station was loud enough to wake you up, but its mystery was bargained by unfulfilled guarantees.

The Center appeared exactly like the dream Lazarus had the evening he soared out of Tessie's window. Everything yes everything was there. He could not exactly remember what everything entailed, yet everything was present in the fullness of time, including Devora, his family, a sky full of bright stars, and happy graveyards.

He greeted the Center by rolling over some pebbles on the front porch. The porch was swept nicely except for a little pile of smooth stones and a few dead Roly Poly bugs. Lazarus rested an hour or so with deep, restful sighs pushing and pulling toward a distinction between capacity and reach. Without his total understanding of how everything jumped in, he imagined receiving those who would welcome him with anything.

On the following morning, he made his appearance. Brünnhilde was preparing to leave when Lazarus was at her ankles. In a sort of bewilderment, she remembered Julius' words, "Within the morning hours a dog will sit at your feet. Receive him as if he were your own person. His name is Lazarus."

It was the end of her graveyard shift when the nectar of the gods and the fading smell of the night forest ascended to the train station. The entrance door of the Center was getting ready to shut when her garment nearly jammed between the joints. It was a little difficult, but Brünnhilde snatched her coat from the hinges and pushed the door solidly, quickly wedging one foot between the door.

"Shut up, Julius' prediction is more than time over an inflated ego on Bourbon Street. This hour underwent a marvel. His words manifested a devoted body under my garment. It's 2:00 am. This must be Lazarus! Certainly, if the dog survived Julius' prediction, one might suppose a great light from the night. It shall give me pleasure to welcome him, he looks eager to please." She pulled the door wide-open singing, "Tra, la, la, la, Tra, la, la."

Lazarus looked as if he had fallen out of someone's laws, and the journey back into their good books would not be easy. Listening to the rhythms of the train station, he thought to himself, "My lips are sealed."

Suddenly, Brünnhilde saw something. It was a little light floating through a side square porch window-seal. A butterfly whirled out of it, like a whisper.

"We are here waiting for you, are you experienced? Nothing can keep us apart." The whisper faded.

Startled she answered, "It was not you that I expected to see."

It was Julius, and his goal was not to show off but to show how.

With four freshly manicured fingernails, Brünnhilde nervously tapped the window seal, dot dot, dit, dit dot. In a dash, the moth transformed into a vampire bat and vanished.

To her surprise, the dog spoke, "Who had given him the key Das moo?"

"A talking dog, I'll be… who died and made you King?" She asked.

Lazarus answered thoughtfully, "I will come to know through your words. I have been waiting for my soulmate, Devora. We are two halves of a circle closed tight around a constellation of understanding, wisdom, wealth, and victory. This Center shall produce a great legacy, a new Egypt. Like dung, it may stink right now, but a new palace is in the future."

"What is your name, and why'd you come here looking like that?" She replied.

"My name was changed but not my tactics. I am Lazarus. One friend calls me Chew. I arrived at this place with nothing, but have walked a thousand miles to find Devora. I love her and my family like no other."

"It sounds like this love is more than the sum of your present form. Is this love the affection to be hailed as a romance for the ages?" She wondered.

He held his head high and scratched his leg, a little skin was showing.

In the distance a bell rung, the toll turned mathematically elegant when a dressed to kill Vampire stripped time from his flesh companion. Once you get into these Vampires' clutches, it isn't so easy to get out of them. The Vampire's companion stood like a loaded gun. His bloodless corpse fell on a passing shadow, and it all was a bit desperate. He would come to be Vampire, fiend of the living dead, night beauty, and the blood son of darkness.

Lazarus' ears dropped to cut off the fading toll of the bell.

Seconds of silence compelled Brünnhilde to speak, "A talking dog, I'll be god... Look forward, head up, you got to have something! My name is Brünnhilde. Indeed, God uses foul stuff, even if it slinks through the streets dripping dung."

Lazarus persisted, "So, everything ends in comedy. You know how much that line cost Madame? It is a shadow of things to come!"

"I must keep my sense of humor while looking at your condition. This is why you're down here, right?

Lazarus' ears perked.

She continued, "Once you get into drama's clutches, it isn't so easy to get out and blend into the background. Fortunately, it's the drama of living on earth with a savior named the Nazarene, who took the center of a cross for all the wrongdoers. He is more than comedy or any creature. Take up your burdens and accept him. The dead are raised in his name, souls are saved to advance God's kingdom, and lives are transformed. If you say that you are a man but look like a dog, you can decide to put on the mystery shoes of faith and let your soul magnify the King of Salvation. If you are his friend, you are not his enemy, but a victor. Indeed, God created every living creature, capable of something, let Spirit guide you."

"Brünnhilde, I am acquainted with the dead, the undead, and the living. You say, through this King of wrongdoers he appointed you to help me find my family? Our lineage is destined to reign in this land because of promises that an eagle spoke in Egypt, my homeland. I will not walk in mystery shoes of the Nazarene, those are his shoes. Through your invitation, I'll accept him, and will get to know you and him."

"Dear friend, I am glad that you have at least found a haven." She half whispered.

"To you Madame, wrongdoings are forgiven and are removed as is the East is from the West through the Nazarene. I expect my lineage to prosper here in this land happily. We are the keepers of mythical and mystical treasure, at present, hidden from view. Once truly unleashed, I will soak the deserts in truth. Ancient enemies that have an ominous pattern of forgetfulness must be reminded that God belongs to all things on earth and in heaven."

"Many who live and visit this Center believe it is not becoming for them to be served by a dog. Are you here to serve?" She asked.

Lazarus answered firmly, "Are you refreshed, let's get rolling! I am not a dog! I was made by an incomprehensible and incomparable race of beings. I have faith and believe in one Creator and a military of angels on earth and in heaven. There are tremendous costs when drawing lines and disregarding tribal kinships on earth. Heavenly beings watched those who thought it is not becoming for them to be served by animals ignorantly believing they'd be served by animals in human form. The highest Being measured what's going on. Men who were given supernatural authority for a limited time turned me into a dog. Their time ends soon. Those who altered my form do not own my soul or me, I am a King in search of his Queen. The pain of my present form has produced a body of vision coming into manifestation. The legacy of human heritage and my Creator's will carried with champions has exposed darkness to the light. I am the direct descendant of the originator of heaven and earth."

"I see," said Brünnhilde, while rolling up her sleeve. "It is rather unfortunate, but in the Center, many humans have also abused their authority. I bless those who bless me and curse those who curse me. This I came to appreciate for the Center's sake. The abusers did not physically alter any into dogs or cats. Nevertheless, their own transformations were kept as pets."

With a hoarse growl, she coughed. Her throat was very sensitive from the frigid air. Tucking a wool shawl closer to her chin, she began counting minutes in her head, hoping she was in a dream. She looked at her watch for one reason: to be built up in truth and understanding.

"Madame, I am positive we were banished from our kingdom because of the wrong attitudes toward tradition and law. I am a direct descendant of the originator of heavens and earth. Yes, I am laden and still here because of God's will and the love my family. In time a great curse will be lifted in the cell of a sting because of suitable history and spirit. I shall be restored because of faith in God and promises spoken by a talking eagle, and I believe that I am a part of a dynamic solution. Wrong attitudes, shall submit 100% and are to be repaired in a place that is shining still."

"Lazarus, I am saved with powers that never diminish, and death can't even break it. The Center is my true family, and our Center is full of grace for those who believe in the blood sacrifice of the Nazarene. After hearing your story, it is my hope that your enemies drop to their knees in humility."

"Meet me at the top floor. I'll be there with one miraculous diamond waiting with a city of refugees brought to the city by God. The Sa's actions in the old kingdom created only a little room for grace or the royal blood offering of salvation. Human and animal blood satisfied the stomachs of many in high places. Blood sacrifices are still poured into a cup of a crystal statute, Alia. The token blood gifts to clerics are at a great price, their life force. Alia has given some diamond smiles, but in the future, many shall beg to be transported through diamond eyes."

"These are tortured memories of a stony dwelling with open hands cupped in blood. I am praying for our souls. Only the Nazarene paid the price for the salvation of everyone who believes in him. There are those present in the Center and visitors of the Center that do not believe in the power of Nazarene and his redeeming blood. The Nazarene's breath of truth is the best vindication." She answered.

"It cost the Nazarene his life force. He paid the price for humanity?" Lazarus asked.

"Yes, for those who believe, and this has been preached. It is a King's blood offering."

"Brünnhilde, I am praying for your soul. Do you recall the situation of faith and the soul?"

"Faith is built up by hearing. Once awakened, it waits like a fierce bid for the soul," she said.

With a submissive grin, Lazarus tail fluffed. "Faith also keeps one confident. Families of God reigns with degrees of peace, prosperous in paradises on earth, and in the heavens because of faith. Souls belong to the Creator. One inheritance enjoys multiple replays of reaping tenure. It perpetually passes the porches of false legacies. Souls carried to heaven or hell are well beyond every breath you take. My future and present are full of gifts from every bit of our past. My loved ones never denied the past, and the best of it has always been our present and future inside and outside of time because of trust. The rulers who thought it wasn't perpetrated a grand evil against us. They hated without cause. This hate went beyond planetary hours. My transformation happens with the spirit of *Justice* who has strict conditions. As long as my animal form remains, manifestations of warfare falls upon those who perpetrated this crime against me. I'll get out of this beast, this creature of imprisonment. My stolen identity must point out the footsteps of wrongdoing. I am from people who will bring *Justice* to of you."

Brünnhilde's voice sounded as if it was coming through the trees.

"If all the trees were one tree what a great tree that would be! Here, here, to the spirit majestic of *Justice*, our clerics took truth to all. As the paintbrush salutes the shadow, meditate and continue to learn the living word of God. Preach, and teach, draw out the truth. To those who believe in the shed blood of God's son on the cross, praise the Lord. A purging will make room for worldwide truth and understanding. This I claimed as I passed through things that passed through me, and I survived. Indeed, there is a primary intelligent cause behind it all."

"Dear lady, what happens next is the life blood from the vein of truth. You see my tail, well I may have gashes on the sunburn side. However, I am not the tail."

Lazarus lifted his tail straight up.

Brünnhilde answered, "Let us make mankind in our image. In our likeness male and female God created them. Have a big appetite for what is really going on in our Center. We commanded what was spoken by his chosen. To pierce passing liars and cunning voices might get you a dog walk. You can wear your dog form for now, and nobody will see your identity. This unique form makes your true body invisible. You are unparalleled. I can't even take your hand."

"Let the whistle sing its tale. I passed a street named Coronation on my way here and made it to the Center safely. I even ignored a bucket of blood." Lazarus' voice softened a bit as he reflected.

"That long winding road is pretty busy. You made it through all the traffic, sound, and distractions, just beat it and go inside. All the other voices outside the Center will be inside for the showdown. Let us observe as we listen for the truth. The Center is similar to a special cemetery, honeycombed with tombs. In the morning it is quiet, but at night you better be prepared. Tomorrow evening, you shall meet two friends of mine. Julius wears long white flying locks. They are very well kept and do not drown him out. Most significantly, his fasting does not allow trouble to get the best of him.

My other friend, I call Fr. Louis. He has a box cut, and lightens silence, leaving us to think about, oh brother where art thou. His presence, voice, and prayers are valuable to us all. He expects everyone at the Center to be on a first name basis.

"As in call him Louis?"

"No, as in call him Fr. Louis."

"Julius, find him at once."

"No need, he predicted your coming. The events that are about to unfold will occur because Julius brought you into his fantasy. He shall find you! Please go inside the Center. A bucket is near the breakfast room. Rest beside it. I shall return with Fr. Louis tomorrow evening. He loves our hamburgers and fried green tomatoes. Our cook prepares him a juicy burger every time he visits. We call'em, celebrated Buzz Burgers. Many humans will not be able to hear Fr. Louis, only some wrongdoers whom he calls sinners. You see, his history is made from the inside."

"I must be a sinner. I am a wrongdoer!" Lazarus replied.

"Don't bother thanking me. So am I. May I call you dog, one time, figuratively speaking?"

"No, why should I thank you? May I call you Lamb chops?" Lazarus asked.

Brünnhilde looked like she was going to bite her finger off.

"The Center will not be left a little less innocent. Its message is like spiritual food. It transmits in every language, a powerfully relentless Spirit finds believers, listeners, and watchers. Hidden entrances are everywhere, and you will not be waiting long. I'll catch up with you when you get your hands back from that menacing threat that is born of every age." She laughed and reached her hand out like she desired to shake his paw.

If it was not for his own tireless faith and hope in a positive future, his paw might have felt like a spiked vehicle.

Lazarus answered sharply, "I'm not a dog! Is the Center full of liberty, equality, laughter, and loyalty?" He asked.

"Can you laugh out loud?" She asked

"Yes, I am laughing now, but it's not funny!"

"It is a secret privilege. No one will be able to hear, though, unless they are within the circle, listen."

Lazarus's ears perked. "Privilege I have, woman, please help me to fight a good fight. I have loved ones to find."

With burning palms and her heart in her throat, Brünnhilde continued, "I have a deal for you. I have one dollar with your name written on it, but there is just a little formality. It's for one burger, and you do not have to pour over a map or Morse code."

"I am not in the map business or changing the name on the dollar bill." Lazarus shook his body hard as if a hatchet was buried into his skin.

Brünnhilde whispered to the air,

"You're all shook up. You're shaking like a leaf. Barreling down a corridor, costumes appear with drama and lies laced with fear. Julius is on his way to collect their tags. One dog, your dog, three dogs, fun. The cloud of witnesses shall all be stunned, in God we trust and will not be shunned."

"Are your palms ok?" Lazarus asked.

Brünnhilde laughed, "They're not itching, they're burning. I'll wet them when I arrive with Fr. Louis. Ice will be prepared to cool our hands off. I am glad a bucket is near the breakfast room. Money is also on the way, but only because healthy donations are given to those who are chosen, the simple who ask with the right spirit, and the messenger with a message of our truth. You see, one gold fund performs like a glass ceiling; it crashes down like a throat full of bloody opportunity. Are you satisfied?"

"Brünnhilde, when I look deeply into your eyes, I see all the things money can't buy, and my eye is wide open in this Center."

"It's interesting in how it just springs up like that, an eye of inspirations."

Lazarus dropped to the ground. Brünnhilde's skirt mushroomed over him.

"Roll your skirt up for me, my lady."

A gust of wind blew. Her skirt appeared suspended in air.

With a dazzling smile of welcome, Brünnhilde answered, "One round is felt by everybody, and it is as rare as rolling up a window in a Rolls Royce. By the way, the Center has three cats. They're friends of mine who bring the Center good tidings. A little birdie, near the line outside the mosaic circle, told me that in the future another birdie who did not sit on its rarified perch shall have lots of seeds to share with our Center's little ones, especially with the help of common light. Lazarus, do not eat them. God knows what's in the weak and drunken hearts of men, but animals whatever! The birdie near the line outside the mosaic circle told me that locking the cats downstairs in the bunker would not be right because, like the catch of the day, it's in their nature to travel freely like a Madagascan Sunset Moth traveling with one empire, the Lilly of the valleys."

Amazed, Lazarus said, "It took a great deal of effort and thought to find a compromise with flowers. I enjoy them on my dinner table, but remember I will never go hungry."

"I hear ya, but do not eat the Center's three cats, and the cats won't eat the little birdies. For envy and jealousy makes the bones rot. Abstaining carries a great deal of freight. The future will make room for a well- portioned garden feast, and you are invited on our hill crest any time." Brünnhilde coughed and scratched Lazarus behind the ears.

She opened the door.

Lazarus walked through.

As the door was closing she crouched forward and peeped through the other side, and said,

"Boo, you are a little dog with a big heart and a unique mind. You sat outside my door, so better watch out for your tail, I do not want the door to crush you."

"Feasting on organs, my lady? My mind does not function like yours."

"Stand aside, life will begin at the tombstone. The eve is on the eye of secret chambers that shall be driven away from you, and common sense will prevail, like a cluster of chord progressions I must strengthen things that are dead, and remember the Center is never more apparent than when you need her. Stay here with the Center. There is a strength, like a back-drum, but when false wings burn I am not to blame, as many burn so brightly."

Their trail split. She went her way, and Lazarus walked inside the main Center.

For several minutes, he meditated. "The human practice is full of certainty and mistakes. There is gold in that woman's grin, but who is it for?"

His eyelids felt very heavy. While inside the Center, he was struck by tomorrow and clenched his jaws. For a reach into the future, he gave up his own pride. To do away with misunderstandings next he found himself in the brightly lit Center. The entrance looked a lot like a monastery. He walked slowly down the main entrance area, and his eye happened to land on the mosaic circle near little birdies. Whenever the birds wanted to, they could fly out of the black wrought iron cage through a narrow slit. Lazarus stared at them long, and silent then began to concentrate on the cosmic flat and deciphered the coming of an enterprise that would stun his present form into giving up its most enduring secrets about the world he was a part of. Into the maze inside the Center were things hidden away. Little things would re-surface to shed light on his own journey of greatness. One hallway path looked cut off. He sulked and was perplexed at things appearing to be in a state of excitement, fatigue, nervousness, agitation, and entertainment. He waited for thirty minutes. "Someone's coming!" Suddenly, his position left those things speechless. He disappeared, and he found himself in the *Labyrinth*. His eyes quickly traveled through it. Images of earth, a wretched world inside an invisible church gifted with burning shoes brought him back to the Center like a tour guide. Back in the main Center, he desired to show off his strength. He felt more confident with his personal relationship with God and continued his search for his family.

He walked along looking for more clues, hoping to find his loved ones. He pondered on what he was shown in the *Labyrinth* and sighed, "I survived visions and pictures of a wretched world. Like bamboo, I am the little line outside the mosaic circle. Time has crawled for me, I will follow my personal faith. It zooms in a body full of love, liberty, prosperity, and *Justice*! And I'll get by with a little help from associates. Our rewards shall come like the talking eagle Darius spoke of.

Lord Give Me A Sign

Tessie pulled out a little piece of paper from her side vest pocket. *Behold, I give unto you power to tread on serpents and scorpions, and over all the power of the enemy: and nothing shall by any means hurt you. (Luke 10:19).*

"Shut'em down, and let the enemy show itself may my God get the maximum out of this place," she muttered under her breath to a group milling about near the garden railings on 2000 Times Cove Street. Unprepared for a toxic gathering, she observed the people. Most were prejudice. A bit different from the rest was one Rabbi and a Buddhist in a Mormon tabernacle speaking about crowd funding for ostrich farms. The cozy posse gathered beside their synagogue singing, "Let's play our music loudly!" Words are lacking to express dress to kill when the pitch has reached its toll. At the sight of Tessie, their unforgettable bill of needs quenched. The cozy posse started to consider things that planned to hide Tessie from her own destination. A young boy from the posse had already revealed the unsuccessful plot to her. The little one was near the side of the synagogue raking muck.

He said, "Hey, Lady in the dead-white makeup. The posse fuels fire and it keeps flaming with their passing. That is what's happening, don't you cry no more, let them put their own fires out with a wave of tears."

She replied, "Little one, are you a wonder twin, talking to me like that because I'm a big old lady rock!"

Together the cozy posse and the little one called wonder twin considered those things supernaturally, and the peoples cried, "Muck this way, muck that way. There will always be muck, go another way, do not cross our path. MOVE AWAY FROM YOUR HOUSE MADE OF LEAD. MOVE TO TOWERS MADE OF WOOD!"

Tessie began to ponder their intentions metaphorically. "Winter is a thief. A moisture thief to shit, but most of the cats in the neighborhood instinctively cover their shit. There were those who left piles of it behind in the open world of watching him duke it out with a different world and uncovered mess. The fading champion's task was left to their own hireling. Win or lose their boy was always occupied. He was their grand fertilizing muck hero. With despairing certainty, the posse's callous glares did not have to utter one word. Their time-honored eye was unable to recognize the frailty of a meek body passing. Her route was taken to reach a bus, and like the treasure under a stone inside their most prized synagogue, she too was dying."

The cozy posse babbled, and continued to brood over the cost to develop a scheme which prevented them from witnessing and honest illusion, Tessie's state of gloom? By rejecting her, their own plot to destroy a system which they deemed to be her hideout grew horns.

"Everyone is welcome here!" They babbled.

Tessie who was plainly in need of everything was suffering. After surviving a few feet of the walk on by, she glanced up at a passing bus thinking, now we are going to look at how complicated it is.

She was not only thinking of herself when she reached her head up shouting, "Dead or alive I will never forget those who deny history and encourage terror. God, prepare Galaxy's thrones of angels endowed with wisdom, strict conditions, and Justice! The guardians of ancient wisdom shall help us make a planet of visions. The universal church read her silence well, for their wall is my oxygen, and if you owe her, maybe all of this will go away!"

Every seat on the AC Transit bus was full. This day was no ordinary day. Typically, there were lots of empty seats. A taste of fulfillment was near the wicket and unwanted black and white section of strange. This is where incorporating various modes of existence miscarried.

She shouted louder and louder at the passing windows of vital connections her pitch echoed, "Nothing meaning anything, will give us all things! Do you want your Social Security? Take a number and when they ask you what you want tell them everything, everything, everything!"

As she saw the back of the bus drive onward, riders gazed back as if to say, "Anything at this point sounds farfetched, just go on and make your thing."

There was the weight of expectation. The people near the synagogue roared back, "You creep, our nightmare, we cannot find ourselves in this wicked generation!"

Tessie decided to walk to the Center, an eight-mile journey. During her walk, she recalled the people near the synagogue.

"Oh seat of reason, let's pull the lever of wisdom, my God dwells wherever my fellow man lets him in. Christ in me is the hope of glory. The cozy posse in front of the freshly plastered synagogue was nothing but a band of selfish babblers, given over to sharks, traps, and preconceived notions. People do not kick dirt in my ear, or shrug me off! As feeble as I be, I would rather walk my way, rather than wait for another bus near your section of drowning. There are rough and sad times ahead for the cozy posse near the synagogue of the spanking that hurt."

She recalled gesturing toward the little boy. "Come along with me young one before they consume you."

The boy with the rake burst into noisy laughter. "If we maintain an honest intercourse with our little ones entrusted to us, then a dwelling place for the divine shall not leave. It is a closed loop system."

Tessie answered, "From a distance, it looked very abrupt. Nevertheless, it was I, with an eye for light that was passed. Like a graveyard of ships, your foliage was a portion of ruin on the empty streets of many, and it helped to break down families, while the after effects hailed what a profitable chew!"

A Mixed Bag Of Enthusiasm

DUSK FELL ON a brief but telling moment. Tessie reached the end of a very long walk. She was dead tired after a month of retirement. The putrid flesh killer cancer was spreading rapidly. Her spirit was simply divine, carrying dead manners and imprisoning the *Flyby Nights* from awakening by day. The truth was harder to absorb than light. *Flyby Nights* rested in their crypts. Even the more advanced Vampire sensed holiness when she pursued her path. Very few of the undead or the living understood the source of her power, so they feared her. She had outlived her life expectancy. Not a moment before her death would one wrinkle tell the story of her degree of earthly suffering. Surveying the Center, she hummed her favorite gospel hymn, "Standing in need of prayer."

Tessie believed everywhere her heels stood was holy ground. Holiness was not a space of land in a far off country unless her feet touched the ground. God was with her everywhere at all times. Speaking with exquisite penetration, she reported to an evening nurse who quickly handed her a social security check. "Thank you, Miss, for me life was a constant overcoming of suffering. I would like a resting room, please. Oh, not so I can hide behind an invisible cloak, going to rest with answers to prayer." She smiled half way.

Suddenly, a loud bark was heard, Tessie's eyes brightened.

A MIXED BAG OF ENTHUSIASM

The leather wrinkly skin nurse shouted. "A dog is battering the door down!"

In between heavy breathing, she sucked on her dentures.

"The bark, a mixed bag of enthusiasm brings good news, and he is here up in everything!" Tessie waved and gently rocked side to side.

In the lounging area, most were startled. Sliced thin eyes wandered, talking heads turned, and one woman, wearing polka dots, hastily rushed out of the registration area like a ghost on a flying saucer. Others giggled and blushed. Lazarus' bark was at the top of every lung.

"What do you say to that? Chew, come here, boy!"

Lazarus obeyed. The on-lookers attention stayed fixed on Tessie, who looked like a living skeleton.

"Chew, I have held my peace for you all night long! Why did you leap out the window? Certainly, God willed you here."

Tessie! Impossible, he thought. Suddenly, a rat peeped its head out from a wall hole. He saw a little piece of cheese, went for it then quickly returned to safety."

The nurse said, "Every blue moon that rat comes out of his hole.

Tessie sighed, "Pushed into a corner, a rat will jump. This is Chew. He is my service dog."

"You're what? Dogs are not allowed in the Center." The nurse answered.

"This one is, you'll see. You do not want the sick to create a scene, do you? I can get super ill with it!" Tessie growled.

"Oh, just go on to room 222. We'll accommodate this service dog, as you call him."

One noisy bark had really taken over the Center.

The nurse cleared her throat. She was not immune to the sight of Tessie. She called out, "Night attendant, Mr. Lipcombs! Over here please, take Tessie to room 222."

Upon entering, Lazarus plopped down by the bed and fell asleep. Tessie looked for a radio and turned it on. Her favorite stations were to the right, where the soul channels were. A blues song helped put her to sleep, but only for a few hours. As she slept, *Flyby*

Nights entered the room. One creature helped itself to some water next to the bedside hutch. It snatched an old-fashioned tablecloth unraveling from the seams. Like magic, the glass of water stayed put. Tessie's barefoot fell to the side of the bed and dangled near Lazarus. He moved a bit as if he had been injected with something. After it quieted and became still, the other *Flyby Night* crouched over him.

Both bit his neck and perceived his entire life, but found him bloodless. Left for dead, Lazarus' body was soon removed by Julius.

A Letter A Number And The Drum Of Ordinary People

TESSIE WOKE UP from a dream about fishing to the sound of music. It was Jazz night. Guests, Live-ins, and visitors loved and relied on the night band Cockpit Cale. Tessie was no different. Before her bare feet touched the floor, she hoped to graze the coat of Lazarus. He was not there. To open space and noble music in the background, she sang, "*I am talking in tongues, and once again you made me feel some kind of way. I just woke up, now have it all, and all it was, was just pretend. Pay me everything or see me in the Ghost of a Fisher King. I can help two thousand men, moving on with all your friends. Truly that's more than change. In the night I found a soul, and it's talking in tongues again!*"

She stopped her foot vibrations, glanced around room 222.

"Feelings often change with women, but dogs? Now, where did Lazarus go?"

She smiled numbly.

"Perhaps he went downstairs to listen to the band."

Lowering her head, she reached for a bedside glass and noticed the contents inside the cup were gone. Before dozing off, she remembered little properties floating around inside a glass cup. She shrugged it off like a dream.

"Hmmm, I remember the cup being half full, and where is that…oh never mind, like money in hand I will get the facts in the end. Rescue me, Jesus, sink or float, just rescue me!" She slipped into some bedside pink slippers.

Simple and straightforward as she was, Lipscomb watched her shuffle down the hall.

"Hey, Mr. Lipscomb," Tessie's voice smoothed over the music, "the beat just changed."

"Yep, I heard it too, but it was not through the grapevine. It happened quickly like a hip and a hop."

"Well, time does not hold up my hip hops, or my noble picks." She nodded and kept moving slowly.

"Well, then you're not letting the days go by. You're moving or wading swallows, not lazy asses. Now, where are you hopping off to?" He asked politely.

"Beats, and those stays in my book. But my ass no, no, no, it doesn't get beat, if you catch my drift."

They laughed with all their hearts.

Under the rumble of faraway train noises, Lipscomb said, "Tell it to the T. and a drum. You're loyal to redemption music. Speaking of loyalty, some night attendants are under investigation for stealing. No one has been caught yet,"

"I am sure the storage lockers are full of hidden things. Everyone down there spends their time squealing and pushing each other, off of things."

She wiped her brow and continued, "If I could only peel an onion. Nurse Chekilla and others have stolen from me for over a year now, nothing big, just a headscarf and a few photos from room 222. They were in a trunk next to a stool. When confronted politely a few nurses protected her. I was troubled that they would do more harm, and don't want no trouble. I know who I am, where I come from, love myself and choose not to keep reminding them where they come from. Just not in the position to warn them anymore. Didn't even tell my mistress of the details, Brünnhilde won't let them sticky fingers forget after they're caught, and their stick, won't stick to my sticky shoes, after all my walking. Those shoes have changed and are now very comfortable."

Lipscomb lit a cigarette and inhaled deeply, "I got news for you. Her, oh be so Majesty Brünnhilde, as I like to call her, don't mess with no stool pigeons. She is about to air things out. In a manner of speaking, she went to war last night and was given a bird. The bird said, "You will never feel the fear of the blackest night."

A visible shine on Lipscomb's, forehead spoke volumes. He answered, "I went to war and let the bird free. Now the bird flies and brings me back seeds from places only God knows where."

"I won't be the one telling. Brünnhilde is not the one, but she is a hero to some. She helped me recover when I was sick at home, and she has helped me here in the Center. I got news for you, plant those seeds in the planet of visions." Tessie said.

"News, may I ask where from? Do you have enough wing or potential in a big world of fake history? My seeds sprout and bloom," Lipscomb insisted.

Tessie answered, "The Center is the real world, and a little birdie told me soon after I am dead and gone, that same trunk in room 222 will tap a message called, squeal like a pig. One mighty knock shall teach grand lessons about stealing from the poor in our Center. It will hit and have the might of no apologies."

With a tiny gleam in her eye, she gestured towards an image of her station to be raised up in an afterlife with Jesus Christ. Inscribed on a wooden cross hanging over a foyer were bold black and gold letter that said, "**Count Your Blessings. I saw you coming back to me, with everything!**"

Lipscomb saw the dwindling gleam in her eyes.

"Words reduced to a sentence like lumber." He tugged on his right black pocket.

She sighed, "If all the axes were one axe what a great axe that would be. Now give me some skin."

"I shall shed my skin off, at *Mach 441*." He tucked in his white shirt.

"How do you shed skin, and where?" Tessie asked.

"It is a secret area in the Center. On a brick wall, it is written, "Life is Love. Love is dream. Dream is Hope. Hope is everything. Everything is nothing." He smiled a little.

"Count your blessings, and strengthen your skin. You turned on life, I am a dying breed. Tessie answered.

"Your enemies did not triumph, T. When you're tall somebody has to be short, and all gifts are not breached. Hounds of love, have a lovely day. By the way, where is that pup-cake that you brought in this evening? He looked more important than the song and dance to catch a thief."

"Aaaah taming the senses with sound can cause them to miss their prey."

"We are all prey, pest? We all die like dogs, there was no mo work for me?" He asked.

Tessie's penetrating eyes held to the cross, while a drum and some everyday people in the distance droned, new dogma! Long live hounds, we're going to miss you. Hounds go to heaven.

Eating Off U Because U Taught Me 2

LAZARUS WAS ON display, propped up in a glass case in the Hiii power brownstone section. He was not rotting. The sides of the case were covered with money. Taped beneath the case were fresh flowers and pictures of all sorts of trees. Like history, the pictures and words on them were captured. His dog form was covered in shades of gray, a round silver medallion, and get yourself out of jail free cards. He looked to be playing dead. Tessie's body was weak. She observed the others, and could not believe her eyes. It couldn't be Lazarus on display glorified like an unaware detainee.

Was his presence in the Center a part of the game of life, or a public practice looking for attention? The thought made Tessie wheezy. Under her breath, she uttered, "Have compassion on my nerves. People he is family not your meal ticket. All my life I felt like food, insisting on hearing bad news immediately to dodge the greasy spoon, but now a fierce thing to behold is eating the Center."

She observed some patients in boxer shorts with their private parts hanging out of their clinic gowns. Some were squashing lit cigarettes. Lazarus on display had won over their dominos and chess games. Nurses were neglecting patients and far from helping on the night shift. The band, *Cockpit Cale*, was glued to the spectacle, playing to it as if the case was inspired by an old mass.

The spirit of Cut was hovering over the scene like an inheritor of a vast estate. Rusty Wagner body had died earlier that evening from alcohol poisoning. An American flag was wrapped around his head. The spirit-man Cut was completely out of Rusty's body, away from the gangs and drugs in the neighborhood. He learned the neighborhood did not want to lose their daredevils because they did not want to lose their positions. The ghostly aberration yelled, "Where is my oozie?" but, it was not there. Every wordless blast of boomtown had called it a day. The living could not hear him anyway. Instead, *The Ghost of Westside* shouted back, "that's entertainment. We're shooting and hustling truth, and it is fierce."

A deep rest and inner peace settled into Tessie; although, if she had any physical strength she would have thrown a brick at the case before retiring. Oh, to get Lazarus home and wake everyone up, but life had taught her blood is a huge expense. Why contribute to a recommended insurance policy. She treasured praying and helping unjustly confined prisoners, meet *Justice*. As she watched about 28 minutes, the second hand on the ½-hour mark determined the entire audience was a part of a vortex called the spectacle. The party went on and on, impelling more nights, and much later in time, the Center became a culture which accepted farce.

She thought, "It must be a mass agreement, everyday urgency might as well send in clowns on asses!" She walked to the case, threw a dollar at it, hoped to die, and walked towards room 222.

She pondered further, "As soon as a coin in the coffer rings, a living soul from heaven springs? Perhaps they'll raise thirteen thousand. Whether I like it or not, Lazarus has changed. Faith must help him transform back to a living body. God's love might keep the others from destroying one another's faith, and worship of the case of the dead. It's unbelievable."

The Holy Spirit was so jazzed the sound of music slowed down. The sound of traditional Romanian music from the room next door sounded marvelous. Completely at peace with everything, in a mysterious spiritual kind of way, she was back in the room, dreaming of quality sausages. She turned herself about and laid her cancer, morphine-filled body on the bed sighing, "My pain is mine. I just got a check and got religious. Pray, we shouldn't talk about it."

Noble Tessie And Scratch My Back In The Center

THE DOOR TO Tessie's room was left ajar. She did not even raise her head to a soft knock.

"Could I come inside your room?" It was the Incubus, on the other side of the door.

"No! Get out of this place and bring me some wood. The Center is going to turn up the heat."

"Friends?" asked the flesh fiend.

"Are friends stronger than Jesus? I never had many friends before, why now?"

"The crossroads of the world, are you beautiful? Are you Bella? No priest is present. Besides, I do not have anything to worry about," said the Incubus as it peered inside her frail bones.

Tessie meditated. This is what it sounds like, I will not close my eyes until that thing is out of this room.

The incubus could see her weakening. Mustering up her last bit of strength, she pulled her wig off.

The incubus had often watched her undress. Julius, in the form of a moth-man, was watching from above the rim on a glass jar.

The incubus repeated, "Are you beautiful? Are you Bella American woman?"

"I can tell you many things metaphorically. There is just one caveat, but plain and simple, the answer is No! No Mo!" She cried.

"Then where shall I go?"

"No need to come any closer. Go to hell, where you were headed anyway! If I am wrong, and I want to be right, we make progress with a sovereign God. The decision to ignore you much of my life when my wig was being taken off is my prerogative. My relationship is a personal one with the Son of God. I am willing to sacrifice you to Julius. In this way, you will know what happened. Truth shall not be buried alongside its corpses, truth is veiled because it burneth, and can never die."

The Incubus departed as if it had dissolved in a puff of smoke. Tessie's decision had a far-reaching effect. An unobstructed view of the universe turned to darkness, then there was light. Her last words were, "They killed your flame, Christ? Angel of Death, go fetch me a priest."

Then, she died. The fight was won, and a huge degree of holiness had left earth. Especially since Tessie believed there is not one friend in the world, or out of it like the Lord Jesus Christ. An hour later two undertakers carried her off. Her rich dad had arranged for the cremation.

Not soon after her death, *Flyby Nights* had a feeding frenzy. The slaves believed it was rage against the dying of the light. The furor over many parts of the Center remained until the break of dawn, just as Tessie said. Julius was there, just as Brünnhilde had said. He was watching the blood bath from the exterior third-floor window while raging slaves were greasing their blades. Vampires peeped the whole scene, and *Flyby Nights* gorged. Lazarus, inside of unbelievable, was as tranquil as an unfound treasure. A favorite Vampire corpse could not size his importance. The beautiful aroma of fear moved in like feet without din.

"Blood is a huge expense, I am quaking in my shoes," Julius heaved a sigh, while his fingernails cuddled the side of the Center's building.

One teardrop of blood slid down his cold cheek as he watched Tessie get hauled off in a body bag by two men in a truck.

Clutched to the building, Julius stared at a window and pondered over his settlement locations. I was not given a choice to become Vampire, *Those Who Must Be Kept* chose me centuries ago. I have remained on earth steadfast with restraint. Finding Tessie was the last thing in the Center that willed feelings to me. It's so amazing, me a Vampire, desiring the salvation claim because of her. Centuries ago in Egypt feelings came and passed to a sea that I floored inside a royal ship. Feelings used to layer wood. Emotions like the wealth the Nile brought were born out of the catacombs. Yet, Tessie could not save me, and on earth, it is difficult for the human to love like Jesus Christ. Feelings come and go; however, she chose to love me willfully with a gift given to her, by the highest God, the God of all gods. She made a decision. If one does not make, a decision one does not have Sovereignty. Tessie was different because she received this gift and freely shared it with a Vampire. She did not deny the salvation claim. Before her death, I watched and heard her tell Incubus the flesh fiend to go to hell! Tessie was real, now she's gone.

Julius primed his ears near the window and then bellowed without saying a word to Nurse Chekilla and the others in crime who were pleading as loud as the Vietnam War, "What's going on? Let us reason together!"

They were testing an answer from a Vampire's anonymous jungle. The scales on their two-faced eyes of wonderment prevented them from witnessing a long affair in hell. When some Vampires' pass on the blood of those that steal from the poor, the thief rapidly recognizes they're in trouble. The platter of sticky fingers on crack pressing on razor blades dipped in bleach swiftly became broken necks on the side, left to the *Flyby Nights* who ate them whole.

Fr. Louis was in the breakfast room, on the other side of the Center. He was eating fried green tomatoes with some sides. Focused on MMM MMM good, he missed the details of his own appointed Vampire kill. The pajama-clad Louis slowly walked over to his palatial little bedroom on the first floor. His ears were plugged with cotton preventing him from hearing the screams of fifty shades of horror. He looked around then noticed his favorite African mask missing from the wall. He scratched his head, and then sat on a plush orange leather chair. "Well now, who could have taken it?"

That is how he thought it would be, silent with fingers raised to Nazarene. After ages of bold pursuits for the eldest Vampire's head, that very night during a chaotic feeding frenzy, Fr. Louis asked God out loud why do Vampires exist? Why are swarms of diamondback moths and bats flying like wheels inside wheels, around the Center? Why the musical voices of coyotes' singing too night and day favorites? Were they created to infuriate mankind?

A shadowy nose pressed on the window. A voice whooshed outside, "Look alive, I said, look alive!" It was *The Ghost of Westside*.

Fr. Louis could not hear him. The *Ghost* said it again, "Look alive, I said look alive!"

Staring out the window into the fog, thinking about all the work he had to do to survive, Fr. Louis grew weary.

The Ghost of Westside plainly heard his question, "were Vampires created to infuriate mankind?"

With a whisper, the *Ghost* answered, "No, Louis. Vampires were not created to infuriate humans. God created people like me to feed them blood. Don't take it wrong but ashes to ashes, and dust-to-dust. I believe God regrets most of the humanity as a species. I also despised the world, wrote poems about it, and remember my little instruction book?"

Fr. Louis refrained from opening the window. Consequently, The *Ghost of Westside,* moths and the music of coyotes didn't inconvenience him. In the city of Oakland, California you really had to listen carefully to hear the music of coyotes. Their howl was faint, but it was as resilient as the shadowy long nose *Ghost* who wanted to see the minds of people vegetate.

As the moon grew brighter and brighter, the silent hunter became totally engrossed with a few Hail Mary's, French fries, and a side of barbecue sauce over a polish dog. With every bite the search for his own appetites churned, then he removed the cotton from his ears.

In a soft-spoken voice, Fr. Louis said, "Always remember Holy Spirit I care. Glad my part of the Center is off- limits, it is the only time I can truly reach people. Over the weekend many have been preparing for our Knott Pete's Fundraiser. We are here waiting. Indeed, human friends, be blessed that I chose you. Indeed, you're blessed that I chose to save you from the Mighty Impaler, who changes through the fair, for I dream in his language."

Fr. Louis began to imagine a blaze around a bird's nest. It was not blazing like a bonfire, but like someone or something had put cigarettes in the nest. He decided to sit on the season for an answer. Like a mother goose would to protect the eggs, he too would bravely sit while the nest just simmered. He concluded he was doing the fatherly thing by taking the brunt of the heat. Besides, as his superiors have always said, "Permit God to do some things, and why not all things, the doom of the wicked approaches swiftly. Ready or not, like hate mail it responds."

God in his goodness had sent him on a mission with flesh eaters. It was a secret scavenger hunt. Beautiful innocent children hid behind his back, and in the scheme of things, this offer was a prayer on a wing to divine power. Fr. Louis reached for a current events magazine on a nearby stool. The magazine was thin, tasteful, and informative. He scanned each page and thought.

"I am whatever you say I am, a dreadful note until there is applause in heaven you are born once again for me."

Julius was still in moth-man form. He flew near another open windowsill. He read Fr. Louis thoughts. "The secret astounds no one. The truth means everything. Perhaps this evening Count Julius might be called to fullness and be kept. But then you must ask yourselves, can the eldest Vampire enter into grace with unmerited favor? Are *Those Who Must Be Kept*, torn between the hunger and their dead placed on seats buried under a pure earth, or rendezvous in the *Labyrinth*, which is in Purgatory? Who shall lift the curse of a Vampire to a vast estate of *Those Who Must Be Kept* toward the fullness of grace?

"Not I said Fr. Louis. It is already flowing toward me."

He laid the magazine down near a small window lightly scratched with age and stared without blinking into a well-lit fog. His light attracted a 3-mile moth cloud. Julius' form hovered within it.

A dove on the windowsill pleased Fr. Louis. Mesmerized by the bird, and her beautiful shrill, he snarled with wretched delight, "Caution, dangerous curves!"

Soon, he was asleep stylishly without consequence in the plush orange armchair. The television ominously whispered shush, the outside howl of wind sank into the earth, and moth-men turned to the stage of fallen angels. After an hour of horror, the Symphony of **Nosferatu** ended.

It is better not to know about it until after it's done. With four bloody invisible claws of Harpia, flying predators agreed wordlessly before they tore into God's creation. The voices of sand, glue and brute force something utterly incomprehensible clutched to bodies of doom. Cells that looked like donuts without holes had received the full impact of its fury.

Fr. Louis muttered in his sleep, "Louis had a dream," slowly raising one long thin finger he pointed to the screen sighing, "If you let it, that thing there is going to destroy the world, but like an eagle's flutter, my crown is back. A King's action released a thinker on my property, and it makes a lot of sense to all who lost their little heads that I prosper for a thousand years."

It's A New Mind

DEVORA HAD LOST nothing in these scenes. All the while she had taken up the position as a neighborhood spy. The content of her favorite book had plunged her into the direction of an open pair of safe hands, *Justice*.

She said, "For Christ sake, there are hunters at the *Camelot Motel*, the Vampire Motel in Chapter 26 of *Machiavelli Rage*."

Biting the inside of her lip, she looked to Darius and maintained,

"I met with baffled expressions and some resistance, yet an entire sea of water nor did running blood enter our part of the ship. I will not allow the heartless thirst of the inhabitants of *Camelot Motel* to get inside of me. Like The Book of the Dead, the best of it trails unveil places of understanding to my awareness and soul!"

Darius fondly referred to Devora as the watcher. She was standing close. Gazing out the attic window, he answered, "I can't speak about the chapter or book until I read it. You say the book is a book of understanding and has spoken to your mind and soul. Then it is like a book born into an age as greedy of epics as this age that humans of genius shall obey, and humans of simplicity may adore."

"Thank you Sir Darius, it is the coldest story ever told. To read it is to plant your feet in the resilient territory. I hate that the prize is increasingly being passed back to *Die Nuss*. I am a simple woman with a fascinating imagination, and capabilities. I especially adore

IT'S A NEW MIND

good reads. The problem with Vampires are those who postpone adolescence until their fifties might find a remedy for the condition, but, they must read it in broad daylight."

"Do you mind, do you mind?" She inquired.

Darius was silent awhile. "If they are dead you certainly do not expect them to come back to life, do you? The condition may just sort its self out over the coming decades as a new generation of Vampire Killers takes charge." He smiled thinly.

"I beseech you, let me have the belief that in time we may yet find a real remedy, for them! A cure appears to exist from the book's vantage point inside well-hidden pages."

"I only need one remedy, Frigates Fire!" He spat in a low voice.

"A remedy is hidden inside the pages of the book!" Devora insisted.

"Then I shall read it a thousand times. Do you mind?" Darius raised and balled his fist.

Darius' supernatural gifts were growing stronger every day. Devora, unceasingly braided and twisted vectors from their ancient world, while daily eluding evil intentions from packs of enemies outside the window rustling about below them. It was natural for her to discern the old ways and explain them to her family. Enemies were at her heels, dying at every turn to assist pure evil in a cluster to uproot another neighborhood's soul. She refused to offer the turns to the system of despair. Sometimes standing naked near the attic window, she'd signal the twilight hour, even gracing it a natural setting for those she chose to pray for.

"Do not be a resident of crack or cocaine," was a chant she'd repeat to herself. A prominent megastructure was going to have the whole world on a plate and would not be grief stricken with addictions or struck deaf and dumb. Those in the know were aware of what it meant to eat off a platter of addictions. One of the worst mistakes made on a watermelon man's plate was smoking the pits of hell.

The older generation had poured seeds of faith. God's word assured Devora countless blessings, which happen to those who just say no to drugs, foolishness, and ignorance. Ultimately that was what life was about, ensuring the next generations, promotion to its body on earth. Heads, shoulders, knees, toes and a few neighborhood children hidden away carried the incentive that would one day strangle-hold a system which daily deserted them, intending to sell their next generation to the coats of new drugs with humorous names to lure unsuspecting kids on the block.

The whole time armed with weapons of mass destruction, Devora pondered over moving scenes and sweet -toothed surveys. At the setting of the moon, she acknowledged that goodness existed when contemplating the well-ordered cosmos. She gestured as if to capture it in her palm. "If I can't fly, let me sing." Love was in her hands, but still, the reflection of the night skies lit a path for her to witness the speed of *Flyby Nights*.

Fr. Louis gave promises and opportunities, a shovel. So, she grabbed one shovel from *Jacobs Garden*, the garden of the great sufferers. Thirty-three thousand nights ago, Count Shylock Gruden named the garden. In the backyard of the Victorian above ground tombs and behind a long steel black gate, it lays sealed off from the dawn of the coming dead.

With far away eyes and a slight whisper, Darius groped Devora and said, "You struggle, they struggle, and the whole world struggles. It's a closed subject. At midnight a chorus cries, "Many many have been slain in *Jacobs Garden.*"

Devora answered, "Our struggles are no small victory." She motioned an angel to approach, then offered to accompany it.

27

Tear Of The Fangs

ON THAT FOOT long night, the moon was covering the sun. It created an eerie twilight. The greatest rock concert of all times had just sealed the fate of some gatherers. All over Telegraph Avenue, a concert would quickly result in abandoned cars and pledges to devour, "The Good Old Days." One Vampire in winged sandals was eager to gobble the concerts legacy of virtue set in stone and poor sanitation. It was out- right war. Devora's angel would not allow innocence to hold a blood cup offering to tears of fangs. Close to a jagged hole with plasterboards near her tall garden fence, she flicked a grain of dust over heads without teeth.

A *Flyby Night* flying about was an extraordinary thing. His *name* was Pho. He caught the dust, swooped down on his Master Vampire's sandal, and untangled a chain. Pho shouted to his Master, "Look upon my hook and despair."

From a few feet in the air, Devora's wildly beautiful angel heard Pho's petition. He had successfully tricked his Master ensnaring him with an illusion. The Vampire hung from a bewitching hook attached to a chain that exposed an illusion of a river of blood. While his Master dangled, Pho returned to his crypt and snooped before retiring, watching his Master swing beneath a changing moon captivated by the false picture.

In the midst of a fast rising sun, Devora's angel saw the chain and hung over the entire scene. Would Devora have lived to tell the tale of one of the greatest Vampire slayers if she hadn't relied on her *Die Nuss*? A champion of style didn't care what people said. Divine blood had never been caring, and there comes a time when angels of the Klip Mountains and the twelve labors of Putin are called to descend into hell to protect God's chosen. At the audible range, an ache of an Appalachian beauty was gliding in black and white golden years of the mysteries of her good old days. The good old days on a Vampire's chain were not at all that.

"Welcome to the good life. Wake up, number thirteen! The Vampire will take your soul if you let him!" Devora would not hold her tongue. She was astonished to see an angel appear above at a distance to ensure the making of a harmonious environment. Minutes before the Vampire was tricked, he had bitten into a mother and child. This is where a conscious effort to observe *Die Nuss* opened to Pho. It happen right before entering his crispy little crypt in *Jacobs Garden*. Devora's angel cut the chain, and Pho's Master dropped hard. Trapped in a gruesome heap of mess, the rising sun quickly turned his controller to ash. *Flyby Night* Pho saluted the sky before retiring. Shaped like a packsaddle inside the garden, he stood in a row between two higher tombs resting in his own mysteries of liberation.

It happened with the drek of dazzling slang. A soaring 500 Mercedes Benz with AC blasting did not break a sweat. The vintage breath of "Three's a crowd," was blasting highway to Hades. Headlights pointed at the dawn guaranteed ashes to ashes and dust to dust. The sun had already been dissolving when a thirteen-year-old girl and her small mother, too small to view the stages of death took a slumber, barely escaping a deadly transformation. Devora, acquainted with the ripple effects of Vampirism, ran over to them. She observed the marks on their throats. In the midst of a rising sun, the mother and child's Vampire marks slowly disappeared as Devora's angel swung them up. Within passing light seconds, the angel also cut the hook of the Vampire who quickly turned to ash and fell into *Jacobs Garden*.

The next day eyes popped out of human terror. The love concert caused the streets to curdle without reason. After Vampire dust was set, gathered, and separated, human slaves of Pho's Master assembled. Before the face of light, in a heap of morning garden ash and tiny bits of skin from the mother and child, neighbors purified the spoil like millet and tea cures from old wild trees. At noonday mother and child were born from another garden called Leballister. Devora's angel had placed them there, where they awakened perfectly sound and perfectly human. Over the years as the child grew more like her mother, she grew free from the taste of blood. An unsaid treaty also saved them from further attacks from *Flyby Nights*. Pho, had a friend, *Die Nuss*. And it grew among its keepers who do not ask why only why not.

In time, mother and child embraced the doors of a richer sky with new and beautiful horizons. Colorful cloth, kimonos, and fine scents rose up to the sky with sincere prayers of thanksgiving to a beautiful constellation. The spirit of *Die Nuss* helped to create an environment of harmony which came before the needs of the bloodthirsty. Far, far, into the future under a bright yellow sun, a concert of harmonies became a beautiful orchestra before them all. The mother saw Devora and sighed, "Shush you better shut your mouth, while the circle of dancers with magical kimonos float up in a dreamy kinda way, as we now know of your *Die Nuss*. They both grinned with mutual respect, closed their eyes and called it harmony. Although, if mother and daughter knew that any *Flyby Night*s had seen the backs of angelic kimonos they'd want revenge on Pho and would expect some towering monstrosity from a legendary Vampire expanse. Devora lifted her veil with a crooked smile and rested better that night.

When We Die And They Die We Won Wisdom

THE FOLLOWING MORNING a church bell struck five times. The bell woke up Devora, inviting her to pay attention to a saintly apparition. There was just no escaping or no place to hide from the simple combinations of vibrations in her atmosphere. Could the apparition be from a perilous fall out of heaven, she wondered?

At first glance, something looked like a black and white scene of strangely deserted shadows and textures. It was moving too fast to register and did not seem that remarkable until Devora took a closer look.

In her dimly lit bedroom, one shadow blurred became solid and took form. A beautiful weeping skinny lady with her hands buried between her thighs was sitting upright on Devora's low-slung couch. The lady turned to her, and in an unearthly voice said, "I bid you welcome. Some say don't hate anything but hatred. Some are busy being born, some are busy declining, but their just your fools, Devora. Give me a number 2 pencil and some paper so that I can figure my time."

Devora was coiled, fully present, and afraid. Hour after hour passed slowly, and she finally mustered up enough strength to get over her fright. The sight of the lady's sorrow appeared to her like thousands of man-hours, which finally compelled her to rise and obey.

Devora sighed, "The things you say," and handed her a number 2 pencil.

"One of us must know sooner or later. Besides, I love you and yours like the good life under the sunshine." The lady answered.

The lady had observed a glimpse of the world that had not been seen in thousands of years and saw that Devora was unafraid. Her sorrow passed just as people listening to music do under purple rain on Sundays. The sorrow was miraculously cleared out of her way, and then supernaturally passed to mortal haters and betrayers under the same clouds. This time of sorrows remained with many for the course of their lifetime. They had rather been sad together than alone. In solitude, Devora took authority and learned to seek holy indifference and understanding. The spirit of starry chambers, the Sistine Chapel of ancient Egypt gave both, like seeds that sprout richly.

The lady was a gypsy. She shared with Devora that when she lived on earth long ago, *Flyby Nights* were a low-level form of Vampire, haters, liars, night thieves, and enemies that had unsuccessfully strived to discount her God- given contributions while venturing to turn the sons of God against her. Their actions empowered her to keep hope alive while enjoying many gifts which came to her in very mysterious ways but always through suffering which she offered to Jesus Christ and his saints, which were rinsed by his blood.

The lady took a papyrus scroll out from beneath her vest. The fragile scroll looked tattered. The bottom edges had been worn away where it had rubbed against her clothing.

She wanted to read Devora her story. So she asked, "Do you want to read my story?"

Devora agreed.

The only way to read the scroll was to unwind it carefully and place it on a desk. She did not see one or paperweights, so instead, she told her story.

"In the beginning, I will refer to myself as *The Lady of megahertz, your fool*, or since this is more than a story and more like an interview. I am a gypsy lady."

"I am not a fool, and so far you certainly do not appear like one," Devora tucked in her lips.

"Then you can call me *The Lady,* or *Ladylove.*"

Hanging on by her brow, Devora experienced *The Lady's* story, "Oh what the?" Devora felt like the wind at double speed she was flying through a dream. She saw a vast mountain pregnant with countryside untouched by time. *The Lady* was climbing up a steep rocky hillside, south toward a park near a secret dwelling called *The Royal Neverland.* The hillside tangled in the wild was known as *The Tower of Hope.* In the south side of the park was a big tall field of grass, and out of the middle, she observed a scene. In the scene were huge outside markets. She watched some haters pecking about like hypnotized chicks. They were performing in circus cages shouting at prey about making it rain and creating massive storms.

Mystery hung in truth, but is was buried alongside beauty and nature which gave her more than any religious ceremony. Because of the Gypsy Lady's presence, beautiful majestic encounters everywhere in every form on the mountain opened their arms. God listened to her as if she was a dedicated and well-intended ruler. *The Lady* could even make rain. Swordfish would raise up like saints and warriors. For her sake, the mere sight of a storm at sea produced eyes on the back of righteous heads. Those heads who lived on the mountain with the undead could dissolve in a puff of smoke at the sight of unrepentant evil. Suddenly, the master of the undead and greatest warrior of three hundred named *Vampire Mountain King* appeared out of a cloud that she named *Apollo.* Untouched by time, he hovered over nine villages inside the high mountain. Hidden inside thousands of clouded Apollo butterflies he watched with the snow and the light of a full moon. His strength was like the death of funeral fashions. On the side of zoot suits on fire, one glove on a hand of chastisement put *Flyby Nights,* hateful night thieves, and their monstrous caged systems on retreat.

The Vampire King took a calculated risk and threw a vampire snowball, and then a vampire mud ball towards the bottom of the mountain. Two thumps were heard all over the mountain. The momentum of the snowball became everything that the snow wanted to make. It got bigger and bigger and became a tall snowman. The mud ball was right behind the snowman. It got bigger and bigger. Roots began to extend out of the mud ball. Then flowers sprouted that could not die. Round and round the snowman and mud ball went. This made their bodies miraculous because the snow gave the tall snowman vital circular attention, and the mud gave the mud ball vital circular attention, then bounced. This peculiar way kept its elements for their Maker in all seasons which produced success. Even more amazing, the tall snowman never lost his form or melted, and the mud ball never lost its form, dried, or crumbled. Both shot upward, eventually making their way to the top of *The Royal Neverland*. The tall snowman and mud ball stayed and thrived. Many followers were also a part of this miracle and began to follow them out of the park. There was even a fireworks celebration in the sky. *The Lady* enjoyed fireworks in the vastness of a sky which could never fall.

To undo the power of the tall snowman and mud ball's life missions, the haters and night thieves in the park made agonizing noises that would one day cost them something that *The Lady* already had. They were mad at those that bashed many simple and faithful ones against the Highland while traveling up the mountain. The haters and *Flyby Nights* boomed, and even fed off those moving up the mountaintop. Through it all, the snowman's surviving loyalist just kept moving and working toward *The Royal Neverland*.

The unseen Creator of the mountain witnessed the hateful hearts of mammon, the fiendish thirst of the undead, and let the *Vampire King* permanently part the snowman and the mud ball from the others who hated their movement. The *Vampire King* ate many haters, and many *Flyby Nights* perished in ways only known to the unseen Creator and the *Vampire King*. After all his blood meals, a huge cyclone set a smaller mountain and a lake which separated the snowman, mud ball, and the loyalist from the remaining marinating haters. Soon after, the *Vampire King* made a smart vampire fox on the smaller mountain, who would advise everyone close to *The Royal Neverland* to look after the snowman, mud ball, and each other. The sun started to shine a bit brighter inside an awesome sky garden and a protective dome.

The tall snowman began to smile a little. What a lucky snowman he was, for a whole lot of good was inside the body of the snowman. The mud ball's flowers grew seeds. What a lucky mud ball he was. A whole lot of lotus flowers sprouted from the body of the mud ball. More significantly both were models of truth, a beautiful weapon. This very much mattered to the *Gypsy Lady's* future. She very much wanted to avoid a certain kind of future.

Meanwhile, the *Gypsy Lady* held her fury like a pause of a weary traveler who hated envy, and common matters of existence. In a time of uncertainty, she sought wisdom and waited close to *The Royal Neverland* with a song that sings to you, and not at you. On the mountain, she had witnessed the making of the snowman and the mud ball. They were not perfect, but she enjoyed and loved them both. On the other hand, she could not make the trip up the mountaintop because of haters who agreed to a plot that desired to block her. Yet, she grew wiser as time went on, and escaped the alchemy of false scenes and death traps. *The Lady* was an outsider. Her desire was to see the haters turn from the error of their wicked ways.

They hated her, the snowman, the mud ball, and the loyalists who were beginning to spread and live all over the mountain. The haters desired to see the snowman melt, the flowers wilt, and the mud ball dry. They also wanted many mouths on the mountain to be sewed shut. Their plot would never fly because *The Lady* loved freedom inside a garden of the sky.

She decided to wait inside a cave of the mountain, a crystal hall. It was where the *Vampire Mountain King* loved to hibernate. She waited and waited.

When she returned to the mountain, there still was no changes among the haters, only an ugly glow of envy with green lips. She returned to the crystal hall. Upon her return, the *Vampire King* awoke. He stared at her for hours and thought she was the most desirable woman that he had ever seen. Her beauty had a strange effect on him and his hair. Everything about him could change except his hair and lovely blue eyes. Her beauty was so pure it could stop centuries of mortal terror, or help to ensure it. Cracked Vampire hearts inside the most fertile ground of risen pureness might properly integrate into the other world at the sight of her. Taking an interest in her, *The Lady* struck him as curiously Egyptian.

She heard an unearthly voice, "Are you French?" The *Vampire King* inquired.

"No, I am Romanian.".

"Curious, your life is not worth death, and you do not fear me." He replied.

"No, I was trained in the mysteries of life and death. I may require warning regarding rites, sacrifices, and mystical unions. Europe is endless, and I am from a mystical Romanian society. Do you speak French, Sir?"

"Europe is endless," said the *Vampire King*, "An obvious point of reference. Yet, somehow I thought I'd be seeing you in a short skirt and leather leggings. Oh well, surprise, I am the Master of this mountain. Come closer, in person, we can read any area and sometimes even hand out free wings, languages, and numbers."

"Well says me, I drifted up here by the grace of God." *The Lady's* blood and face turned cold.

"The only free substance I was ever given was the body and blood of Jesus Christ who offered salvation and promises to earth and heaven." Suddenly, she felt like a helpless wounded wolf. Many unseen eyes throughout the cave looked to her like cold looks to autumn.

"You believe in the discovery!" said the *Vampire King*.

"Do you believe in feeding gremlins or trolls after midnight?" She inquired.

"I loaded four packed-cows with them! You look stimulated with nothing. Why have they awakened thee?" He asked with a charming grin.

Suddenly, glim yellow flames came out of narrow slits of the cave. The *Vampire King* was the most beautiful being that she had seen in her lifetime. His hair was long and white, like that of a lunar bow, rare and magnificent in color. He then said, "For your sake, the beautiful daughter of Eve, *Flyby Nights* and dark forces shall gobble up multitudes of envious haters and thieves who have stolen from you. It shall happen on earth. Wherever you are we share in your triumph and hardship with love at first crunch. I am lucky to have you and shall devour your enemies' for god sake. I shall take your enemies lives on the day they steal your crown."

"Finally there is someone who understands me. It suits me and my style. As the blood of Christ gave his life, the night he wore my crown." She said.

"I sense your human pain, and you have returned to my cave. The only thing you must now do is go fetch me a mule," he said.

There were no stalls anywhere on the mountain. Instead, she gave Rhine wine from her hip flask tucked inside her vest decked with tiny jewels. *The Lady* hoped the *Vampire Mountain King* would accept her gift of wine. He did, and then gave her a piece of bread and a little salt.

She sighed, "Thank goodness, a good piece of bread with you is better than roaming around looking for stalls or watching others being eaten by forces and hateful entities around the mountain."

Toward evening she ate the good piece of bread he offered her. After spending time with him, and much thought and consideration, she realized that making the haters turn from their jealousy and wicked ways was not her or the *Vampire Mountain Kings* job. It was her Creator's will to call them to revelation. The *Vampire Mountain King* was content on the Mountain because he required nourishment, and killed the wicked. At times he ate *Flyby Nights*.

He said to her as he watched her very feminine eyebrow raise, "If my kind had souls, or even once had a soul it may not enter hell to be organized by Lucifer or his minions. We shall leave spiritual decisions to your Creator. Your helper Jesus Christ set you free and has offered virtuous blood. He shall help guide you in all you're getting."

With eager eyes, she answered, "I trust my Creator as he created your kind to roam the earth, and you are my kind of creation because my Creator did not permit you to destroy me. Only to give me back what my enemies have stolen. It's the look on their faces, which make it all worthwhile. In old times the haters invaded on horseback. Today we ride on eagles and travel throughout galaxies.

The haters did not come together in peace. Now we can live their victory, on earth. Indeed, I am quaking in my shoes as I have not gone after any gods, nor served their God. The Lord Christ shall open good treasures up to me, swearing it, to my forefathers to give to my future descendants and me."

"Proof again, capitalism works wonders, and my kind shall submit out of obedience to your inner beauty and virtue, given to you by your Creator. We shall take your enemies' life force, then throw them into a lake of fire if they do not return everything that they said the Devil has stolen from you.

Far off in the way distant future, your descendants are destined to become members of the ruling class, in a reign of prosperity miracle workers will be ready to defend their Kingdoms Sovereignty," answered the Vampire King.

"Perhaps in another time of peace you may leave this mountain and serve as a commander and chief in another part of the universe," said the lady.

After spending time playing parlor games with him, she began to understand his thirsty dilemma. With a twinkle in her eye and brow raised she imagined, "I have always had a flair for the dramatic, although perhaps I am living in a dream world of very shrewd grins, and trails of blood tears. Oh, Holy Spirit shows me the way, the pure way. I shall offer you song and dance which Jesus Christ must have loved as well."

One god cold awful night, she observed the *Vampire Mountain King* speed off like bats out of hell to do what he had to do to survive. Under a blood moon outside the cave overlooking a few daffodils, she stood unscathed by squirrelly winds and anger that was palatable in some parts of the mountain. She gazed over the mountain into a vast prolific scene of nature while the *Vampire Mountain King* took flight and became a thousand bats. About ten hours and 42 minutes later, he returned from his night bleed off wild hogs. Scraps of shredded meat laid at her feet.

He drew close to her and shared that another Vampire from an Ancient Egyptian civilization named Julius Florian, had made and named him, *Vampire Mountain King*. *The Lady* admitted that in her fatherland Rumania, she had also met Count Julius, the handsome. He is the very first of his kind to leave a vast civilization. High cascading jet-black curls, great height, and long thin fingers tell the stories, a dream weaver would one day sing about.

"Please do not get too thirsty. I know him to be Julius the handsome, and he will find us. I always recognize him no matter how he chooses to change his looks, hairstyle, or hair color. He has the capability to dissolve in a puff of smoke, yet longs for something better. He would never harm me during the fall." She cried.

"I bid you welcome and will catch you. In our time, a mythic time, for you are a loyal and confident human being from good domestic well-to-do stock."

The Vampire Mountain King agreed that he would follow his Maker's suit, and not destroy her or those she loved. He would not make them Vampire or *Flyby Nights* blood companions, but due to his unquenchable thirst, he shall only destroy bad men, thieves who steal from the poor, unrepentant serial killers, murderers, and selfish criminals out of necessity.

She answered, "The enemies' anger is palatable on the mountain, and the grave cannot hold those of the righteous spring, in the happy garden of remembrance and laughter. *Vampire King* my eye has been in the center of it all, and especially on the tall snowman and snowball who I freely love like family. You say you will catch me, but do you hear the snow?"

The *Vampire King* saw that she appreciated free will. Free will drove him to throw the first vampire snowball out of love for the game.

As a substitute, he made for her a yellowy-eyed mule and then gave her a silver Egyptian bracelet from his treasure trove of antiques. He kept a matching gold relic, and then swallowed it. The relic mysteriously played pretty music when she was not in his presence. In this peculiar way, they would always stay connected. She had come into Vampire territory and would need the strongest protection for her journey around the Mountain. When pretty music played inside him, the *Vampire King* was reminded of her acceptance, beauty, and uniqueness. The special relic inside him would also signal him if she were in trouble or needed help. Ordinarily, he was a cold-blooded reptilian kind of creature and enjoyed the silence. However, the relic inside him awakened a soulful stir and a wall which produced a soft spot for many living on *The Royal Neverland*. The tall wall had a quartz crystal door that poured pure spring water from holes that many who were close to *The Royal Neverland* could drink. These innocent humans were not food, they stirred with a soulful stir and drank. A beautiful statue on the other side of the wall submerged inside clear spring water laid quietly. Like layers of sea flooring full of the good life, many could not take that water it had to be given. Many ate fresh fish from this water, and it was purest on the entire mountain. Sometimes droplets scattered to the four winds and mysteriously created little rivers. Natural Crystals reflecting beautiful purple light mirrored these waters, and only a few who saw the light could live to tell about it. On one special occasion, the beautiful statute saluted *The Lady*. She saw the statue's light but under the modern value of great loss. The *Vampire King* did not want *The Lady* to awaken the Vampire within herself. It was the darkest part of her nature and stronger than all of hell which could even provoke grown men to cry and hunger.

"I shall never substitute my free will for the un-dead. Although we have known one another, I shall warn many about your tactics." She said to the *Vampire King*.

"Suits me, you must survive, and you shall survive, securely. You have a flair for the dramatic, including dramatic escapes. I just want to be here with humans on the mountain. When the Christ comes looking for you, I will be right by your side, silently killing time on beautiful green lush earth," said the *Vampire King*.

The Lady's eternal life and liberty were placed in the sacred blood of Jesus Christ. She believed his cup offered her promises of eternal life, good food, water, and a royal place prepared for a kingdom on earth and in heaven. That place the *Vampire Mountain King* envied. He had known her, and it was only a matter of time when the discovery happened.

It was a windy September 10th. The haters of the year would not make any guarantees, but the wicked witch of winter did. Most of the snow had melted when *The Lady* left the cave and sat with the mule inside a majestic scene of lush nature, bird songs, and wildlife. By golly, the Vampire King was a friend and wanted to make himself helpful to her and her loved ones. He pardoned her debts, counted out 700 pieces of gold, put it on a checkerboard and said, "A gift for you, picture me rolling and don't you ever mess with me, for I shall also help other humans near the natural hot springs from destroying the springs with plastic."

The Lady of infinite charm closed her eyes and promised that she would not mess with him. Clasping the bracelet around her wrist, she rode the yellowy-eyed mule through a big tall field of grass.

Suddenly, she noticed the bracelet was missing and was very saddened. However, she had to do her work, as another gift had awakened within her, hunger. This gift called for her to put all her wishes in one mediator's hands, the redeemer and savior of souls of the fiercest loyalty, the Nazarene.

In Jesus Christ, she hoped the multitudes of haters and spectacles were released from selfishness and hateful ways. Saving them for God's ultimate work in their lives would be a wonder that might even happen on the Vampire King's Mountain Ocean of tinkling alliances. The grace of immortality was also kept there inside the beautiful statue who merged with many until the hour of death.

The Lady accepted a belief in seeking and to save those who are lost. For years and years after her own sparks of goodness were blocked and prevented from hitting good tinder outside of the mountain, she went to war. With this understanding and her heart on her sleeve, her enemies' sparks were extinguished inside a blood pot of pumping oil, for blood and water do not mix.

Having told her story, *The Lady* looked dead into Devora's eyes and said, "Tell em say's I placed hand mirrors in their hands, and out of the voice innocence sang, see a woman in the mirror. These mirrors are befitting ornaments for Kings and Queens of the earth. God's children will be the joy of my crown of glory, not inferior gods of twist weaving into the natural roots of unbelievers. Do you believe in the discovery?" *The Lady* inquired.

"Why should that weight fall upon me as something called discovery?" Devora answered.

"The adoration of angels and saints sing. Make me as nice as a girl can be! In heaven and I am setting up thrones for righteous judgment on earth," replied *The Lady*.

"Wait until I turn the light up a bit. You are beautiful, we must not lose this virtue, and the discovery affirms God's glory." Devora answered.

The Lady had a beautiful long braid that was like a global arch. The braid began to grow longer and then right before Devora's eyes, the *Vampire Mountain King* appeared. The light was low, but Devora could see them both clearly. The floating Vampire Mountain King introduced himself, altered his size equal to a thumb, and sat upon *The Lady's* head. He poured a silky golden liquid into her crown, pulled the relic from his mouth, and laid himself down on it to rest. This prompted Devora to whisper, "A pool of golden liquid. The light suits you both."

Into Devora's third eye the light exposed more about *The Lady's* time on the Mountain.

The Lady continued, "It began with one obedient knock, four ice-cold stone knuckles, a chuckle, and a scratch. In ninety-two degree weather, night thieves were not prepared. In seven twilights my rage around *The Royal Neverland* was activated in the form of a cap and a nut. The pleas of mercy's thirst were on a rampage. A blood mystery had knocked on the *Vampire Mountain King's* door."

"The vision is unclear. I am afraid, please tell me more!" Devora insisted.

The Lady answered, "Be of good cheer. It shall be well, with you. The *Mountain Vampire King* reminded me why he chose never to bite into my neck and make me his own. He mystically took me back to the mountain through the relic, and he reminded me that a part of me was a voice rider. That night message was special, an overfed world did not have to use AK's. The next day empty promises snuck in for a last attempt to starve my reason for coming to the mountain. It was out to destroy body and soul. Something bad was happening that was frightening many on the south side of the mountain. Lurking in their midst was the smell of blood, rage, and corruption. Their daddies said shoot, my daddy said to save a life instead of taking it."

A very interested Devora said, "You're riding through a relic. Sounds like you were on the move and our time can be controlled, or is our time an illusion?"

"The mysteries of time are supreme, definitive, and nothing is stopping The *Vampire Mountain King* except God, his Creator. He showed me five-minute epics. Inside were skeletons inside luxury items who masked themselves within an interdimensional portal. Later in time, there was a true resolve to explore the vastness of *The Royal Neverland*, and a door to my future opened. Like moth men on a revolution with a mortal man, it was as easy as A for always, B for ball, and C for the cat with the roar of a lion, not the purr because its sound was too quiet. Other exceptional cats joined us inside the Crystal Mountain hall to play, and at all times these cats, like God's sons, were greatly conscious of their qualities and powers. Born imperfect, as the sons developed, they became perfected by God. After manifestations of balances had been complete, the lazy bones of children from all around the mountain cried out, "God bless the dead!" and fled from the undead of the great divider to those who held the fiercest loyalty. Not the dead in spirit, but the living in spirit were defeated."

The Vampire Mountain King woke up, swung from *The Lady's* long braid, and landed near her ear. The relic remained clutched on top of her head. He whispered, "Why did you awake thee? Why were you born?"

The Lady answered, "To find out, and this I will come to know. So watch, and listen."

"Do not back down, not one weapon against you or the angelic sons shall prosper. The sovereignty of your God secured your right to exist on earth and on my Mountain in *The Royal Neverland*," said the *Vampire Mountain King*."

The Lady continued speaking to Devora, "The fairest of ten thousand shall be protected, and peace is with them through faith in the Nazarene and one all-powerful God."

WHEN WE DIE AND THEY DIE WE WON WISDOM

The Lady trusted the *Vampire Mountain King*. She knew that she could accomplish all things in the One who came offering blood so that she may have life more abundantly, and they all fared well in difficult smoky trials. Heartfelt prayers went with distance to subterranean chambers, and even up to a portal called the mothership, a football field-floating phenomenon. On its wing tip under vivid sunset was the bluest part of the sky. *The Vampire Mountain King* showed to her that the snowman was still standing strong for all the right reasons. He was within a vortex of supreme and inconceivable intelligence that had two directions, one way was true peace. The other provided wonderful fat vessels of multiple flourishing components. Most extraordinary comfort was with those who were taken to the *Vampire Mountain King* and given back to heaven through *The Lady's* faith. Sweet smoke rested with a ghost, while prayers descended and ascended- to and from the blood of Jesus filled all their veins sometimes even filling the tall snowman who from time to time appeared crimson red overcoming the first Vampire throw.

The Lady had living sons. They lived God-fearing lifetimes on earth and had access to the *Vampire Mountain King's* garden in *The Royal Neverland*. This garden permitted better nourishment of mind, body, and soul. When the death god and enemy sparked the killer wrath or came with the intention of stealing their land, *The Lady* always reminded her sons to eat a hearty lunch. It was not going to be a cakewalk. With eager eyes, she held her glasses and said, "Our land is God's land, and the Skyland was made for those who we desire to share it with. Rules don't apply, learn that enemies submit like bread from heaven, and like a well-received stalk God shall defeat your enemies on your behalf, but you must learn the methods of *The Royal Neverland* for it is a long-standing tradition, lurching back and forth. When enemies come against your dignity, dog them with the discipline of the original self. Don't be afraid of a rare layer of white, tangled with frozen neglect. Your face will be as adamant as stone. We are free like birds in a tree, who wait patiently to receive the early and latter fruits nourished by a good snow or rain. As ripe fruits are born from a well-nourished garden, your inner man will lead you to many green pastures, and your fruits shall never spoil. You're created for friendship, God's glory, and sharing kingship as this is in its will. Every gift given and received is fertile like a valley without end. As chosen vessels, the Nazarene called you. Apart from God's grace, all are like the walking dead. I get around, therefore do not give me over to men or things who have no capacity for faith, mercy, or enhancement. Clear out the walking dead, clear out their honeyed untrue words and deliberate rebellion. Clear it out of the way! Make rules of truthful engagement, my fruits of righteousness are sown in inner peace, and justice, from this place blessings, extend outward. Here I racked up only to hear the real word revealed. You are not to become stumbling blocks to the corpses on the Mountain or work with the tromper of the downtrodden. Let God be the judge of seeds of their own kind, and thank goodness for a Creator of all things made in its image. We are children of promise through a personal relationship with the blood of the Nazarene that filled our veins with his holy spirit."

In the course of time, her sons' received great profit, delicacies of understanding, and the golden *Midas Touch*, which would one day be used to help the tall snowman meltdown fresh beginnings, successful endings, and principles that pledged to the truth for those who were created for it. If the sons wanted to, they could walk the earth as immortals. Their presence, extraordinary gifts, and talents crushed every enemy. The sons ruled and triumphed in every kind of war on earth. Blessed as the most powerful spiritual warriors in being and time, one door knock of honor, respect, and honest conduct kept their souls and protected them from evil. And evil tempted them and evil watched.

After returning from the Mountain, upon their Mother's handiwork and tears they watched sadness turn to joy. Once her works were long established to the satisfaction of her Creator, she no longer troubled anyone's delight. *The Lady* believed the saga of the inner circles of *The Royal Neverland* who cried, "Get it! Get it! Get it! There she goes, and she is looking good, so be of good cheer!"

Many came to enjoy laughter, understanding and accepted correction. The spiritual awakening on the wall of *The* Royal *Neverland* was well worth the wait. The tale of things to come has only been half

WHEN WE DIE AND THEY DIE WE WON WISDOM

told. These are the mysteries of life with the *Ladye of megahertz,* the best spy on earth. And her mirrors never died, for the Knights always come running to her delight.

Let Vital Engery Absolve Me

"I BEGAN REFERRING to myself as the *Ladye of megahertz*. Now let me introduce myself in total. My name is the mighty *Ladylove*. At present, I am spirit working with *Lord Justice*. I appear when I can no longer tolerate the lust and strength in the networks of webbed lies, corruption, senseless killings, or the burden bearing for those who refuse to change their old ways of deliberate disobedience. I have come to you to reveal that change for the betterment of society must take place in large numbers and to prepare you for your visit to the Center tomorrow. Your experience there will be beyond your total understanding."

With each word, *Ladylove's* form grew more solid, her voice was like satin.

"Is it judgment day?" Devora became a little nervous. She remembered *The Ghost of Westside*, telling her to prepare for the day of the *Mighty Ladylove*.

"In time I shall give you a new species, a Galaxy 200 million light-years away, where new intelligent, beautiful life forms exist in harmony around fountains of life. At the hands of divine beings I was created free, once a Christian loyalist, now I float above a constellation. We call the constellation *Baby Galaxy*. The Galaxy is celebrated for it is a sea of goodness, cosmic milk, truth, and justice. For a short period when living on earth, my weeping served as an offering to those on earth. My tears spewed to serve as a sign of what is to come if there are no changes on this earth full of evil and hatred. I change, have changed, and am changing in a mystery inside and enigma. Yet, I am unchanged and have returned as a mark in spiritual history, and shall pull off all historical upsets. Mark this, *Baby Galaxy* hates evil on earth but loves to see any evil transform into goodness because of what Jesus Christ did freely on a cross. He offered his body and blood so that mankind might be healed of its wretched conditions. The way mankind evolves dictates the shape of our future relationship.

"Your faith and beauty are pure. Trusting in God we are joined by respect for the law, and human dignity regardless of our many difference," said Devora.

Ladylove answered, "After my short time with the *Mountain Vampire King*, One Mightier opened the clouds and called me into his fold. I heard, "Awake, oh sleeper, arise from death, arise and go forth in faith, for you are alright with me, and forgiven. When the call in the spirit of God occurred, little by little I changed for the better."

"On the mountain people of schemes sought my beloved sons and me in a nasty world praised by mammon. Some people turned to the bloodthirsty. Some became Vampires, others devolved into *Flyby Nights*.

I had confidence that both species would turn to gold dust and elevate from the ground, to be free in the Nazarene. Tribes and forces of a hate feast gained ground because of broken and bloodthirsty unevolved beings. Later in time, I left the system of muscles and bones that only let me move in a world of moneymaking schemes.

In the world of materialism, I was hopping mad and wept for a long time because those in powerful positions sought to deny my dignity and steal my contributions of God -given gifts and talents. With patience, the spirit of favor came over me like a patch of blue skies. Favor came, and resources formed blessings. One can only imagine a seed of faith. Its anointing spread to my faithful sons. I continued to sow stories of the circle of life with the *Vampire Mountain King*, and exalted the King of Kings, my Lord, and Savior Jesus Christ."

Devora sighed, "I have suffered too, and lost a twin named Future. The joy with my family has overpowered my grief."

"I have seen a fiend, a *Mountain Vampire King*. When I slept, my eyes saw words and visions written on pieces of stones. A delight filled a day world that I'd leave behind, with a good night's sleep. With the spirit of delight, I sowed seeds to the salvation of souls called Y Geezzz sons. A Sovereign Creator planted these seeds in my head and heart. Filled with the blood of the Nazarene, and pretty music, I could hardly think of anything else. And the relics of a *Vampire King* poured forth a mystery adorned inside an enigma."

Devora ecstatically replied, "My mind is filled with work to serve my family. This too is a mystery because we are growing together in an opera of evolving feelings and honesty."

With a horse whisper *Ladylove* held, "That much we owe each other, good family values. The *Vampire Mountain King* told five-minute tales and allegories about hypnotized chickens, stories of churches that did not grow, and of rain that had set out to drown human goodness. On *The Royal Never Land,* we did not want the tall snowman or the mud ball to melt, so time stood still. It felt like the heart of the mountain was in my shoes. It was difficult to part from the *Mountain Vampire's King* Crystal Hall. It is one of the most beautiful caves ever created. Before my eyes, he showed me night thieves that tumble and crumble, men of error drowning in greed, lust, violence, defiance, and jealousy. Many suffered from reprobate minds filled with obsession producing defamations, and accepting evil capital from a group called, *those who never forget*. That bunch pushed bids for the souls of many falling sons who enjoy producing and looking at unspeakable horror. I was ready to close my eyes permanently, but heard some poor spirit cry, "I'm on one for new slaves."

I answered, "So I must be going. With that I took my departure on the mule made especially for me, I was saddened that I would never hear about the curious stories or see the *Mountain Vampire King* again.

I rode on the yellowy- eyed mule until I crossed a mulberry bush lodged deep in snow. Suddenly, the Mountain shook. It was a knock from the *Vampire King*, and it forced the mountain to cough up another bush out of a hole.

Drenched to the bone, I sat comfortably by a laughing fire, picked five handfuls of berries from that amazing bush, and like fine china, set the table for wedding guests."

"With what, and who were you expecting to entertain?" Devora asked

"A couple, I set out stones and berries," answered *Ladylove*.

"Did the couple arrive to join you?"

"Not at that time, but I had faith that in time I would see them producing beautiful, and wise descendants."

"How long did you ride around the mountain?" Devora asked.

"Sometimes I rode sometimes I walked, when I reached the bottom I left the yellowy-eyed mule with a herd of healthy cows. I thought this was a good place for the mule because the mule would have some company. He looked thirsty, so I gave him water from my pitcher. The water was from the wall that offered pure water. The mule happily drank. Anyway, the *Vampire Mountain King* made the mule, so it probably ate the cows too.

Never shaken off course, I looked up into the sky. It was about ten minutes after four. I could feel the *Vampire King* breathing, but could not see him. Then there was another knock. The call had the authority of London. All of a sudden, the *Vampire King* spat out one son. He was in a defensive crouch and covered with tattoos and stories about many unrighteous things that the *Vampire King* had discussed with me. Then the son rolled to my feet and said six words, sorry that I was on one.

I never much felt like a pure Vampire, so I did not eat him or skin him alive. Instead with one long breath, I forgave him. Then revealed how to move forward in a wide-open world of anything is possible through faith in my God. One good action from the *Vampire King* prepared us. I also told him I thirst, and the water was within me and advised him to tell the others living in dry places to prepare for the water flow. It's wise to remove all mountains of impossibilities. Some might listen. Others not right with themselves might be carried away by the undead. It wasn't nothing new to just cut them off, shake them off, like a berry bush, or cry a river inside frost, and build a great fire until thaw came. Lack of faith threw clouds over many on the mountain who were hungry for things, trading in family values, and morals. *Flyby Nights* were created to bleed humans and their gifts dry. Humans must not let them, even if they are in a moral mess, living in chaos. Your human DNA from heaven could only come from an intelligent Creator. Respond to God's love. By any means, necessary you must prevent Vampires and *Flyby Nights* from altering your bodies and destroying your soul. Faith in God is an absolute must.

Devora answered, "Many lives have sacrificed, and been sacrificed." She kept her knowledge about her experiences in Egypt with Vampires and *Flyby Nights* private.

"After leaving *The Royal Never Land*, that one son, painted with stories of unrighteousness prospered with the good hunt and told others about the predicament on the mountain.

Many others who loved loyalty, truth, wonder, beauty and faith opened their eyes to the hunt reserved for paradise. They stocked splendid riddles for my favorite constellation which is full of light to the world, a friend of God, and positive like an eight hundred wonder."

Ladylove drew closer to Devora.

"Many believe life is found in a person, not an event. The substance and essence was the blood, so we pointed to the King of Kings. I said to my sons, "do not to let your nets or tabletops get taken by the enemy. You may wobble from time to time, but don't fall down and stay down. Get up and get understanding. Do not let the evil one lay your souls to waste. Fair well with healthy appetites, and believe God prospers you. Be willing to build for all that is offered, was prepared, because you're saved for a purpose. Learn to receive favor. Those who desire to impart blessings took in provisions and understand good cheer because we believe all things are possible through faith in the flowing blood of Jesus Christ. The blood offering was grace in action.

"If my descendants were not favored by these spiritual and earthly promises, the earth would become barren and lost. All the same, we shall reign, mightily on horseback, Mars, and other planets that have created new life. One cannot have peace and prosperity if they are evil liars. For it was through faith and hope in Jesus's blood that we are blessed; Remember, the *Vampire Mountain King* did not plunder my soul. Thieves carried away into darkness tried."

Devora rubbed her sleepy eyes, "On earth, every family has good and bad memories."

"The degrees vary." *Ladylove* sighed.

"Rest in pieces, *Ladylove*, the universal church, and prayers will make atonement for the dead."

"A rainbow has draped its arc of beautiful pastels. The sky is the limit. You will bear a secret. It is our constellation with immeasurable power, love, and treasures," said *Ladylove*.

"Tell my son, *Future*."

Reason for nostalgia passed over Devora.

"It will be known among the living and the dead that in all times your son's reign, all around the world. My spirit, like *Future's* spirit, was made for *Justice*." *Ladylove* grew even more humanlike.

"Devora, you have been blessed by *Justice*. Far into the future, the sky knew you. Your womb shall bear many strong, and vigilant, sons, with Lazarus not by an Immaculate Conception. I have learned that you believe that you are to conceive in this manner. You are mistaken. Like a tree that bears much fruit, you shall produce blessed children from blessed seeds given to you by the blood offering of Christ, our Savior Jesus. History will take note of your sons and their good works. They shall prosper on the earth mightily and shall love and help common people. Their wives shall be faithful, producing beautiful, prosperous children. Their families will grow stronger with time and shall remain with mankind. Any power that rises up against them or their good works shall be rooted out. Your sons have a cosmic intelligent governmental universe, called *Baby Galaxy*. Many on earth shall enhance these sons and preserve the goodness of their Creator. This is good, and the wise and those who prosper, shall share in it."

Suddenly, the *Vampire Mountain King* resting on top of *Ladylove's* head, opened his deep blue eyes, and then swallowed his long gold relic. Both vanished. And she was. He was not for the taking.

Devora was positively convinced that Fr. Louis would further shape her visit to the Center tomorrow. Hearing the good news from him first, that one mediating god head who manifested in the flesh wasn't any other man.

30

Love For An Egg

THE FOG WAS lifting when Darius, Devora, and Galaxy arrived at the Center. Fr. Louis considered it a great honor that the family had allowed him to tutor Galaxy for much of her childhood and young adult life. He considered it his duty in fact. They all were the darlings of his vision on earth and heaven. Fr. Louis believed prayers called them to the universal Church. The family carried an air of mystery. One full circle of delights in intercourse with time and space. Darius was wearing a humble white robe with an embroidered design on the collar. He had always been a man of excellent taste. Devora smelled of sauces tinged with mint, saffron, and garlic. Her cheeks glowed like a moonlit Moroccan countryside. Galaxy was barely twenty, not exactly glamorous but more attractive. Her bone structure was chiseled rather than soft. She had a face that was not to be studied or compared to other women. Her beauty convicted most, except those who had made a pact with the devil and even then God was not robbed. She kept her Yu reserve, which destroyed every myth or legend about the endangered beauties coming as cursed specimens. Her loveliness gave life or took it away.

It was never too early for Fr. Louis to receive friends. His attitude was upbeat. He patted his heart with expectations. The sound of the family's footsteps were close, giving his mind a little time to bring the second dream about a dozen eggs and ashes into view.

"Winks and nods do come, but I refuse to walk on eggshells in this Center!" He sighed.

Fr. Louis felt unhatched, as an egg-burdened by crooked fingertips must. Many Catholic churches managed to resist his lectures on mysticism, spiritual warfare, and polytheism by forming a human chain of legalism. For years he was unable to share his knowledge, gifts, and talents on these subjects. He reminded himself daily to hold his ground and hoped that one-day church superiors would concede. By way of cooperating with church superiors, he'd dress in customary fashion. The ageless return was his own security. It never compromised. Reactions to his crushed ambitions remained a source of conflict until the day he ultimately relented and studied privately at the Center. It was the likes of an unearthed Utopia in the late sixties, many made a difference. Drugs, sex, and rock and roll had become natural opiates, a substitute for spiritual food. Many were looking around at what was unfair in society, and boarding on that as a cause. He had plenty of reasons for hope, and would never give up soul searching, with the main meal. Consequently, in the presence of ten minions unprepared for duty, a single knock left one to lean on. The last man standing in rotten tomatoes raised his hands and quietly sighed, "All we need is someone to lean on. I got my mind on my minion and my minion on my mind." Many of the superiors drank dark elixir from the necks of field rats.

His daydream broke.

"Soon the family will be here to celebrate, and we will have some real food, this is a glorious page in our history. Most of the 20th century belongs to the Devil and mumbo jumbo. However, I was not an absentee landlord with this family, the biggest mystery of the 20th century."

He joyfully walked over to a closet to gather his preparations for an extraordinary ritual, a Mass. The initiation embodies the body and blood of Jesus Christ. Devora, Galaxy, and Tessie often joined him. From the time he had accepted the collar, he'd perform Masses in a little side chamber in the Center. *The Ghost of Westside* faintly whispered near Fr. Louis's left shoulder, "The hour for the initiation into the highest mystery is? Game, game are you there, in the Mass, one moment the eternal moment where some have said nothing is past or future."

Before Fr. Louis could finish a thought, the ghost continued, "You're not making sales, why waste time? Why waste your time and my time when they can just observe free will."

Fr. Louis's memory flashed. Admiring the mounted deer head on the wall that he had killed years ago, he wiped off the dust from his suit, adjusted his white collar, and Bravo, he was new again, a renewed faith. Just like good old traditions, the ones that are preserved, and refuse to fade. His turning stomach stirred, he turned his head upward and then to the right, whispering, "Aah, those fried green tomatoes, and hunks of grilled lamb on the bone, nothing compares!"

What Is The Name Of Your Front Porch

SLAVES OF THE *Flyby Nights* had quickly cleaned up the bloody feast. Shadows of crisis rolled like tongues on fire competing for the meaning of the truth. Heaven and hell were open, the earth was open, and every sprinkle of blood passed for spirit burial. This was the true reason Fr. Louis had been assigned to the family. Their association and timing were not a coincidence. It was time for them all to take their God- given positions at the Center. A short walk pointed them towards the middle of the mosaic circle.

Galaxy asked, "Why is the Center in such a stage of excitement?"

"It's Knott's Pete's yearly fundraiser," answered Fr. Louis.

Many were facing Lazarus, including one exceptional kid in elegant handmade shoes. He was accepting donations, others were in bits of conversations. Darius saw Lazarus propped up like a gunnysack and was stunned. He held his tongue out of shock, then gently landed his hand on Fr. Louis' shoulder.

"Darius, Christians preserve what is good. Thank God it's Lazarus! I'll give a heart for a penny when a man really loves a woman. Look at Devora's face, it is shining stardust."

Fr. Louis touched his chin gently.

Darius responded with an engaging incentive to labor, "Lazarus' survival serves as an example of her patience and long-suffering, even if she does not yet recognize him. Our talking eagle was not about magic formulas, but a whole lot of love."

A few exceptional men dressed in metallic suits overheard their conversation. One jumped up and met Devora with a double handshake. Another noticed how she was sadly staring at all the trinkets and money near Lazarus.

Fr. Louis interrupted, "My friend Darius, like a caterpillar beneath the open sky, transforming power from Jesus Christ awaits. At any moment you can accept his body and blood sacrifice, and begin a personal relationship with him. Devora and Galaxy have no regrets. Look what their faith has brought back to them."

"They are definitely in Agreement about their personal relationship with Jesus Christ and his blood offering on a cross. After all, it is far better to linger there together, than to be cast down by uncertainty. However, I must be sure that what I see around and outside of Lazarus is not an abomination. Look at him. He is propped up like a spectacle." Darius answered.

"You all have found Lazarus, and we all are imperfect outside our true love. I am glad to see you out again! Have faith that the dog will change, while what is around him might change," said Fr. Louis.

Fr. Louis was aware of the ancient spell that transformed Lazarus into a dog. In many ways, the spell turned an army into London, which was not denied witnesses to conversions inside pink-tinged wings of an arch of safety.

Many years had elapsed, Darius remembered the words of the young man at the Port of Oakland and then set himself on the ground. With a gesture of his claw, he wished to manhandle Lazarus. "It has been years, dog. I am a walking museum."

The dog's eyes blinked. Darius quietly wept, as he had the day they first arrived in the teeth of America. "Your blinking eyes are greatly and widely admired, a true sign of life."

The glass case and a piano on a long delay were absorbing the putrid smell of dead flowers and paper. Devora approached the crowd. She stared long at Lazarus suspended inside the case and then peered inside the thoughts of onlookers and strangers. Some outside the case were thinking of the sky, others were thinking of the sun. One was thinking of a bloody show. Only a few longed for the divine and desired to know where the glory was. Many believed to know where the glory was. Julius was near. Devora and Galaxy could hear his thoughts. He was thinking of the Ship's long journey to America. "That reminds me of my own case, today what is absent is the great sway of night wind and rough seas," Julius smiled starvedly.

The present helped Devora to remember a hazy past. It prompted a vague recollection of living with the consequences of human cargo, and the smell of blood on the ship across the sea from Egypt to America. For so many years she and her mate had been separated from everything that they knew in Egypt. The memory of the smell of carnage and unpredictable seas hung in the balance of her own future. As she stared at the case, the borders around it symbolized a system of slavery. The offerings, reminded her of the vile side of idols given to lure someone into a false position or a dream bid.

The family moved toward Lazarus suspended in the glass case. The reek of full-throated waywardness became a great reminder that signs of bad news is better than no news. The stench of the Vampire aftermath lingered like accepted sacrifices passing through the portals of hell. What were these sacrifices for? Devora thought of *Ladylove* and the magnificence of her life's story.

The daughter of an ancient race knew the stench of Vampires well. Like Egypt, it was all too familiar. Unwilling to spend much time thinking about the deadly chaos of what had happened the night before, Devora turned to Fr. Louis. He was nodding and whispering sentences from *1 & 2 Timothy*. Flipping through a few pages of a King James Bible, he shook it.

Busy collecting donations the boy in white buck shoes seemed to float rather than walk. He quickly glanced up and saw an object drop like a coconut. He cried loudly, "Shake, shake, and shake to the arithmetic!"

A small silver spoon had fallen from the Bible. Galaxy stooped down to pick it up, then handed it back to Fr. Louis. He placed it inside his Roman cassock, the outline of the spoon bulged.

Contrary to popular belief, Vampires can move about during the day, their powers are just weakened. Julius, standing tall near the mosaic circle, was gazing at the entire scene through the black wrought iron birdcage. He saw Galaxy cover her neck with a khaki colored scarf.

"Thank you, dear child,' said Fr. Louis."

Scanning the area, she sighed to herself, "Sacrifices have to be made for a cause, tell me, and I will make them too. It's hard to imagine heaven sighing. Many might be destroyed for lack of knowledge of a Vampire epidemic. God must work out this predicament. A solution must be sought in this Center because by belittling its crisis, we make creation a monster!"

The boy with the white buck shoes stood staring at the two birds in the wrought iron caved- in, birdcage. The birds were free to fly away through a narrow slit, but instead, they sat silently on their perch.

"The little boy, gazed upward as if he was looking at a wide open blue sky. He asked Galaxy, "Are you tired of looking at those birds?"

She sank to her knees and took his hand. 'Why do you think these birds are here in this Center? And, what happens in the zoo, circus, and dog pounds when everybody goes home?"

"The boy said, "To show us that we have gained a night."

Galaxy had not realized that the dog in the glass case was, in fact, her father. She suddenly experienced a quick supernatural vision of the subterranean chambers. It was a mystical projection from Julius' pendant concerning *Those Who Must Be Kept, Flyby Nights*, and the living. Blood was pouring into the cruel waters of indulgence. She reflected quietly. Many of the sons and daughters of Eve have been unkind to me. They were mothers before I was a daughter of Eve. This is not my war, it was a dream. I gave myself to it, yielding to my Makers authority. When fully awakened, I shall not have to fight. My warriors will fight on my behalf.

Galaxy projected to Julius, and asked, "How much does the Center want for those birds, in the bird cage?"

MACHIAVELLI RAGE

Those Who Must Be Kept sensed her projection. Two from their source in the mystery were in hibernation.

Julius answered, "They are not the Center's birds to sell."

Many *Flyby Nights* in the subterranean chambers below were from camouflaged rock- pockets of dull, stiff anemics. They were thumping, "Let us out! Let us out," but were unable to rise for service. Their crooked feet were twisting and curling inside specially designed crypts. Unable to fly freely, the footsteps of passer- byes were shouting, "Welcome to the cognitive era of *Those Who Must be Kept*. Galaxy is awake."

Galaxy's projection continued, "Wisdom has become a nudge of thoughtful import. *Those Who Must Be Kept* were once living gods riddled with flaws, blood oaths, and sins. Their mystery door opens to me an ocean of souls for the sake of life, and it is united here with the past and the future's highest outcome. Divine conversations revolved around both. Thereby grace, I went, and like a harp of the Holy Spirit came back around with treasures of green pastures on a trolley of faith. Fr. Louis' preaching about eternal power can only be achieved by a sinless unconditional blood offering. The Nazarene was born and has already died for those souls, among all that there ever was. I have only asked Julius how much does the Center want for those birds?"

Those Who Must be Kept interrupted, "All of your tears and sweat!"

She answered, "I once heard you don't make peace with your friends, you make peace with your enemies if peace is to be made. Peace is not my role. It is the precious blood of Jesus, whose sweat and tears shed willingly. It is the same, as it ever was, free to do what you like. He is forgiving.

"From a narrow slit, the birds fly out of the cage. They come back only to show us it could be done, you can do that. Do what you like." *Those who Must be Kept projected.*

Julius preferred meeting with Galaxy. She was a quieter more persuasive speaker, preserved presence, persona and a kind of unmistakable pureness in time and space. Like Tessie, the tread of her honesty satisfied him. She was similar to a small town he once lived in, where ordering locks were considered witchcraft. But still, his course trembled, and his hair smoldered when Fr. Louis preached the gospel. At times he felt like peeling the day away. It could be done when his skin felt the burn.

Galaxy continued, "Long ago, in one of the ancient constellations, my Creator had a plan that I am still learning about."

She pulled a little snag from her tweed jacket and brushed her pleated skirt.

"It is a perfect plan, a perfect picture, and what you see is really what you get. Yet, its perfection is in its imperfections. You have to know how to talk to Vampires, who don't float on sound or water. Most roll or fly about on hungry shady highways. There is only one Julius in the world. If it was not for the headship of the eldest, and his sole inclination not to feed in America, God only knows what would have happened. Julius has helped balance the city of millions and the Center for the leadership of his species. My family was born to hear the word of God in America. It has protected and suited us. The Nazarene is free, young, and has an endless life, so am I in this world. We fight good battles. Even though I wanted to leave America, pack up and live in Fr. Louis' Old Country, even return to the holy pyramids, my family refused. Fr. Louis said, "Evil has to be brought to its knees, and made to be our footstool. Make a good living here."

"We shall watch. And the light went into darkness, and the darkness did not understand. I was called to wake up those who sleep. Arise from the dead, for those who believe, the Nazarene shall give you light!"

Breathing heavily, Darius took a closer look at the crowd and cringed. He said, "Within Galaxy's DNA is courage, wisdom, and *Justice*. Her understanding is timelessly allowing for extrasensory perception. Like music, her mind a non-static phenomenon is the same phenomenon her forefathers used to better the world. Among other missions, Galaxy's *Die Nuss* employs the intuitive, swallows divinity, and nourishes parts of the *Labyrinth* called "Moog." The warmth comforts predictable spiritualized entities with hearts that never thaw. Her legacy shall take pink tinged angelic spirit forms out of Egypt's indestructible. The monsters of her generation, will war against one another and melt like marmalade on the palate of her generational legacy. She shall expose magic, Vampires, and dark forces. The Yu willed it into her to succeed in the supernatural hunt. Wrapped in her *Die Nuss* and friendship with the Nazarene is a land with a great deal of velocity. Evil powers will learn to submit, as the molecules of her body and spirit are destined to thrive at missions involving life, death, and resurrection mysteries."

"Fr. Louis, I know it's not my place to ask right now, but I need a cup of coffee."

Suddenly, thunder began to rumble. Romanian music on a transistor radio bellowed. The quiet creep grew faint after someone quietly shut a door. Immediately, Vampire bats near the Center transformed into moth-men. On their abdomens were peculiar places, spheres of activities begging for hope in the Divine. Countless surrounding the outside of the Center were peering inside to witness what would take place. There was something in it for them beyond the thirst for blood, a liberator from evil, the Nazarene.

Darius inquired, "Some here looked to be devoting their time to Lazarus' destruction. His suffering will not be in vain! What is being concealed? Is Lazarus being kept as a pet?"

Raising his speech to a gawking audience, Darius bellowed, "I am invited to where people are hungry on many levels and must protect my neck from evil, by any means necessary! Some of us are salivating while watching my brother in dog form. This can't be tolerated under my family's watch!"

With a rolling of the eye built like a freezer with a head, the mysteries of *Die Nuss* snapped. The hiss set with the sun, rain, and thunder. The Eyes of sixteen Vampires from Egypt and Europe simultaneously awoke. *Die Nuss* slung low, like a powerfully sucking vacuum into the subterranean chambers, causing Julius whole body to plummet inside shattering tombs. The speed of light pulled his form from the mosaic circle through time. Speed defied the Moon, Venus, Jupiter, and Mars. The explosion and colliding planks throughout woke up Count Shylock and Birdie Collins.

When the collapse ripped through the tombs, it aided Julius' fingernails to stab through their filthy hearts of coursing fluid.

Julius was able to supernaturally read their rebellious past. Count Shylock and Birdie Collins had tasted *Flyby Night's* cells. Their loads surged with a vengeance, disclosing lessons of blood memories. Ages of deceptive religious discourse and visions of innocent body parts afforded a reason, as to why they could not remain with the pure Vampire race. Their filthy hearts had revealed what they had become during their time at the Victorian in the 1800's. Julius had warned them for ages not to feed on aborted flesh or *Flyby Nights*. Count Shylock and Birdie's actions defied ancient Vampire laws and treaties sending them into a long hibernation before a final collapse.

At one time Count Shylock was a pure Vampire, but one night the fiendish entity licked *Flyby Nights* matter from aborted fetus from the Victorian's basement floor. During pricks of despicable experimentations, he sucked cells between his teeth and shared the great disadvantage with Nurse Birdie and his daughters. The Bishop, a creature of the institutional church, understood all roads led to the secret archives of the Church. He was also aware of Count Shylock and Nurse Birdie's incentive to labor with the shine of swine and became very close to participating in those experiments. The famed Rabbi, the Count's head assistant, bottled plasma when at last the Bishop decided to slowly pull the entire foundation out from Count Shylock and Nurse Birdie. The violation of Vampire laws which were older than soot guaranteed them sealed crypts in the dampest part of subterranean channels. There they would remain like molded mannequins for thousands of days and nights.

It was many seasons later, at the Friday night entertainment bashes, when the Bishop observed the famed Rabbi reading his poetry and handing out pocketbooks near Hiii Power Brownstone section. During these festivities, the Rabbi visited comatose patients. The entertainment distractions made it very easy to steal blood from transfusion tubes. The Rabbi quickly bottled the plasma.

The Bishop enjoyed entertainment, visiting with patients, and watching the Rabbi, mouth poetry. His unperfected inferior and shepherd of the Church, Fr. Louis conducted Friday night Masses inside a side Chamber, which he attended often. Some nights the Bishop witnessed the famed Rabbi enter comatose patient's rooms.

Soon the Bishop was on to the Rabbi's activities. One late evening, after all the doings, he secretly followed him to the Victorian. The Rabbi was stashing several bottles of fresh blood in a private storage area of the basement. Near a darken doorway door, he sensed the Bishop's breath. Squirming he gently asked the Bishop, "How will I eat without killing? I was just a poor assistant to Count Shylock and Nurse Birdie. They had need of me. Please do not take the bottles of blood."

"Please follow me upstairs to the library and take a seat," said the Bishop whose breath could cloud any basement during any times of wonder. He began to read from a journal outlining abortion preparations. The Rabbi grew fainter as the hours went on. Finally, the Bishop sat the Rabbi's journal and pocket books promoting Eugenics on his lap and punched him in the chest, then he tied him to a rocking chair, and bolted the rocker to the floor. With this mild but deserved rebuke, the Rabbi sat and pondered for hours. Yet, at sunrise, he died of a massive heart attack.

The Bishop had full intentions of freeing him. Upon his return the next morning, he instead found the Rabbi dead, like a bent twig.

The Bishop said, "You've got a foot movement like molasses. But would you mind giving me your new name?" He asked while untying the Rabbi. An appropriate silence followed. The Bishop prepared to quietly have *The Ghost of Westside* buried in *Jacobs Garden*.

Julius perceived those blood memories, and then suddenly the Rabbi's shadowy nose appeared. He whispered, "*I am the Ghost of Westside*, and this secret shall not be kept from you, Count Julius, the handsome. Before the Bishop left me for dead, he asked, "How will I eat without killing? It is true, Vampire blood was transfused into him. At the Center, he also fed on the blood of patients in commas. Let the blood feuds begin, Julius Florian."

"Who would you like to play you? Julius asked.

"Organs and parts are unknown, for I am a ghost, and you are a Vampire with more power and can share scotch or water with any human!" He quipped.

"*The Ghost of Westside*, you question me about the degree of blood sins? You stole blood, and have confessed that the Bishop drank Vampire's blood. Where is the woman with the issue of blood, who has freed her? Birdie Collins agreed to treaties that this world would no longer brood her and Count Shylocks blood feuds again. Now, they are powerless like you, and like a ghost may not roam for blood any longer. Their crypts have been sealed. But before I consume them, you will hear a whisper, "Do you know who I am, *Ghosts of Westside*?"

"A whisper you say? Count Julius."

"You are a whisper *Ghost of Westside*, but I am the highest Master of the Vampire species. This difference shall no longer cause Count Shylock, and Birdie Collins to suffer from the thirst again."

Suddenly, Count Shylock and Bridie whispered, "It's peculiar *Ghost of Westside*, tell the *Flyby Nights* that our hunger has left us to groan and moan. Do you hear their activities?"

Instantly eight Vampires emerged from pieces of wreckage, some immediately flew through the passages of the subterranean chambers, others clinging to walls, they required a night kill, leaving Julius a choice. Destroy Count Shylock and Nurse Birdie Collins. In union they groaned a final moan, "It hurts no more!"

Julius inhaled their ashes and the best of what Vampires offer took up residence in Julius. The worst of what Vampire's offer, was spat into the air like raisins headed into a child's lunch box. And yet the lies of Count Shylock and Nurse Birdie remained with the ignorant until forgotten by most.

Julius emerged stronger from the subterranean chamber. Seeping through the Center's structure, floating right back where he was, near the mosaic circle, the floor immaculate. It was as if the hours behind him were up against the finest run one has ever seen in the subterranean paradise. His skin and hair sparkled.

The Ghost of West Side was hovering not far behind Galaxy. He whispered in her ear, "Every Vampire knows you now. The lesson of Julius' mirroring see me, to be you, was as visible as a giant tilted mirror providing sunlight within your secret *Die Nuss,* and it can never be defeated in death, life, eternity, not even on planet Mars."

With that done, Galaxy believed she saw a glimpse of movement on Lazarus' right ear. She whispered, "Just be yourself!"

Shocked As Hell

Fr. Louis lived within a rotation of incorruptible light, believed his spiritual warfare lacked nothing. He had come to know that through right choices and preaching the Gospel as a weapon, a Vampire could be overpowered without cutting its head off, pinning it down with ties on heavy objects, rocks, burying it, burning its body, or even piercing a stake through its heart. Secret *Die Nuss* was and is a mystery.

He believed the power of darkness was not worth missing all the wonderful blessings that God's word had promised through the sacraments of baptism, matrimony, the chalice, worship, and confession, where he waited like a Maytag salesman, for people to frequent. Confession helped many at the Center. And it was a lot cheaper than any private counseling session. Here was an order of true territorial integrity.

Fr. Louis determined that every problem, including Vampire hunts, were wisdom problems. The time had come to demonstrate it. Preaching, knowledge, and wisdom would compel his declared enemy Julius to willingly show himself and surrender in God's chosen way. One toothsome master transformed into a black and yellow Monarch butterfly. Julius' ability to bring humanity to a landing strip shrouded in mystery through a glass case is what a good Vampire does. The tips of his wings picked out the thoughts of men, and the eldest, capacity to pimp the human race was unmatched. Julius hid, watched, and continued to listen. And, so it was, terror behind one doorway landed on the Center's front porch. Within hours most of the Center was drunk with it.

Julius thought to himself, "If there is a God, forgive them for going where I do not want to go!"

His silence was unequaled, for God had created Julius.

The last sixteen hours in the subterranean chambers were adorned in hunger. Its dead were sitting on seats buried under a pure earth, and sensing the beginning of a battle for souls.

Alia's ethereal body awoke, her eyes were blazing like fire. On her head was one crown, but her true form was still hibernating with *Those Who Must Be Kept*.

Alia projected an image to the family. They were still standing staring at Lazarus. She said, "You may call me Queen Alia. Your eyes tell me you have good questions. Yes, God is just a thought away. Make teeth, sometimes life surprises you."

Hear my riddle. Alia projected her voice loudly to the others, "We are waiting for the ones who are responsible for pulling the messages out from the blood. It was meant to be pulled by the strongest spiritual warriors on earth. These fighters in city streets hold sauce. Like the original recipe of fishy grits, Cointreau, and puff the dragon Swisher, the whys, why nots, and wherefores are also known to *Those Who Must Be Kept*. Many of these warriors are not even acquainted with one another, in the flesh, yet."

A few Vampires were present and lurking around Lazarus. They perceived the riddle and hollered, "who dat, who dat be?"

A thug in the life of a tattoo hollered, "We know, we know. The soldiers do everything, anything, and nothing at the same time for love."

Some of the slaves to *Flyby Nights* with gaudy smiles perceived Alia's riddle and almost broke their necks wondering who the soldiers might be, yelling, "Hell yea! Let them introduce themselves, nobody can pen them down! They never give up, and they taint sorry."

Galaxy had an eye on the future. Pondering long while listening to Alia, she asked herself, "Am I a gift made for divine conversations?

One fully armed to stand against evil schemes and things of graceless molds? Or, has a mighty sword reared its thorny scent?"

Suddenly her mind's eye mystically became a part of a cyclone which safely assisted her in perceiving a massive Vampire-producing event. Hour upon hour passed away in their company. It was a vision to behold. Slowly fear disappeared, as it was shown to her that their Creator had chosen them as if they were songs of positions against forces and enemies. There was a message that helped guide her. After hearing the message, the battle against evil became evident. She opened a mouth of a cave then climbed over a glass ceiling within the middle was the *Labyrinth*. Inside was the most stunning area, behind an arch formed a lovely iceberg. Stunning Vampires once on earth had fasted from drinking human blood. They were cut off from the rest of the world sitting on stools, singing happily. All of them were visibly pregnant with loyalty to song and melody. They caroled offering songs from the other side to their Creator and her twin's, vast Kingdom. The traveling sound was extraordinary and even reached the celestial Nile. Future absorbed the music unconditionally and then shaped the extraordinary into a vast Kingdom of eternal creative power that was mysteriously mirrored to Galaxy on earth and back to the *Laby*rinth. All there were happy and content.

A lovely voice swung her high up for a ride into many parts within the *Labyrinth*. "Duck your head, you are not dreaming! You are in moog."

Galaxy saw one body, *Saint*, a place inside the *Labyrinth* where wolves and lambs play freely with precious flakes and snow bunnies. They'd howl back like content wolves' from a hill with diamond eyes. Gates of blue sapphire created a kingdom on ice brimming with beauty. There were green pastures as far as innocence turning comfortably in high gear with fine fur and wee chickadees on green acres. It was the place to treasure, and to store up things for heaven.

Something tickled Galaxy's ear. It called her. She landed in a soft garden. There, she was a heroine and was asked to bring back knowledge from the great *Labyrinth*. When her mind's eye returned, her skin was translucent with light. She was a bit dizzy, her head was kind of cloudy, but she quickly planted her focus back to the present moment in the Center. She immediately thought of Future and herself, one day living in an abundant, glorious heaven together.

She glanced at her father in the glass case and howled with laughter at what she saw as an outfit. To Alia, and the others she said, "Do you see what I see here, a movement standing on the shoulder of a Vampire's chessboard?

A peppy older gentleman with ramrod straight posture said to Galaxy, "A thousand welcomes. You have traveled so far to join us to stand here in the Center. Tell us about the *Labyrinth* and the Diamond Cross."

"Mr. your interest In the *Labyrinth* points to three bodies of water, an opera stage on top of one body of water. On the other body of water, crystals shimmer light, like you never seen before. A garden grove of treasures offering new life is there, and the preservation of eternal life, beauty, and understanding exists on the third body. There are lots of wiggles and giggles. All they to whom that water came were saved because in all their getting they got understanding. And so did I, in this very long game of eternal life. So, there I was as if I were in a very long opera. Given a heap of miraculous bricks, many angels helped me to build wonderful towers slowly and carefully. When we reached the top and quickly finished building the magnificent towers of brick, a gratified Vampire hemmed in a hill stood in front of me and said, "Look at who is hemmed in the hill. It's Julius the handsome, and he does not belong to the game. He is resting in his work, and there are plenty of openings. And what splendid towers these are, and way up high. May I come in?"

I answered, "No worries *Vampire Mountain King* we have got them surrounded. Except myself and the family, it is up to you. I depend on God, no magic spells here! Then I blew him a kiss to make him free.

"What shall you say to your forefathers according to the flesh in this matter?"

"Blessed is the one who sinned. The Nazarene will never count against us." There were very strong golden and red bricks in the *Labyrinth* of heavenly substance which provided peace, joy, and a community of indescribable satisfaction. An angelic astral arm projected to the tower and everything within it. After seeing the arm of goodness, I jumped back into the living with the Nazarene and gracefully came out of the *Labyrinth* back to the Center. I heard someone calling. In the day of death, do not ask any great menace about salvation. A dark experiment near the undead living inside a shell-shocked cap invented false authority. It was where the Vampire comfortably hemmed in the hill lived. Instead, ask the Crystal Angel Emelia. She is a Sovereign Queen, has a flare for the dramatic of different circles of influence inside an endless balancing structure within the *Labyrinth* where she found a spring of water and drank. The *Labyrinth* meant freedom, not cooped up. The Nazarene did not impute sin, crediting Emilia's crown and righteousness with those who love and partake in offerings. When I asked about the spirit of *Justice*, I saw the Nazarene, and kept him company and heard his word. He snatch iniquity out of the musical Vampire *Labyrinth*, because I believed in my heart and counted it as His promise. Everything God created us to become happened, so I was gifted a life estate that allowed me to live on earth and the *Labyrinth*. There were many fun Countries, the chicken was delicious, and I received many awards of the highest degree. Then I died and came back so I could tell the others about a book of deeds storing up treasures and life in heaven. Others, yes indeed you are the others in this Center, I am all tired out, as we aim to live at the highest level in heaven after a living God and my Creator's promises on earth all arrive and are long enjoyed. I am here with eyes wide open, now sharing with you that there is really no place like Galaxy's world. Now my brains are on my feet, and I'm faster, and not ashamed of my conscience. The journey through the *Labyrinth* was fast, sweet, fresh, flexible, and short."

Galaxy's bold look assured Alia that *Those Who Must Be Kept* had chosen her. Sometimes a friendly invitation is simply an invitation.

33

Puff, The Color Con, And Dinero

ALIA'S SPIRIT GROANED, divided itself and went inside the *Labyrinth*. She hovered in the air above the celestial river surrounding the tower. There were 200 million budding light beams waiting for their maker's mark. Why is the *Labyrinth* and *Die Nuss* a mystery? You can ask a mystery to please stop smoking the La La, but then in man-years, one more drink will get a revelation. Alia began to turn her mind to things to come and perceived Devora's read on *Machiavelli Rage*. Devora had received a life-changing message. It paved the way for birth in many special dimensions. Like plucking tail feathers, if you pluck with conviction, the mystery helps you from destroying yourself. Another revelation leaked, it said the Center of Galaxy is void. At the void, you will walk into the Center, its theme, free falling. When you land do not question your worth. Awake oh sleeper arise, get everything in alignment with understanding. The actuality is required to bear the values after its form emerges out of the void. The Creator has determined that outcome in the public offering. The shadow of a ladder, a hidden face resembling the shroud of Turin, squeezed into skin. It pressed against the glass case. The movement was a new timeline. The open sky was not the only one that recognized its designation, for nothing new is under the sun. Stars within a future Galaxy were thirsty champions for Justice in the American way, and so a queen puffed and drank a cup with horsepower mercy because that is what solid rocks and bad chicks do while carrying one on a stairway into the void. God's word is a commitment beyond time and does does not treat the imminent like castoffs.

Returning from the *Labyrinth*, Alia asked the crowd at the Center, "Who delivered them from the issues of blood? Did the slaves ocean of enemies serving *those who never forget*, or the axe from Estupinan deliver them? Was it an unseen rider urging her horse into a canter while she halted another horse disguised among men? Was it an avenger coming back to bleed enemies' dry? Was it void?"

The Axe from Estupinan's reward was conditional and its reward certain. Once in the jungles of South America, it was now safe with other relics in a perfectly hidden setting behind the *Paramount* door. The hidden place enhanced the shroud of mystery near Devora's ancestral box, which had a license to drive hope to buckle up mankind's future.

Alia was ecstatically conscious of her inquiry. Continuing to question on all fronts, she said, "Who delivered us from the issue of blood, not what, and not one shall steal God's glory. Was it void?"

A few faithful people hearing her in the spirit looked to Fr. Louis and hollered, "Please don't go, and we need a national exorcism. Many have rejected the revelation and the word in one body."

Devora replied, "Why do you ask my dear ancestor? Who was chosen to paint the human canvas? Have the wolves of the sea vanished with the centuries of layered glaciers? Have I died and come back? Is the theater of inquiry shut?"

Tangled in her memories, Devora began displaying hand symbols of the past.

Devora persisted, "Alia, you own your questions, and I own my answers. The fellowship of the sun, the moon, and soldiers are in America. Many creatures were given to Jesus, who ain't scared to catch no bodies. The glory of Christ represents one body, one time, in all."

Alia replied, "But, I wanted to measure the full effect of his glory in a Vampire who has fasted from drinking human blood. Lazarus suspended in the air is a conception. The *Flyby Nights* have not grasped anti-gravity. This is *Those Who Must Be Kep*ts Holy Grail.

PUFF, THE COLOR CON, AND DINERO

The *Flyby Nights* destructive slaves are dry empty vegetables for *those who never forget*. Among you, *those who never forget* have gathered around the dog for everything, anything, and nothing. *Those who never forget* flatter and lie about, lying for bloody gain, seeking profit for its sake only. The basement's blood bank and the slaves of *Flyby Nights* merciless exchange of blood for money are the roots that awakens evil. Slave selling their values has no real value. Their actions are enticing simple ones at the void to compromise their integrity in the Center. Vampires say they know of no evil when it comes to fulfilling appetites. They know profit."

Alia continued, "Many humans in the Center are poor. Consequently, they offer themselves as food. *Flyby Nights* have mostly fed off whatever they can outside the Center in the city. Many nights when pretty music played to human hearts and the *Queen* of song, Julius observed them drink from willing and unwilling bodies. Last night after Tessie's demise, the *Flyby Nights* consumed a bleeding gore of greed and skin right here in the Center. This morning I observed you, Devora. You entered the Center with your family and perceived the aftermath. The smell reminded you of why you departed Egypt. The same odor is that of those who followed you. When the death of *Flyby Nights* start with a celebration, it is the death gods that turn the lights off, and it is the purest Vampires who sometimes retreat into the quiet, helping many in the Center to turn to Jesus Christ. This institution has become alive in its own hunger. Last night was different, Vampires passed on blood and chose to watch *Flyby Nights* eat their slaves' whole inside the Center. This from the view of *Those Who Must Be Kept*, has not been done in 700 years, human time. The eldest Vampires in Egypt and Romania perceived the feast. Slaves of *Flyby Nights* robbed the Center's innocent inside the assembly. Tessie was acquainted with the thieves. Julius, our watcher, observed their bloody show after she offered her final breath in prayer. At the void, you walked into the Center. Her beautiful aroma, you didn't whiff, but I was there, in the celestial and saw the majesty in her death given to the love of Jesus Christ," Alia claimed.

Up until now, the family had not heard of Tessie's passing. The quiet of their moan knocked the core out of sorrow as trouble had an end.

Alia continued, "Listen everyone, and surely Jesus Christ's anointed stand here. Winning the heart of your people is challenging, and all can hear lingering hearts. Julius understands one very important factor. Do not wake *Those Who Must Be Kept*! Some say do not wake the witch or the alchemist of time travelers. Many titles throughout history stand the test of time. *Those Who Must Be Kept* do not need titles or differences to come up with love or hate for blood menus. They can be the guards of dignity for all people if you let them, and rest assured they are like one people in favor of loyalty beyond human understanding. *Those Who Must Be Kept* invented Vampires in your human likeness. The most significant difference is that Vampires travel the earth seeking blood, *Those Who Must Be Kept* rest with pure organic crystal. If awaken they shall swallow oceans. Like towering limestone cliffs posing in uncharted icy waters, if unnecessarily disturbed by unwanted intruders or strangers, all in heaven and hell shall be loosened. If awakened, humanities plan and faith must be unshakable to survive. Humanity, like agents of Babylon and its baits, hangs low like ripe plums on a branch. Most ripen too fast to register on their selective palates. Unlike a scorpion, their strike brings anguish, healing, and new laws. Long ago, as a pawn sacrifice, I saw the need for Vampires, because Julius bit into me to preserve my purity. But he did not get it. I am not Vampire. The blue twins, inside *Those Who Must Be Kept* preserved me for *Justice*. I am kept for *Justice* while the *Flyby Nights'* identity has worsened. The earth's crisis has rattled signals. We have come to learn through close observation in this Center, that humanity requires a special priority. It is essential because human identity can get lost so quickly in America."

Devora sighed hard, and the lights flickered. She responded, "This is true. Humanity grows cold. Its need for blood worsened. I watch the warfare from the Victorian window! Some days I have distracted Galaxy with newting in the back yard pond, we feed newts lunch while covering glass jars with seals. At night with my own eyes,

I have seen red liquid trickling down into the city which brews like fire."

Alia answered, "Humans must learn how to guard their identities if they do not want to lose body and soul. When an identity is not guarded, it might become an occupied vessel. The rate of *Flyby Night* turns are accelerating, and it has become extremely rare for Vampires to make Vampire."

Devora changed the subject, "An intercessor named Jesus Christ, the Nazarene gave humans more than can ever be imagined. No entity on earth has ever offered anything like the savior. He said to drink his blood and has died for human sin. People can just call out his name, for help no matter what race, color, or creed!"

Alia replied, "Has Jesus Christ returned? How shall Vampires make him?"

"I am afraid not," answered Devora?" The crowd cried, "Satan is here!"

"From our view, fleshly bodies become more than protein when they truly embrace and receive the Nazarene. Centuries after *Those Who Must Be Kept* returned to their original form, Jesus Christ came out of a grave to die and forgive sins. Very few followers truly believe and receive him according to the Christian Gospel. The law written on their human hearts naturally nudge them to exercise self-restraint and righteous judgment. Jesus Christ is the grace of a living God for some humans in real time. Even *Those Who Must Be Kept* might submit to this grace, in and outside of human time. When taking the form of blue twins, *Those Who Must Be Kept* existed among humans and communed with several channels on every existing planet. Brief communications were like centuries of sacred text inside one amulet and tubular bells. A watchful Darius refuses to work with the bony claws of a fiery abyss. He was born into the ancient Sa tribe which existed long before the Nazarene.

In much the same way nets gather fish when crossing the great ocean belt, Darius and *Those Who Must Be Kept* silently watched flights of Vampires and Mummies unlawfully taken out of Egypt. The silent *Die Nuss* piercing deeply into living Lapis engraved on my ancient sarcophagus, found no limits while we crossed the Nile into Europe and America. On the ship, Darius knew the limestone sarcophagi held royal mummies. The Lapis carries great and powerful energies. However, the dynamic power held and exercised within your ancestral box Devora, inherited from the Yu, brings stronger channels to a living God. Your inheritance is eternal and was chosen for reasons only known to your Creator!

Devora cried, "Who am I?" She pulled some butternuts from her coat pocket nervously placing a few in her mouth. "The ship, yes, it is all starting to come back. We must be the refugees of the flesh of royal gods who helped protect the legendary vessel of preservation. One cup inside my ancestral box brings words, time, and events into manifestation. This is a holy gift, an enigma inside a mystery. *Die Nuss* has assigned roles from the beginning of time and is beyond any ring of power which interferes with our God-given legacy. If our peace is undermined, there will be worldwide consequences. Have mercy on our past with false gods, who sat with deceiver's attempting to dupe us. Our Creator's talking eagle prepared and sheltered us under a wing of protection and prosperous our chosen ones! Thank God we were brought up out of Egypt and shall be restored more powerfully by all enemies who hated and blocked us! We are eternal survivors!"

Alia's and Devora's convincing words caused Darius to look up. His eyes welled up with tears as he stared at Lazarus.

Devora continued, "The will of the Creator has the final word. Our family harvests what we plant. Our view looks toward one supreme power who has planted its self into us, exercising its understanding beyond ordinary measure."

A presence whispered, "Er-h'rm. Are great and little list of offerings included?" It was *The Ghost of Westside*, nose meddling inside the ring of power. He was sniffing from the window. His end was near. Everybody stopped talking.

Alia replied, "There are rough times ahead for you. Go away from the window and go away from our light. You have been soaked in banners of operations which escalate evil practices. Truth and Justice have abandoned you. Many in this life and the afterlife believe *Die Nuss* can manifest ancient strength written on the tiniest of Egyptian papyrus. Without total understanding, the Sa have absorbed very little traits and powers of *Die Nuss*. A chosen Darius and Devora came to America because unaccepting priests did not bend from law; they practiced magic and urged the journey on an extraordinary ship from the earliest Egyptian times. From the beginning, this cosmic ship, a warrior epic dream soul, was carved, painted, and placed inside *Die Nuss*. The condition produced worldwide and spiritual phenomenon because of a sitting messenger draped in black, not a little singing tongue born to manipulate a two-faced family affair feeding aborted flesh to a gathering while profiting on the back foot."

Alia continued to weigh in on everybody present. Hell and humanity were in the shadow of *The Ghost of Westside*. His crew shepherded into the camp of Hades.

"All on planet earth better be prepared when this messenger is awake. The means remain open to the messenger everywhere. The legendary cup and relics behind the *paramount* door in the Victorian are like the Axe of Estupian only passing to congratulate the messenger's decree, *Justice*. Without faith, family unity, and wisdom inside *Die Nuss*, Darius you will never discover the biggest part of your mission. It was inside the weighing of hearts of bad men and women turned good because they were open to a message that reached them. Everyone, it's an emergency and Darius might wake up as a rescuer, or maybe only a pawn floating in a casket wading back to Egypt. Fr. Louis, your backstroke enjoys liberty so greatly. You have helped prepare a room where Devora's ancestral box, legendary cup, and Holy relics remain. Devora, you can open the door. In the course of time, the box will allow for time travel, but your memory at this time will not permit the entire contents of the mission without the help of *Those Who Must Be Kept*. Since the beginning, the Yu tribe guides from one spirited pyramid. Galaxy is the chief deity of this generation's message. *Those Who Must Be Kept* used the ordinary on earth to make extraordinary inside their planet. Galaxy's twin brother, observes the stages of life on Earth from his vantage point absorbing the sacraments every time truth on earth are given. Future is death and life. One floral clock of eternal peace and happiness soars peacefully Chariots and ships made of pure gems and stones triumphant. Passages bend the oceans' invisible wraps. Swimming pools of fragrances are beautiful, spirit is holy, wise, precise, and abundantly drunk with the history of many souls' victory and *Justice*. The preservation of the earth's kings, queens, martyrs, or saints cannot compare. Tender is the ghost who we love to love the most. It helps to keep Earth for unknown reasons. Some call this place the *Labyrinth* inside *Those Who Must Be Kept*. When remote tactics entered the Center, and wicked creatures offered blood to idols and false Vampire gods for their own debaucheries, *Those Who Must Be Kept*, time on earth draws nearer. As they prefer to rule in straightforward superiority, not false flags appealing to Vampire Wars. Your daughter Galaxy seeks and brings *Justice* and truth. *Those Who Must Be Kept* passed the eternal gift to her. The Nazarene inside Future leaked pure light, has snatched cloaks of darkness and greed from their enemies. So far together they have left five hundred thousand enemies humbled. These enemies obediently and willingly serve Future as subjects in the afterlife. Galaxy is the grand inheritor on earth of understanding and power of their Living God. In heaven and in the *Labyrinth a* sovereign God split universal and interstellar prosperity into degrees of goodness inside their created will. Do you remember your midwife?" asked Alia.

"Yes, before Daciana left with Future she looked at us quite benevolently. Has she been turned into a crystal statue, returning to *Those Who Must Be Kept?*" Devora asked.

"Daciana was designed to sail from Romania to America. Her sixth sense was programmed to awaken the life force of *Those Who Must Be Kept* in Transylvania and Slovenia. The greater plan is unfolding in their sphere. While in America she awakened your twins to produce a message and a voice of reason. She has now become the voice of reason. Upon contact, a mysterious conversion connected *Those Who Must Be Kept* to your delivery process. The procedure is incomprehensible to mankind. The midwife has turned safely to the hands of a living golden tree heavily invested in anticipated rewards. Daciana is now a crystal statue, a voice of reason and kept in peace with others like myself around the golden tree. If enemies awaken her, she shall consume Julius' *Flyby Nights* in a pool of blood according to their bloodthirsty ambition drench in pain. If awakened Julius shall consume her. Within him, she returns prosperous and at peace with Galaxy growing stronger in understanding, sober, wealthier, and ripens with those who seek *Justice* near a majestic constellation of stars that shall succeed in God's ultimate plan for life on earth, the *Labyrinth* and Heaven. They shall fare well in all times in every dimension on Earth, Mars, and Heaven. If they are called to raise hell, satanic forces shall submit by a power of the Nazarene and Vampires all over Earth.

In Egypt and Romania, Chosen Vampires wait for deliverance. Within them, coursing blood mysteries live forever until *Those Who Must Be Kept* return to them. For who shall make the one Creator known to Vampires in need of salvation? Its purpose must be comprehended through experimentation and advancement. One was heard laughing saying, "Can't say, you're still drinking blood!"

The eldest Julius passed on that one's dynasty of death beams, overcoming his desire for blood offerings. The *Mountain Vampire King* developed a mysterious malt inside the Carpathian Mountains. Charms may be influential in his courting process; but it is not a proxy for saying, "I do!" The *Mountain Vampire Kings* expansions shall doom most Vampires. *Flyby Nights* like a pathetic witchery of doomed charms will be consumed. They broke the eldest Vampire laws which have protected innocent human bloodlines. Before the pursuit for cures, Julius waited for a message, a voice of reason. Abstaining from innocent human blood was discovered to be the beginning of his successful cure. However, there is another tribe, which functions differently. So differently, that it should not be written about unless the messenger is prepared to awaken the destruction of Mankind. Love is the greatest thing of all, and for that reason alone, if *Those Who Must Be Kept* return to earth in their fullness, the law in its totality, shall consume earth as humanity know it. Desolation shall be the world's new little friend, and then they shall rebuild, with a constellation of majestic. Think of a brick wall, and compare them to it. They hold together. However, if you keep pulling bricks, eventually one will give way to a final fall. Mankind's fragile prints will lay under that fall, penalized."

Suddenly Darius pointed, "Alia, the dog! See him in the mirror. The law can be like a mirror which this day shows you the strength of injustices done against my brother, Lazarus! The priests' actions in Egypt were rebellious acts against God's desire to permit love between Yu and Sa."

Alia interrupted. "Darius the flowers, see them in the mirror, they are dead. The cut flowers symbolize dead flesh. We believe the Nazarene gives true life."

Alia's twist in the spirit, veiled under a thick cloud, spun quietly. Many gathered could hear her spin. She refused to become flesh, remaining pure in spirit.

"Although you are correct, the strength of injustice is reflected in the mirror. *Those Who Must Be Kept* refuse to look into it. They are not copycats," insisted Alia.

Her voice entered into the hearts of everyone present. "This is not the dog's original form. Very powerful Vampire priests ordered a curse. They have since fallen asleep and are detained until the final judgment."

Galaxy roared, "A man in the mirror just turned backed the hand of time. A change has come. Do you see him? The power to recognize through the spirit of truth is excellent, and apart from the priests' doings, curse, and law. The man's true form is a gift given by God, sent by living grace. His real form is beautiful! Quickly, let's bind the acts of evil who participated in this monstrous act done against him. Everyone must have mercy on the dog's form gifted by something the priests did for purposes that are to come if recognized and not blocked."

Darius cried back, "Shall Alia will Lazarus into her presence in eternity past?"

Devora smiled. "Please, take notice of me, Alia. I offer you a choice that I was never given. The 100-year-old Axe from Estupian is behind the *paramount* door! It brought its stench to the Kingdom of Vampires. As must be obvious to all by this time, I, daughter of Yu, was covered by a fleshy cloak of the Sa. It shielded my youth from perpetrators. Vampire stench can be suffocating in a world where there is a lot to see. We sailed, they sailed, and we all are here now in America."

The stench in the Center aided her in recollecting the spirits who spoke in thunderous chants before leaving Mint of Zeb.

Devora went on, "I deciphered the tongues' message. The Priests said, "Leave Egypt, the law does not want you or Darius here! The priests or law will not redeem you! The chants were decades in the making even though the priest's laws are not truly God's law. One day we shall return to Egypt, to prosperity, wisdom, heath, and goodness. Egypt will welcome us with open arms, as we shall help restore and rebuild what was stolen. When we were at sea, pressing fingertips and one thumb under sleepless nights in Brooklyn assisted in creating my new identity. *those who never forget* sailed with us on that fated journey, they gnawed and then drank their own death inside a mug called forty, so that they might ascend to the next day. The cup represented a King raised out of Brooklyn. *Those who never forget* threw their birthright into the cup and arrogantly looked into the mirror of the strongest death god on the waters. Nightly, bodies were thrown off the ship into the sea, burial shrouds mounted on walls were left behind. One floor on the ship's quarterdeck was the area were vastness, and exotic silence existed. Everybody was having a wonderful time up there, enjoying one another, quietly. In an organic thirst to feed, the eldest Julius always credited *Those Who Must Be Kept* for their sheer power not to feed on an altered kind. He learned that no one is above their law. *Those Who Must Be Kept* must awaken to help the Yu to survive. The tribe is barely reproducing. I am one of the last ones left. Your kingdom also has a man in the mirror. On earth, just any mortal eye does not know his reflection. Only the immortals might recognize him. Like oxygen you know him well, his name is always Julius Florian, the eldest creation. On the ship, Darius sensed your presence inside ancient wooden sarcophagi. My psyche and disenchanted energies also recognized it, even while venomous seeds competed for my total memory."

Darius feasted his eyes on Devora's creative vitality, breathlessly declaring, "Her memory has really returned."

Devora sprinted toward Alia's ethereal presence. "I am talking to you at the suggestion of the eldest Vampire created in Egypt. Since our arrival from our motherland, Julius has secretly met with me three times a year in our Victorian's library. I have known him to be a Vampire, and have never shared his secret or our meetings with anyone."

Galaxy racked her hair, she thought the hardest part was not sharing her meetings either, sighing, "Ta Er-h'r'm! Dream on mother boo! Julius has met with me, as well."

Darius remembered the precise times of those meetings. He recalled those years when Devora and Galaxy carried a gleam of privilege in their personalities.

Devora went on, "Julius assured me that when the lights go out in the city, not to fear the worst about the neighborhood or Center. He claimed Holy particles given to me through my relationship with our helper Tessie and Fr. Louis would facilitate in creating a bright future. The seeds that were given to me in Egypt never detoured me from our bright future. The Holy Osiris and ankh are also fertile, fortunate, and loved by the shed blood Christ. Do you know what I am talking about? When Fr. Louis serves the Host, the body of Christ I believe that his bloody sacrifice was an ultimate gift despite our circumstances that bound us for a little while. Our temporary suffering shall pass. In one eternal moment, many share the Host in his past, future, and present. Through it all, Darius and I hung on to the words of a talking eagle. It has spoken in its advent and welcomed us upon our arrival. We hope that you have been listening.

After hearing the position of Julius, I understood why he quietly aided us throughout our mission across the sea. Darius' written destiny remained safe in the Victorian. In all his getting, the Yu has always got understanding in these matters. Julius' responsibility was designed to protect our lineage and those of similar fate from the enterprise of *Flyby Nights*. They are also enemies." Devora sighed.

Alia answered, "Friends and enemies shall come to visit. It's written, Thou preparest a table before me in the presence of mine enemies. With the knowledge that I hold, enemies were made to submit to 2 powers, the blood of Jesus Christ and Julius. By appointed death on the cross, Vampirism was given the power to know the blood of Christ, to feed on it, or bow down to it. There was too much deviltry in the world for the king of darkness himself to show up!"

Confidently, Devora replied, "Yes, it is true, the eye of Julius Florian. His destiny written by the kingdom of *Those Who Must Be Kept*, like pig bristle handwoven within the threads, though altered, he may put on the garment of Jesus and so can Osiris. But Julius is not Jesus Christ Today, I perceive you Alia, my ancestor. The body of *Those Who Must Be Kept* are among us here in the Center and the *Labyrinth*. My daughter Galaxy has reflected a vision of unmerited grace. When my veil touched American soil, and the people sang this land is your land, this land became my land. Galaxy became its future, and many shall soon fight for her. I have watched the city with its manifestations and evils of *those who never forget*. The multi-faceted unclean degenerates professes its nature is with all of mankind. Therefore, it does exactly what it is supposed to do, lick the stench from the bleeding heels and asses of the melt. The price only God knows when the axe favored by mammon cuts through the sole soaking the bleed for its fight and the right given over to death, and we all die, I suppose." Devora turned solemn.

"What about the return of Jesus Christ?" Alia asked.

Devora sighed, "One warrior on the ship remembered the long- kept lure of its despair, and passed on plates of flattery. Once revealed, dangling on one chain, not two, misery lost its company. A savior birth by a universal prayer birthed light in the sky. Goodness was ahead in a constellation with angels. A plane of hope was in the wings. If its body remained unopened in the least deal with the devil keepers of *those who never forget*, the givers of their own deception and its entrails of sellouts paid the highest price, their life, freedom, and soul. All eyes on Lazarus are singing, "Turn up the volume in its pursuit of perfect pitch."

"Hear them! Alia" Devora insisted.

Alia's whirling spirit provoked a breeze. "Yes, it is rather a mixed metaphor. Coming from the right direction I can sense *Justice* a mile away. *Those Who Must Be Kept* do not hear the voice of the queen of my song. I caught a glimpse of an angel's foot, and a dark Antarctica inside of Julius, my brother's keeper." Alia was perplexed.

Devora replied, "Alia, I am my brother's keeper in the constellation of hope for the future. The present has made known to me the ways of life and makes me full of joy. It pays to be born into the right family. I am putting you on warning. The playback, you must be out, awakened the memory of off the grid homestead and one fall for heaven's sake. Both snatched back from eight days a week throwing pure energy to my present, back to the past, and to Future. Hear this, *Those Who Must Be Kept* under the pure earth, in crystal, so fresh and so clean, the new world is no longer brave. In its rage, it has become extreme battles on many fronts. Make a stronger army, in time the Nazarene and your own nakedness shall do the talking in the family tree of gold. You are more than human, more than Vampire, until the last days no one knows that hour. Alas, your enemy still feeds from the root of trickery, and I ask myself, was it an imitation game? Who is the bigger liar, begging to be eaten with stacks on stacks?"

All eyes turned to Lazarus.

Devora barked to the sleeping Lazarus, "I refuse to lick the pie off your dog face. What am I? As the kingship for Christ sake plead its case to the natural man, although invisible, and propped up like a dog. God's firstborn angel, awoke a mystery to a promise of the righteousness of Christ who said you can do all things permitted by God through him if you believe in a family tree of a G."

Alia answered, "Devora, this story does not seem to make sense. The human race lies. And you, once veiled one, offer *Those Who Must Be Kept* a choice that you were never given? They made Julius! Thier order is fierce, their tresses ice!"

One man shouted, "As fine as Galaxy is, no one will want to deny her."

The slaves of the *Flyby Nights* moved away from Devora. One yelled, "What is your name hoe? The dog does not know Christ, the untouchable, unsinkable, uncrushable."

A stone statue with a touch of greyscale on her wrist became flesh. She instantly manifested in front of the scene offering Devora a rotten pair. Connected closely with the worst of the undead, she advised Devora to crush the glass case so the blood of Lazarus would feed the soil like a healthy insurance policy.

"Here is an education, cash his life out, we believe that dog is dead." She squealed.

Fr. Louis, bravely interrupted, "We do not need her hopeless education from the dead. It pays to be educated by the best from way back in history before the dinosaurs roamed, and to love the one your with, a Jesuit sealed in the Holy Spirit, near the richest gold vein in the State. It pays to listen to the call of one body of faith, understanding, and instincts. Our hearts stay healthy this way. Lazarus has heard of one Savior and accepted Jesus through faith. He is no enemy of Christ! At his acceptance of the Nazarene, Brünnhilde planted a living tree, near a tree of life that bears ripe fruit in *Jacob's Garden*."

Many eyes dropped, and many jaws popped.

Fr. Louis had learned through Brünnhilde, that Lazarus had accepted faith in the Nazarene.

He continued, "Here is a metaphor, there is only one crack. Do not disturb the sanctity of our secret tombs. The Center anticipated its coming and covered them with golden glitter in anticipation for our royal gowns. This line inside the case has not broken apart. It's still in one full piece. No matter where I'm at, I got T crack! Our golden age is long lived. It was pieced together out of an immortal galaxy where the future majestically sprinkled the darkness of gold dust to rein over the bones of darkness. Let there be light, and there was light which sewed up and pieced together the forms of majesty. *Justice* breathed, as she has awakened the best. Like harmony or a perfect picture, love runneth over them, for bones and the heavens rejoiced with Life. It is good, and it is a war that should be avoided."

Suddenly, Julius transformed into black and yellow monarch form. He flew over to the glass case and stared at Lazarus, whispering, "Man does not lack toughness, he shall work with internal happiness and not suffer too much."

With a balled fist Devora knocked on the glass asking, "Why is this dog alienated behind a glass case, propped up for this Center to behold? Witnesses help him. Doesn't God have a need for a faithful dog, a futuristic dog? Have your hearts grown cold?" She looked up.

MACHIAVELLI RAGE

Word spoken by a stranger from the crowd peered inside the heart of Galaxy, "And now you know the rest of the story, a living thinking being who reflected about vital energy, and an ordered spear that pierced the side from the best of *those who never forget*. Life, is all we need, Life!"

Suddenly, all became crystal clear, and Galaxy saw her father's true form.

She pointed and shouted, "Look up at his body. He is a man apart of a collective identity. Righteousness and faith rest upon his spirit, given as a gift from God. Let our lives unite in solidarity."

"A few dozen of slaves, to *Flyby Nights* gathered with ancient scripture in hand and shouted, "No, that is a lie. He is a dog! Caught by a dogcatcher, enslaved, and serving *those who never forget*. Their so-called rightful gains keeps him displayed like caged monkeys with small thumbs. This way is for their very own profit. We are sure that the dog is aware of this agreement. "

A long wind whispered, "Make that change," and then parts of the earth shook violently, but the Center remained.

For once, some people wanted to make a difference. They looked around at the scene in the Center and began moving away from *those who never forget*. Many were afraid and sensed something was out of their control. *Those Who Must Be Kept* also began to experience something. It was more than a feeling and hadn't been experienced in a thousand years. No human, Vampire, *Flyby Night*, on or away from earth will ever know, until two become one.

Galaxy sighed, "Remember the goose who laid the golden egg? Never forget to say thank you. It is easy: I have been taught moral restraint in the halls of the elect, and null."

Suddenly some began pleading, "Galaxy, do not caste another reflection into a bottomless pit of the *Labyrinth*. The egg is binding. It must remain in the *Labyrinth*, many are prepared to do anything to possess it. Its calling faces the twilight *of Those Who Must Be Kept.*"

One Vampire in the crowd cried out, "Tessie tried to warn the Center for months, about null now she's gone."

Galaxy interrupted, remember? Please don't fail me now. When Tessie was in one pair of distressed jeans, all she wanted was some money for some pajamas. She stood on the corner sometimes in her robe, with distant black crow calls, followed by bells of an invisible church, crying, pray pray, pray! A few took heed."

The slaves of Flyby *Nights* cried, "Puff, the Color Con, and Dinero, we shall do the right thing, and accept that Lazarus is free and the plan belongs to God."

Galaxy relented with the swords of many angels and said, "Before there was the Word, God was with us. The perfect lunge from the *Labyrinth* into the Center has gone heartless. Many are afraid. I am awake, unafraid and called to help, Lazarus, the eagle, and Funk given to feet only known by my twin in miniature are guardian angels in the Center and on assigned missions. We do not know fear, I do not have to pay my rebels, and the glass shall not be broken! Preserve it, make it big, and great. Take your human understanding and don't claim to know about this dog's future. Lazarus' dog form does not feed evil things. He conformed to the invitation of the Nazarene, the true sin offering who delivered us from evil. Lazarus is a man who shall rise out of the glass with many stars carried by one living womb on earth. It is my faith that the eagle has hatched, and spoken. Out of heaven, the anointed one came down. Christ is eternally glorified on earth in the *Labyrinth* and in heaven. Powers of three in one divinity gave a throne of righteousness to him. If you do not know this, look to your rhymes of old. This is a gift, revelation handed down to those who love God and see truth in the living word made manifest through the void."

Suddenly, the child with white buck shoes and fire in his veins yelled, "The sky can fall down, the wombs of death traps can collapse. I am love who pointed to God, and the hearts of many. I sang my run toward life in the word, but the sky did not fall down."

The boy began tapping his buck shoes loudly. Suddenly, Alia inside a veil of a culture rotting from the inside out, sighed to the boy, "Your visibility is limited, but your squalor was made reputable."

Suddenly, Alia returned to *Those who Must Be Kept* affirming, "No one knows the hour or the time of the return of Jesus Christ."

Within seconds, the sound of white buck shoes tapping to the fruits of century-long traditions earned a little appreciation from a dozen of ancient Vampires. The shoe-tapping lure could bring down Satan. The good ole melodic taps, dancing across the mosaic floor unchanged by time, compelled Julius in moth- man form to drop on the little line near the wrought iron birdcage. The Vampire Monarch yielded to a daring escape into the darkness.

Many *Flyby Nights* decomposing on backstreets of surrender quailed, "Now we are no longer blind!"

They turned to gold dust inside a glorious secret garden. The two birds that Galaxy asked to purchase, well they returned to their perch, chirping, "Many are blind to who we are, and indeed we too survived with all the best, in our talking eagle."

Everyone's head tilted. The glass did not shatter, and Lazarus fell softly on the flat stone patch near the massive desk. The crowd experienced a real light and were astonished as they observed him return to the wonderful specimen of God's handiwork, himself, his own person, a provider of trust and faith of the sacred heart.

Galaxy sighed, "Father, father, why have you forsaken us? I did not die for you!"

Suddenly, Lazarus' human eyes opened, just before Julius' eyes closed, he enquired, "Why are you bawling?"

At the sight of these changes surrounding Vampires wept blood, moaning, "It hurts no more! Julius has returned to gold dust. His battle was won, by him, he owes us nothing!"

Everyone was astonished at the orchestra of musical warriors, which were more to them than any wailing angst, or Vampire death. An actual transformation serenaded to Devora's tears of joy. Suddenly, her favorite book *Machiavelli Rage* fell near Lazarus' rib. With a peculiar look in her eyes, Galaxy stared at her parents. They knew the book was different and hopes you won't mind, that one pig sat down on some of the pages by mistake. But all of that pigs skip to her loos were in order, just like the law of supply and demand.

As Devora caressed the brow of her soulmate, their blood vibrated. Some tears dripped inside Lazarus' mouth. He smiled wide with handsome choppers and restored eyes. "My salty one, this is what became of my search and what it took to bring me safely back home into your arms, an epic adventure on high seas," he whispered.

With this miraculous transformation, Devora gave a thankful clap on her knee sighing, "Whatchu say honey turned back into a man, my guy!"

Devora had the same faraway look in her eye that Galaxy had when they were not going to answer the question about mysteries. Truly, black magic spells were no longer a part of their lives, and any jinx on their family's future miscarried. The *Queen of Song* started again, time passed, and love did not fade.

Indeed, some of their stories are true, and some are not, which part is which, one forgot. A few characters are going to level with you. They are just a boring version of *Machiavelli Rage* where no one gets killed except Jesus. Other characters, well instead of creating chaos to manage it, or wage war against great enemies, they satisfied themselves with a little bickering from time to time. Mostly, about what nice shoes to wear or attire flops.

All the characters are forever tied and untied to shine a little light on the coldest story ever told. At this juncture, *Those Who Must Be Kept* pose no serious threat. They found somebody imperfect to wake up, and wish you well.

The End

Acknowledgements

GRATEFUL ACKNOWLEDGMENT IS expressed to R.F, Dr. K.M., and to the spiritual force within all the characters inside this book which uniquely revealed to me a key that opened freedom, hope, historical discernment, and theological exploration.

About the Author

YLOND MILES-DAVIS EXPERIENCED a powerful, illumi-nating, and sometimes frightening childhood growing up in Oakland, California just steps away from the Black Panther Party and Women's Liberation Headquarters. She is committed to Christian Mysticism and inspired by her world travels.

www.ingramcontent.com/pod-product-compliance
Lightning Source LLC
Chambersburg PA
CBHW030321100526
44592CB00010B/518